THE MAN QUESTION

THE MAN QUESTION

Visions of Subjectivity in Feminist Theory

KATHY E. FERGUSON

UNIVERSITY OF CALIFORNIA PRESS
BERKELEY   LOS ANGELES   OXFORD

Parts of Chapter 1 are taken from Kathy E. Ferguson, "Interpretation and Genealogy in Feminism." *Signs* 16 (Winter 1991): 322–39. © 1991 by the University of Chicago. All rights reserved. Reprinted by permission of the University of Chicago Press. Parts of Chapters 3, 4, and 5 are adapted from Kathy E. Ferguson, "Subject-centeredness in Feminist Discourse," in Kathleen Jones and Anna Jonasdottir, eds., *The Political Interests of Gender* (London: Sage Publications, 1988). Reprinted by permission of Sage Publications.

University of California Press
Berkeley and Los Angeles, California

University of California Press, Ltd.
Oxford, England

Library of Congress Cataloging-in-Publication Data

Ferguson, Kathy E.
    The man question : visions of subjectivity in feminist
theory / Kathy E. Ferguson.
        p.   cm.
    Includes bibliographical references (p.   ) and index.
    ISBN 0-520-07939-6 (cloth : alk. paper).—
    ISBN 0-520-07991-4 (pbk. : alk. paper).
    1. Feminist theory.   2. Feminist criticism.   I. Title.
    HQ1190.F49   1993
    305.42'01—dc20   91-48337
                                                         CIP

Printed in the United States of America

9 8 7 6 5 4 3 2 1

For my mother
Laura Ferguson Rinker
and
my grandmother
Marie Badgley Sears

for their courage and
their love

Contents

Preface

This book is about contending visions of self and clashing claims to knowledge in contemporary feminist theory. It reflects my own odyssey through and around feminism for the last twenty years. My goal is to connect theories about politics and the self to metatheoretical claims about reality and truth. This connection raises a question: Why concentrate on the latter issues if one's primary concern is with the former?

I understand metatheory to reflect the impulse to ask questions about questions, to inquire into that recalcitrant yet (for some) irresistible realm of inquiry into the thematizations of one's themes. But is metatheory not hopelessly "academic" in the negative connotation of that term, an activity irremediably disconnected from the world? I think not. There is a less than subtle class bias in the belief that only academics inquire into their inquiries (though we may have particularly perverse ways of doing so). My metatheoretical focus forces me, as one reader commented (complained, actually), "to treat theories designed to change the world in terms of how they understand the world." The point of doing this is to draw into view unarticulated assumptions and expectations that operate silently within one's theories. Knowing how theories of change understand the world helps one to understand how these theories can act in the world, what they may accomplish, what their unintended consequences may be, and what possibilities may lie unexamined within the terrains they inhabit. Metatheory is irresistible to me because it is so important politically: political and ethical differences ride on, reflect, and produce the metatheoretical differences they then disguise. Poking around and prodding within those disguises strike me as significant feminist tasks.

The two central metanarratives I am exploring I have named, perhaps unfamiliarly, *interpretation* (articulations of women's experience and women's voice) and *genealogy* (deconstructions of the category of women). The arguments for and against these categories come later. Here I want to respond briefly to the charge that I am (secretly, perhaps dishonestly) favoring genealogy while pretending to bring the two into dialogue. Certainly my intellectual debts to Nietzsche, Foucault, and their contemporary fellow-travelers are evident—but so, I hope, are my debts to Aristotle, Marx, Arendt, and the anarchists, to name a few. I am pushing genealogy in the sense that I am privileging an anti-foundational perspective. I am also pushing interpretation in that I insist on the need, first, for stable points from which to practice politics, and, second, on criteria to distinguish the differences I advocate from those I oppose. The "mobile subjectivities" for which I argue in Chapter 6 are the products of interpretation in the sense that they are standpoints of a sort, places to stand and from which to act. But they are also fluid and multiple; they are informed by genealogy's desire to let difference be; they are hard to essentialize because their concreteness resists abstract formulations. To those readers firmly rooted in either of these metatheoretical positions ("Women's experience is . . ." versus "Stop talking about women"), I may appear to be advocating only the other. But it is this rootedness in one position or the other that I am attempting to problematize. I don't want to give up the tension-filled dialogue between them by making one the primary position and the other a footnote. Two decades of feminist critiques and visions rub elbows in this text with genealogical suspicions about the reliability of critique and the self-destructiveness of vision. I want to show how to live and work with the tensions between them, how to gain intelligence and energy through the friction their conversations generate.

Enter, irony. I came upon the concept of irony as though rediscovering an old friend. My efforts to hold onto some versions of both interpretation and genealogy initially reminded me of a toy from childhood, an apparatus made of two wooden balls attached to each other by a hidden string running through a central frame. When you tug on one of the balls, the other recedes from view as it disappears into the frame. Dropping the first to pursue the second yields the same result. The challenge was to keep them both in view. The usefulness of this toy as a metaphor is limited, since I ultimately figured out that the best way to accomplish the task was simply to hold the toy still, while the imbalancing act between interpretation and genealogy requires a lot of juggling . . . and dancing around. But my dilemma reminds me of that toy in that I confront two different and valued perspectives, each of which disappears when I grasp the other too firmly. The doubleness of perspective that irony provides allows me to smile at the contortions required to keep both in view, to shrug a wry "oh, well" at the impossibility of definite resolution while keeping at the task. I am advocating irony not as a way of ridiculing others' beliefs but as a way of problematizing the coherence and completeness of all beliefs, including (especially) one's own. Sustaining an ironic view of commitments one continues to hold is an imbalancing act crucial to feminist theory and practice. If there is an "essence" to "woman" perhaps it lies in an ironic recognition of the eternal recurrence of the claim to embody essence.

But how to talk about irony? Even more troubling, how to write irony? I am tempted by statements like "It's time for feminists to get serious about irony." (Well, maybe not.) Shall we be earnest about irony? (An old family saying goes, "You be Frank and I'll be Earnest.") Can I get irony straight and communicate it properly? (This is getting worse all the time.) Dammit, how to talk about irony?

I have no resolution to this dilemma. I believe that an ironic sensibility is crucial for feminism, that it is indispensable in negotiating tensions without being immobilized by them. Yet I continue to struggle with the question: Can one truly be serious about irony? Oh, well.

Acknowledgments

The writing of this book has provided an intellectual journey with many companions, a number of detours, and not a few surprises. Its genesis occurred during William Connolly's National Endowment for the Humanities Summer Seminar in 1984, when I was first introduced to the interpretation/genealogy debates in political theory. My thanks to NEH for its financial support, and deepest gratitude to Bill Connolly for his intellectual leadership during that seminar and since, and especially for his timely assistance in my struggles with Hegel. Thanks also to Tom Dumm, Alex Hooke and Kathy Jones for their contributions to that extraordinary seminar, for their subsequent help, both supportive and contentious, and most of all for their friendship.

Since coming to the University of Hawai'i in 1985 I've been privileged to work with some fine colleagues and some excellent graduate students. Carolyn DiPalma has been a treasured intellectual companion and friend, and her unstinting attention to this book, in its many drafts, has been invaluable. Mike Shapiro provided cherished intellectual sustenance and personal support and gave his time generously to a thoughtful critique of the manuscript. Phyllis Turnbull and Valerie Wayne were helpful in their remarks on the manuscript and in the infusions of life they bring to feminism and critical thinking on campus. My deepest thanks to all of them for their intelligence, their humor, and their care.

Two old friends from my days on the East Coast, Jane Bennett and Mary Bellhouse, gave this manuscript the kind of close reading that makes meaningful revisions possible. I'm grateful to them both for their help with this project, for the intellectual stimulation their work has provided me, and for their lively and sustaining friendship.

The students in my feminist theory courses, graduate and undergraduate, have provided very special intellectual and personal challenge and support. Our feminist theory reading group, now in its sixth year, has been a vital stimulus to creative and critical thinking. My thanks to the Office of Research Relations, University of Hawai'i at Manoa, for its financial support of this project. The unique intellectual and political environments of the Department of Political Science and the Women's Studies Program at the University of Hawai'i have usually been hospitable, and, lacking that, have at least been interesting. Hawai'i itself has been a challenging venue for shaping political arguments and posing questions about identity.

My deepest appreciation to my family for their support in the midst of some puzzlement about exactly what I am doing, and for their care: Mom, Mac, Steve, Julie, Roger, Gary, Connie, Barbara, Susan, and Diane; and special thanks to Lisa and Moe. My greatest thanks of all go to Gili and Oren for their unfailing support, combined with their constant interruptions, for their good humor, and for their contentment with the lives we have made together. And thanks to Ari for timing his arrival to allow for completion of this book and for his *in utero* contributions to family life.

Chapter One

Interpretation and
Genealogy in Feminism

What could it mean to pose "the man question" in political theory?
At the most general level, to ask the man question is to call political
theory into question with regard to gender, to call the question of
gender in political theory. But there are different ways to put gender into circulation as an analytic category, different ways to problematize the social, political and linguistic arrangements of sexual
difference. Many of the most heated debates in contemporary feminist theory, and many of its most troubling and promising possibilities, can be seen as disputes over the proper way to frame questions of gender in language and politics.

   In some respects the man question is a reversal of the older and
more familiar "woman question," particularly as elaborated within
nineteenth- and twentieth-century socialism, wherein a certain ordering of the world is established, reflecting male experiences and
understandings, and then women are problematized and fitted into
that order. For example, in a small tract entitled *The Woman
Question*, an unnamed editor marshals selections from Marx, Engels, Lenin, and Stalin to indicate the proper role for women in
the unfolding of socialism. Clara Zetkin's interview with Lenin,
also included, indicates that women too can ask the woman question: "We must win over to our side the millions of toiling women
in the towns and villages," Zetkin declares. "Win them for our
struggles and in particular for the communist transformation of society."[1] Women here are the problematic others, the unreliable,

troublesome, and/or dangerous ones that "we" must cajole or control.

Many significant western male thinkers have framed their inquiries implicitly around "the woman question." Freud is a nearly unavoidable target; perceiving women's sex to be defective because it is hidden, presenting, as Luce Irigaray remarks, *"the horror of nothing to see,"* Freud relentlessly establishes the male to be the norm, then shrugs his shoulders at women's incomprehensibility, their essential mystery.[2] Julia Kristeva makes the same point: concerning women's sexuality, she says, "Freud offers only a massive *nothing.*"[3] Hegel's account of the modern world articulates a notion of subjectivity that he then denies to women, defining them as "plants" vis-à-vis the male "animal," as " 'ironies' in the life of the spirit."[4] Lévi-Strauss posits an exchange of women that assumes polygamous sexuality on the part of men, and asserts that there will always be a shortage of truly desirable females; meanwhile the possibilities that women's desire might also be polygamous, or that men might not all be equally attractive, go unremarked.[5] In the terms of the woman question women are the problem, men and masculinity are the unnamed norm, and gender is silenced as an analytic category. Irigaray's characterization of Freud could easily apply to all who pose the woman question:

The "feminine" is always described in terms of deficiency or atrophy, as the other side of the sex that alone holds a monopoly on value. . . . In short, they [women] are deprived of the worth of their sex. The important thing, of course, is that no one should know who has deprived them, or why, and that "nature" be held accountable.[6]

Feminist responses to the woman question have been complex and varied. An early and still common response is to claim entry for women into the worlds that men reserved for themselves by hurling a loud "Me too!" at the wall of arrogance and exclusion. While there are still good political reasons for retreating to this position on occasion, the response challenges only the answers to the woman question, not its terms. In order to shift onto the theoretical and practical terrain of the man question, many feminists have pursued a re-framing of the inquiry via a reversal of its terms; that is, they call for the overthrow of male-ordered thinking in favor of a discourse that privileges women's experiences and wom-

en's perspectives, that puts women in the center. But this reversal
is not a simple reversal, nor an uncontested one. It is not simple
because it does not retain the hierarchical structure of patriarchal
discourse, substituting women at the pinnacle. Most versions of
feminism reject the idea of simply reproducing phallocentric discourse or patriarchal society with women at the top.[7] The vexing
question is, then, What exactly constitutes patriarchy's reproduction? In pursuing this question, some feminisms move to contest
the reversal itself by arguing against any arrangement of margin
and center, against the very principle of a center at all.

The relation between efforts to put women in the center and
efforts to deconstruct centers is complex. Both frame the questions
of political theory around the problematic of gender, but in different ways. In the first stance men—male power, male identities,
masculinity as a set of practices—are problematized; in the second,
the gendered world itself becomes a problem. Both stances bring
gender into view as a powerful organizing principle of social life,
but the former reverses patriarchal gender priorities while the latter explodes them. In some respects these two ways of asking the
man question seem simply to contradict one another. How can we
simultaneously put women at the center and decenter everything,
including women? But this contradiction, while acute, does not
exhaust the possible relation between these two theoretical practices; nor does naming the contradiction preclude searching for
creative strategies to negotiate it. One approach to relating these
two theoretical projects is a temporal one: the woman-centered
discourses can be seen as paving the way for gender-free analyses;
putting women in the center, then, would be a step toward decen-
teredness.[8] While this formulation is inviting in some ways, it does
not explain why any group would seek to destroy the center once
they have occupied it; nor does it explore the ways in which the
two theoretical impulses depend on one another.

Debates between feminist reversals and their discontents offer
a dynamic if unstable field for examining feminist discursive and
institutional practices. The creation of women's voice, or a feminist
standpoint, or a gynocentric theory, entails immersion in a world
divided between male and female experience in order to critique
the power of the former and valorize the alternative residing in the
latter. It is a theoretical project that opposes the identities and

coherencies contained in patriarchal theory in the name of a different set of identities and coherencies, a different and better way of thinking and living. The deconstruction of gender entails stepping back from the opposition of male and female in order to loosen the hold of gender on life and meaning. This theoretical project renders gender more fragile, more tenuous, and less salient both as an explanatory and as an evaluative category. Women's point of view is created in order to reject the male ordering of the world; gender is deconstructed in order to reject the dualism of male and female.[9]

The contrast between reversing gendered practices through interpretation and exploding them via genealogy is not (regrettably) as neat as I have just suggested. Genealogy too employs its reversals. Frequently the switch entails relations of cause and effect. Foucault, for example, argues that the category of sex, rather than causing behavior and directing desire, is in fact the effect of a historically produced regime of sexuality.[10] Gayatri Spivak refers to the "subject-effect" to establish the juridico-legal subject of modernity as outcome rather than cause.[11] Reversal is a seemingly irresistible move of displacement, an effective strategy to dislocate the center and challenge its claims to self-evidence. Yet differences between the ways that reversals are deployed remain: approaches affiliated with interpretation tend to use their reversals to provide an alternative resting place for understanding and action, while those employing genealogy tend to undermine one's ability to rest at all. Genealogical reversals do not restabilize cause/effect relations in the opposite direction so much as they unsettle any effort to conceptualize singular or linear relations between events and practices.

Efforts to give voice to women's perspective(s) sometimes emphasize the need to speak with and listen to women in their own terms, and sometimes go on to recruit women's perspective(s) to provide direction for political change. Arguments for both approaches usually call for some founding source for women's experiences: sexuality and reproduction, the political economy of the gendered division of labor, the practices of mothering, or the telos of nature. Sometimes the defining category is conceptualized biologically or innately and suggests an essentialist form of argument in which the meaning of women's lives is lodged in the female body

or psyche. Sometimes essentialism is eschewed in favor of a historical account in which *woman* or *women* is/are produced through
and against the operation of political, economic, and social forces.
Whether the arguments emphasize what women *do* or what women
are, the construction of the category *women's experience* requires
some coherent notion of what sorts of persons and what sorts of
experiences count as fundamental. Realizing that the foundation
they seek may not apply to all women or exclude all men, expressions of women's voice usually call for respect for differences among/
within women (and sometimes among/within men as well), but the
logic of the search for a founding experience tends to elide difference nonetheless.

The deconstructive project comes to the defense of difference,
in opposition to "the founding of a hysterocentric to counter a phallic discourse."[12] The deconstruction of gender is done in the name
of a politics of difference, an anti-foundationalism defending that
which resists categorization and refuses to be corralled in the categories of male and female. While nearly all feminist theory opposes binary opposition at some level, the deconstructivists are the
most radical in their call for an opposition to sexual dualism itself
in the name of "a choreographic text with polysexual signatures."
The voices in such a chorus "would not be a-sexual, far from it, but
would be sexual otherwise: beyond the binary difference that governs the decorum of all codes."[13] Deconstructive strategies focus
on the multiple meanings that could reside within terms or narratives, attending to the many residing within the appearance of the
one. Yet the deconstructive project is itself parasitical upon the
claims it seeks to unfound, including claims about sexual difference, both those of the patriarchal order and those of feminists. So
these two projects cannot be neatly separated. They are like contrasting themes that run through the fabric of feminist theory.
Sometimes the two projects meet head-on in debate, but more
often they coexist within a particular flow of argument, encountering and evading one another in subterranean fashion. Advocates
often speak as though the two projects were totally separate and
antagonistic endeavors, but within the general fabric of feminist
thought they appear more often as connected, yet contrasting,
themes. Although the relationship between them is not harmonious, conversations are nonetheless possible between them. Inter-

pretation and genealogy are contrasting voices that create different, albeit related, possibilities for knowledge and politics.

The purpose of this chapter is to explore the political and epistemological opportunities made available by these two contrasting theoretical practices, as well as to clarify their relationship to one another. Here they are mapped out as metatheories, that is, as theories about how to do feminist theory, or as questions about how to ask the man question. The various efforts to name and to act upon women's voice can be seen as differing versions of the hermeneutic project within political theory. Within this project the task of theory is to interpret appearances properly in order to uncover an underlying meaning, a reality distorted but not destroyed by the power of those able to construct the appearances in the first place. Most theories that carry the imprint of Hegel or of Marx, and often of Freud as well, participate in some version of the hermeneutic project. Correspondingly, the efforts to deconstruct gender take the form of differing expressions of political theory's genealogical project. Here the task is to deconstruct meaning claims in order to look for the modes of power they carry and to force open a space for the emergence of counter-meanings. "A theory," says Gilles Deleuze, speaking for genealogy, "does not totalize; it is an instrument for multiplication and it also multiplies itself."[14] Genealogy is more clearly an activity than a theory in the interpretive sense in that it takes up a posture of subversion toward fixed meaning claims. Yet its emphasis on subversion positions it at odds with authority and inclines it to the side of the powerless and marginal. Nietzsche and most of the theorists labeled poststructural or postmodern participate in various ways in the genealogical project.

Just as the woman question has very little to do with women, and everything to do with filling in the gaps in male-ordered claims about reality, so the man question has very little to do, directly, with men. It has to do, rather, with making it possible to view male power and female subordination, and/or maleness and femaleness per se, as phenomena in need of explanation and redress. In its hermeneutic version, pursuit of the man question entails the valorizing of women's experiences as a privileged locus of discursive and institutional insight. In its genealogical guise, asking the man question entails calling into question the field of meaning within which man and woman can be understood as stable categories at all. One of the ironies of the woman question is that women tend to disappear from its central terms, to become troublesome mysteries (for example, Freud's "What do women want?") or recruitable auxiliaries (Zetkin's "millions of toiling women") attached to a firmly male-ordered story. The man question reverses and maintains this irony in that it is not directly about men, but about the dislocation of male-orderedness in inquiries into gender. The hermeneutic move effects this dislocation by shifting women into the center of the analysis, while the genealogical approach interrupts the stability of the terms *men* and *women* (among others). My central concern is not with the substance of western society's understanding of masculinity but with the kinds of thinking and acting that are necessary to dislodge masculinity from its claims to normalcy and to make it a problem that requires explanation.[15]

Engaging feminist questions at the level of metatheory enables us to ask what Heidegger and others have called the question of the frame. The questions we can ask about the world are enabled, and other questions disabled, by the frame that orders the questioning. When we are busy arguing about the questions that appear within a certain frame, the frame itself becomes invisible; we become *enframed* within it. The frame makes claims upon our questioning that we have trouble hearing: "Man [*sic*] stands so decisively in attendance on the challenging-forth of enframing that he does not grasp enframing as a claim, that he fails to see himself as the one spoken to." The dominant frame orders our thinking in such a way that alternative orders are silenced: "But enframing does not simply endanger man [*sic*] in his relationship to himself and to everything that is. As a destining, it banishes man into that kind of revealing that is an ordering. Where this ordering holds sway, it drives out every other possibility of revealing."[16]

It is possible to be enframed *within* interpretation (feminist or otherwise) or *within* genealogy, seeing only the battles each practice names as worthy and missing the ways in which contending interpretations or rival deconstructions cooperate on a metatheoretical level to articulate some possibilities and silence others. Within feminist theory interpretations and deconstructions of various kinds constitute different sorts of meaning fields, and within those fields certain debates flourish while others fail to take root.[17] Enframing is challenged when elements on the fringes or in the basements of

a particular frame (say, feminisms as fringe or subterranean elements of modernity) become more audible. Further, the fringes of
an argument can come to offer a hidden enablement to the frame
from which they are excluded: it is the fringe's prohibitions or silences that allow the explanations of the frame to do their work.
Paradoxically, the woman question is enabled by the exclusion of
women from its central terms of inquiry, so that the male-ordered
accounts can continue their operations with minimal disruptions
from the margins. Enframing, then, is also challenged when the
"intricate and interanimating" relation of the fringes and basements to the frame is named. [18]

The man question is a kind of frame for feminist metatheories; it
invites inquiries into the arrangements and terms of gender by
marking the dominant configurations as strange, demanding explanation. As a frame it is not exempt from the problems of enframing.
Feminisms too have their fringes and their basements; while it is
probably impossible to know one's own fringe completely, one can
at least know that the fringe exists and stay open to its disruptive
effects. Attention to clashing metatheories, opposing ways to ask
questions about questions, can help bring into focus the frames
within which questions normally reside and the fringes those frames
both create and repress. Articulating the debates and dependencies between interpretation and genealogy in feminism may help
to agitate into livelier existence the terrain that is unoccupied or
underoccupied by the debates framed within each practice.

Three preliminary points need to be made about the constitution of interpretation and genealogy as categories for inquiry into
the man question. First, in constructing them I have disregarded
important distinctions within each set of practices. Advocates of
hermeneutic inquiry may take offense at the inclusion of historical
explanations of the emergence of meaning with religious forms
of essentialism, or of idealist with materialist analyses. Champions
of genealogy may object to the conflation of the textual practices of
literary deconstruction with the historical project of denaturalizing
the claims of power. I do not mean to suggest, for example, that
Marx is the same as Jung, or Foucault the same as Derrida, but
rather to group them according to their overall participation in two
fundamental and opposing activities: the discovery of truth in an
ordered universe versus the imposition of meaning on a disordered

one. The advantage of these categories is their ability to thematize questions not readily askable within the more familiar oppositions of feminist theory, such as socialist feminism versus cultural feminism or radical versus liberal feminist politics. When arguments about the nature of order confront arguments about whether there is an order at all, differences within the two positions are minimized so that differences between them can make an appearance.

Second, I trace contending strategies of argument rather than fixed positions or established schools of thought. By referring to interpretation and genealogy as strategies, practices, or impulses, I mean to suggest both their activity and their fluidity. As ways of comprehending the world, both stances are selective and active engagements with that world; as theories they are also practices. While they are perspectives evinced by individual thinkers (that is, they are things that people *do*), they take their power largely from their status as already existing linguistic/political practices into which we enter to make our arguments. The genealogical impulse is ill-served by efforts to capture it within the docile walls of an academic school of thought; to create a stance called "post-structuralism" that one can then espouse or reject is fatally to tame the rebellion against categorization expressed therein. Nor does hermeneutics as I use the term refer to any single ideological argument or school of thought; rather, it names a stance toward knowing and acting that depends heavily on a stable appearance/reality distinction. The opposition between interpretation and genealogy is not a reformulation of the old war between idealism and materialism; interpretations, for example, can look either to ideas or to social structures (or both) to critique the misleading appearances that disguise underlying realities. The question here is not whether language or institutions are more real, but what to make of claims about "reality." In reading contemporary feminist theory through the lenses provided by interpretation and genealogy I attempt not a taxonomy of positions but a tracing of threads that weave around and chafe one another; not a complete account of a stable field but rather an unraveling of two persistent impulses within feminist discourses. In reducing feminism's many faces to two, I risk failing to capture all the significant debates, but perhaps I have found a way to think about a stubborn and persistent opposition that marks much of our thinking, writing, and acting.

Third, my own account of the interpretation/genealogy story seems to rest upon yet another version of that old foe of feminism, the binary opposition. But distinctions are not always dualistic, and dualisms are not always and necessarily antifeminist. One can make or find salient distinctions that do not negate one another, and one can contrast two ideas without claiming that they exhaust the possible field of meaning. Through interpretation and genealogy two potent truth/power practices in contemporary feminist theory come into focus; these practices are contrasting pairs within a complex field rather than exclusively binary couples. To the extent that the two are in binary opposition (that is, when one emphasizes the ways in which they disqualify one another rather than their interdependencies), they are not necessarily enemies of feminism; while two are usually not enough, some either/ors persist past patriarchy. On the one hand, dualism becomes deadly when it is accompanied by hierarchy, so that one is declared primary and the other subordinate. Oppositions between unlike equals, on the other hand, provide a fruitful field for building feminisms that give up on transcendence and harmony in favor of partiality and irony.

Ontologies and Subjectivities

Interpretation usually employs an ontology of discovery, assuming that there is some order in the world that stands on its own and that can be discovered or at least approached by human knowing. Truth is discovered by employing a hermeneutics of suspicion, wherein one is suspicious of the various disguises that can cover up and distort reality. Interpretation values attunement with the discovered truth for its liberating potential: "Ye shall know the truth, and the truth shall set you free." Confident that knowing can at least to some extent apprehend being, the interpretivist seeks a home on the other side of appearances, where, for example, the power of the bourgeoisie to obfuscate the understanding of the working class, or of patriarchy to control the understanding of women, has been transcended.

Genealogy tends to employ a counter-ontology, one that denies there is any order "out there" to be discovered. The world is a place of flux and discord to the genealogist; it offers, as Foucault remarks, no legible face and is indifferent to our need for a resting place in truth. The genealogist is suspicious of the hermeneutics of suspicion, seeing underneath the disguise laid down by power another layer of disguise. We make up our claims to truth, Nietzsche argues, then we forget we made them up, then we forget that we forgot. Claiming that there is always more to being than knowing, the genealogist sees the interpretivist's search for attunement with higher unities as dangerous; instead, the genealogist opens herself to the discordances and discontinuities discernible within a field of meaning. Interpretation tends toward the construction of a "big picture," one that seeks fully to represent the world, while genealogy moves toward "the affirmation of the particularities that attend any practice, and perhaps the activity that permits new practices to emerge."[19]

Interpretive thinkers usually start from the (undemonstrable) presumption that there is a fit between human desires, human categories of understanding, and the world that humans inhabit. Genealogists, starting from the (equally undemonstrable) position that there is no fit, that instead there is resistance and slippage between what we want, how we think, and where we are, do not necessarily scorn the desire for an order, only the assumption of it. "Their mistake," the genealogist might say of interpretivists, "is not in expressing the desire to find a home in the world; it resides in the demand that there be a way of life or afterlife which synchronizes with this urge."[20] The genealogical insistence that the world does not come made for our categories, that there is no necessity unfolding itself through history, or science, or the goddess, can be radically disturbing, since it destabilizes the "reality" side of the still necessary but now problematic appearance/reality distinction. As Donna Haraway notes, "We [feminists] would like to think our appeals to real worlds are more than a desperate lurch away from cynicism and an act of faith like any other cult's."[21] But this escape from necessity could also be radically liberating; Roland Barthes revels in the possibilities that open up when "by refusing to assign to the text (and to the world-as-text) a 'secret,' i.e., an ultimate meaning, [one] liberates an activity we may call countertheological, properly revolutionary, for to refuse to halt meaning is finally to refuse God and his hypostases, reason, science, the law."[22]

Finally, the genealogical claims are also radically humbling, since one's own truths are seen to be no less connected to power than those of one's enemies; a deflation of hubris is bound to result from confronting questions such as those William Connolly poses: "But if the world were not created, and if it did not mesh neatly with human capacities for cognition, why might not every human theory encounter slippage and undecidability in its structure?" And again: "What political theory today does not lean upon fragile and unstable suppositions bound together by insistence?"[23]

Most feminist arguments for a women's perspective, voice, or standpoint call upon some version of an ontology of discovery and an epistemology of attunement. Nancy Hartsock, for example, strives to create a feminist standpoint that builds on the achievements of Marx's analysis of capitalism while transcending its limitations. Hartsock speaks of knowledge as either advancing toward or incorrectly straying from its totalizing goal. Knowledge generated through a feminist historical materialism makes visible a "still deeper level" of "reality," "the real material ground of human existence."[24] Just as the proletarian standpoint was an advance over market analysis in its completeness and accuracy, Hartsock's feminist standpoint advances further toward the completion of a historical process of liberation.

In contrast, much of contemporary French feminist theory is heavily influenced by the genealogical project. For example, Luce Irigaray urges a disruption of systematizing strategies of inquiry, a "jamming of the theoretical machinery itself." Viewing all coherencies and unities as produced, as the artifacts of analysis rather than its finds, she rejects the question "What is woman?" as excessively metaphysical. Rather than looking beneath the surface for an underlying reality, she takes the surface itself to require reading, looking to the play of bodies and pleasures to provide a "disruptive excess" within onto-theological inquiry.[25]

Often the ontology/counter-ontology disputes within feminism are woven together in complex ways. Sandra Harding, for example, embraces the partiality and open-endedness that accompany an anti-totalizing project; looking at the tension between endorsing a political commitment and deconstructing the ontological grounds upon which such commitments are traditionally founded, she counsels that "this particular apparent tension in feminist thought is simply one we should learn to live with." Yet Harding's "fidelity to certain parameters of dissonance with and between the assumptions of these discourses" is compromised by her hope that all this will be resolved in the future: "Feminist analytical categories," she states, "should be unstable at this moment in history." But this instability is transitional: "we will have a feminist science fully coherent with its epistemological strategies only when we have a feminist society." [26] Here the tension between interpretive and genealogical approaches is resolved temporally: a genealogical impulse necessary now within feminism will give way to a settled future feminist interpretation.

Sometimes the interaction of interpretive and genealogical approaches within an argument resembles a subtextual tug-of-war. In her analysis of gender in Islam, for example, Fatima Mernissi stresses the production rather than the discovery of sexuality. "Muslim sexuality," she claims, "is territorial: its regulatory mechanisms consist primarily in a strict allocation of space to each sex and an elaborate ritual for resolving the contradictions arising from the inevitable intersections of spaces." Yet the regulatory strategies produce the behavior they are intended to eliminate. Her argument, paralleling (although not, seemingly, based in) Foucault's claims about the production of masturbation in modern France, holds that "sexual segregation intensifies what it is supposed to eliminate: the sexualization of human relations." [27] However, this genealogical argument sits within a very conventional appearance/reality distinction. Reality is to appearance as action is to discourse; the reality in the Muslim world is, Mernissi claims, rapid social change, while the appearance is religious stability. [28] Her formulation of the argument could effectively counter an irritating form of orientalism that attributes timelessness to eastern societies and rapid-paced excitement to the west. [29]

But could orientalism not also be challenged through a metatheoretical approach that names rapid social change and religious stability as two clashing practices, rather than crowning one with the foundationalist claims of reality while the other is relegated to the realm of mere appearance? Mernissi's analysis rests upon an argument for a gap between "the realities of everyday life and the ideas and images stamped into people's minds." Why can't these be equally real or equally the realm of image? Mernissi distances herself from the interpretive project through the following assertion: "My modest aim in this research is not to irritate the reader by claiming to have uncovered the *truth* about the new male-female dynamic that has emerged in modern Moroccan society. I leave truth to those who seek certainty. My own feeling is that we move forward faster and live better when we seek doubt." But her appearance/reality distinction is designed to quell doubts, not to stimulate them; it is better suited for reassuring us, for establishing what she refers to later as "the real direction of trends."[30] By figuring the opposite of ideology to be reality she obscures the possibility, which elsewhere she wishes to retain, that what counts as real is the outcome of ideological practices.

The ontology/counter-ontology debates that respond to the question "What is real?" are accompanied by a complex set of subjectivity/counter-subjectivity debates that emerge in relation to the question "Who are we?" Interpretation is usually a subject-centered project. Its search for truth privileges the self-understanding of either the individual or the collective (or of some individuals or some collectives), while at the same time acknowledging that there is always more to the self than the existing self-understanding makes available. Interpretation always has to balance the ability of power to distort the worldview of the powerless with the ability of the oppressed to comprehend and transcend their confinement. For example, in *The Theory of Communicative Action* Habermas distinguishes between modernization, which he defines as "colonization of the life world," and modernity, or "modern structures of consciousness."[31] Habermas sees within the second a potential for reason that can be called upon to critique and transcend the first. Most analyses that call themselves phenomenological are premised on the priority of the speaking subject and on that subject's own accounts of her/his experiences, including Hegel's complex phenomenology in which the emergence of the individual to true self-consciousness is a manifestation and reflection of the same process in the life of the species. In contrast, the genealogist problematizes the subject, claiming that our notion of the subject is itself an outcome of the disciplinary practices of modernity. "We knowers are unknown to ourselves," Nietzsche declares.[32] Subjectivity and intersubjectivity are themselves the effects of power, and thus provide no secure foothold for struggling against power. "It is only the snare of language," Nietzsche declares, that leads us to attach "urge, will, activity" to a speaking, reasoning subject; "But no such agent exists; there is no 'being' behind the doing, acting, becoming; the 'doer' has simply been added to the deed by the imagination—the doing is everything."[33] Genealogy does not abandon the subject, but examines it as a function of discourse, asking "under what conditions and through what forms can an entity like the subject appear in the order of discourse; what position does it occupy; what functions does it exhibit; and what rules does it follow in each type of discourse?"[34] Genealogy takes the modern subject as data to be accounted for, rather than as a source of privileged accounts of the world.

Feminist theory entails both problematizing and embracing subjectness. Those struggling for equity within existing structures and theories have done so in part by claiming entry for women into the world of the subject; Simone de Beauvoir, for example, stressed the importance of sharing with men the activities of transcendence and creativity that mark the uniquely human arena. Beyond the primarily defensive posture of "me too!" feminism lies the struggle between efforts to redefine the gendered subject by centering it in women's experiences and efforts to deconstruct the gendered subject altogether. Some feminists, such as Nancy Hartsock and Carol Gilligan, have redefined the notion of the subject to emphasize persons-in-relations rather than autonomous selves, and have urged greater attention to responding to needs than to defending rights. While this position rejects the prevailing notion of the subject as excessively masculine, it holds onto the practice of privileging women's self-understanding. This reversal identifies as the problem conventional male self-understandings and the power/knowledge practices built upon them; it looks to women's self-understandings, modified to account for the effects of women's subordination, as keys to a better way of knowing and acting. Other feminists, such as Irigaray, recommend abandoning efforts to define *woman* or *women* in favor of "repeating/interpreting the way in which, within discourse, the feminine finds itself defined as lack, deficiency, or as imitation and negative image of the subject . . . [in order to] signify that with respect to this logic a *disruptive excess* is possible on the feminine side."[35]

Irigaray rejects the gynocentric move even while recognizing that "we do not escape so easily from reversal."[36] And her critics have pointed out that she seems to posit *woman* as a unified category in precisely the way she wants to reject.[37] Similarly, Hélène Cixous moves uneasily between a rejection of the binary opposition of masculine and feminine and a reconstitution of that opposition through a language that locates women's voice in "the deepest layers of her psyche," in the voice of the mother.[38] Still others, such as Julia Kristeva, call for a decentering of all social identities, including the (for others, primary) dualism of men and women, which she considers to be excessively metaphysical. The semiotic and symbolic processes that Kristeva discusses are not confined to differences between bodies or subjects; thus she looks not to women but to avant-garde artists for resistance. Kristeva speaks of a subject in process in an effort to capture a difficult balance between the deconstructive subversion of the subject and its psychoanalytic reconstitution.[39]

Teresa Ebert further develops this posture in what she calls "postmodern feminist cultural theory"; following Foucault, she "theorizes the subject as *produced* through signifying practices which precede her and not as the *originator* of meaning."[40] The tension between calling upon and problematizing subjectivity is an acutely political one because it brings one face-to-face with the issues of resistance and domination. In "My Father's Country Is the Poor," Alice Walker writes about her encounter with young Cubans whose notions of themselves were national, not racial: "we presented ourselves as 'black' Americans (they presented themselves, unselfconsciously and without words, as Cubans, of course), and their faces changed. For the first time they seemed aware of color differences *among themselves—and were embarrassed for us.*"[41] Walker and her companions emphasized their blackness in part because of their political commitment to their "own" cultural identity, and in part because they live in a society that never lets them forget their color. The complexity of claiming an identity that is also forced on them is highlighted by the contrast to the dark-skinned Cuban children, who were, in a sense, in but not of their race. Walker acknowledges the implicit rebuke to her assumptions about racial identities, while still cherishing the precious subjectivity and solidarity that blackness makes available to her.

Languages, Histories, Politics

Interpretation usually embraces an expressive view of language; while a particular language is expressive of a particular worldview, it is also capable of transcending the limits of that worldview through careful use and in the appropriate circumstances, as Habermas claims of the ideal speech situation. The genealogist views language much more ambivalently as a necessary set of falsifications that is doomed to (or perhaps blessed with) partiality and incompleteness. The genealogical project calls out the semiotic dimensions of language, those that slip and play in nuance and ambiguity. "We extend ourselves by force of play" against the limits of the already said, Derrida argues.[42] With Derrida, most genealogists see language as an evasion of finality, an endless deferral of meaning. Toril Moi articulates this position clearly: "the interplay between presence and absence that produces meaning is posited as one of deferral—meaning is never truly present, but is only constructed through the potentially endless process of referring to other, absent signifiers."[43]

The debate here is not with positivism, since both interpretation and genealogy reject the conventional correspondence theory of truth, by which truth rests upon accuracy of correspondence between the name and the thing. Both views accept the active role of language in clarifying and completing that which is articulated, and both see language as a social practice, an intersubjective web of shared understanding from which some material always escapes full articulation.[44] But the interpretivist concentrates on the liberatory potential of language to discover or at least open the way toward some unities of understanding, whereas the genealogist stresses the tendency of discourse to constitute that which it then claims to have discovered through the operations of the "mobile army of metaphors, metonymies, anthropomorphisms" that mediate our interactions with the world.[45] Significant debates rage within interpretation over the extent of the world's availability to human knowledge; but to the genealogist these are in-house debates among believers. Gayatri Spivak, speaking here for genealogy, notes that "the possibility of explanation carries the presupposition of an explainable (even if not fully) universe and an explaining (even if imperfectly) subject. These presuppositions assure our being. Explaining, we exclude the possibility of the radically heterogeneous."[46]

This search for assurance reveals the intimate link between the metatheoretical gestures of interpretation and the assumption of a reliably speaking subject. Reflected here is an intellectual strategy pursuing "a project to integrate things into adequate and encompassing explanations. The integration is sometimes explicitly, and always implicitly, in the name of the sovereign mind."[47] Foucault expresses the genealogical suspicion of any reach for closure in the outline of his project as a "questioning of language by language . . . the still silent and groping apparition of a form of thought in which the interrogation of the limit replaces the search for totality and the act of transgression replaces the movement of contradictions."[48]

Irigaray sustains the genealogical stance toward language in her stress on women's evasions of linguistic closure. Although she strives toward an articulation of the feminine rather than a deconstruction of gender, Irigaray does not believe that woman's difference can ever be fully articulated:

Hers are contradictory words, somewhat mad from the standpoint of reason, inaudible for whoever listens to them with ready-made grids, with a fully elaborated code in hand. . . . One would have to listen with another ear, as if hearing *an "other meaning" always in the process of weaving itself, or embracing itself with words, but also of getting rid of words in order not to become fixed, congealed in them.*[49]

A good interpretive counterpoint here is Gilligan's account of the little girl Amy in her rendition of Heinz's dilemma.[50] In her response to Heinz's need but inability to pay for an expensive medicine for his wife, Amy departs from the male narrative about the right to property versus the right to life; instead, she assumes the need for some response from Heinz and the druggist and then considers what form their responses should take. The interviewer, well trained in Kohlberg's arguments about moral development, lets Amy know through the repetition of questions that the way she construes the problem is not correct, that her responses are not heard or not accepted. Prepared to heed only a discussion of competing rights, the interviewer is deaf to Amy's narrative about the fracturing and mending of relationships. Here Gilligan and Irigaray would agree that one must listen "with another ear" to discern the pattern in Amy's story, that without this ear Amy's story seems "somewhat mad from the standpoint of reason." But for Gilligan, Amy's language expresses more or less forthrightly the female voice, a coherent and complementary alternative to the male point of view; for Irigaray, however, the danger of fixity and the impossibility of closure always disrupt the stability of expressions of sexual difference in language.

Kristeva also reflects on the limits of language, specifically on the paradox for semiotics in postulating a heterogeneity that it then denies in the process of speaking about it. Like Nietzsche, she tries to deal with this paradox by making use of the heterogeneity in her own writing, "poetic language making free with the language code."[51] For Hartsock, in contrast, language is an unproblematic vehicle for the conveyance of meaning, and the feminist standpoint represents an advance toward greater human liberation. Hartsock hopes that "a feminist historical materialism might enable us to lay bare the laws of tendency that constitute the changing structure of patriarchy over time."[52] Similarly, Marilyn Frye calls on a notion of intelligibility that attributes to feminist discourse a certain transparency and completeness vis-à-vis women's lives:

One of the great powers of feminism is that it goes so far in making the experiences and lives of women intelligible. Trying to make sense of one's own feelings, motivations, desires, ambitions, actions and reactions without taking into account the forces which maintain the subordination of women to men is like trying to explain why a marble stops rolling without taking friction into account. . . . The measure of the success of the theory is just how much sense it makes of what did not make sense before.[53]

While nearly all feminists would agree that their feminism is valuable to them for the enhanced insight it provides, there are important differences over the source and the status of this insight. In Frye's version the phrase *makes sense* carries a great deal of unspecified weight; feminism is seen as unproblematically apprehending the true meaning of women's lives, and those women for whom some other discursive agenda makes sense (Christian or Muslim fundamentalism, for example, or positivism, or the law) are swept out of sight.

A suspicion that the unities interpretation trades in are posited rather than discovered animates genealogy's evasion of linguistic closure. This suspicion inspires, among other strategies, the substitution of verbs for nouns in genealogy's rhetorical practices; to speak, for example, of *valorizing* or *privileging* a point of view or table of values is a way of calling attention to the act that one is performing in valuing that phenomenon over others. This linguistic move denaturalizes the attribution of worth by emphasizing that the higher status has been accorded rather than discerned. Interpretivists tend to resist this rhetorical move for fear that it will pull the rug out from under the epistemological and moral foundations they seek for their political commitments.

Interpretation tends to seek explanations that rest on a search for origins: the origin of particular modes of domination, such as capitalism or patriarchy, or of foundations of knowledge, such as history or nature or god. Genealogy, in contrast, looks not for origins but "beginnings—numberless beginnings whose faint traces and hints of color are readily seen by a historical eye."[54] The search for origins seeks to articulate the basis from which things grow, to find in the outlines of early circumstances a unified pattern that gives birth to what comes after. The search for beginnings focuses on discontinuities, on the "profusion of entangled events," the "exteriority of accidents."[55] Foucault offers a clear explanation for this shift from origins to beginnings in his analysis of Nietzsche's view of history:

First, because it [the search for origins] is an attempt to capture the exact essence of things, their purest possibilities, and their carefully protected identities, because this search assumes the existence of immobile forms that precede the external world of accident and succession. This search is directed to "that which is already there," the image of a primordial truth fully adequate to its nature, and it necessitates the removal of every mask to ultimately disclose an original identity. However, if the genealogist refuses to extend his [sic] faith in metaphysics, if he listens to history, he finds that there is "something altogether different" behind things: not a timeless and essential secret, but the secret that they have no essence or that their essence was fabricated in a piecemeal fashion from alien forms . . . what is found at the historical beginnings of things is not the inviolable identity of their origin; it is the dissension of other things. It is disparity.[56]

The search for origins inclines interpretation to encounter radical otherness in a posture of inclusion by positing umbrella categories such as *rights* or *humanity* through which to draw the other into the discourse. It has the advantage of addressing the other as equal. The genealogist, on the other hand, fears that such equality is achieved at the price of sameness, and seeks instead power's diminution so that difference can enjoy greater safety within our accounts of things. The search for origins tends to postulate some prior wholeness, before language, or before conquest, or before writing, to which the interpretivist wishes to return or at least invoke. The shift away from origins loses the claim of a "fall" from innocence or completion; no original unity has been forfeited, so there is none to reclaim or to mourn.[57] Origin stories can also provide the justification (in the eyes of the believer) or rationalization (as seen by the skeptic) for the rules and regulations that follow the alleged end of innocence, thus making "the constitution of the law appear as a historical inevitability."[58] To look for beginnings rather than for origins shifts inquiry toward a history of accidents, disconnections and disparities; it initiates a mining of fields of meaning for the many possible stories they hold rather than the excavation of the one true story.

The kind of theorizing done in interpretation relies on the constitution of conceptual unities such as the category of women. Thus Hartsock states that "in addressing the institutionalized sexual division of labor, I propose to lay aside the important differences among women and instead to search for central commonalities across race and class boundaries." Justifying this move by appeal to Marx's similar oversimplification of capitalism into a two-class model, she is both troubled by "the danger of making invisible the experience of lesbians or women of color" and convinced that "there are some things common to all women's lives in Western class societies." The basis of this commonality is the sexual division of labor: "Women's activity as institutionalized has a double aspect: their contribution to subsistence and their contribution to childrearing. Whether or not all women do both, women as a sex are institutionally responsible for producing both goods and human beings, and all women are forced to become the kinds of persons who can do both."[59] Much of the power of the socialist feminist analysis comes from its insistence on the centrality of categories, of political economy, and its persistent pursuit of this single theme. Irigaray's evocation of multiplicity and contiguity contrasts vividly with this singleness: "But if the female imaginary were to deploy itself, if it could bring itself into play otherwise than as scraps, uncollected debris, would it represent itself, even so, in the form of one universe? Would it ever be volume instead of surface? No."[60]

Here the important point of contrast concerns the different strategies of theorizing. Both authors acknowledge that women have some experiences in common, and some important differences. The question is, How shall we ask questions about these commonalities and differences? The interpretive strategy sets aside the differences as less important than connections among women. Implicitly, it is a strategy that constitutes women as a unity in order to compare them with men. The genealogical strategy features the differences as central, using them as vehicles to break apart all unities. Judith Butler calls for "a critical genealogy of gender categories" as the "best way to trouble the gender categories that support gender hierarchy and compulsory heterosexuality."[61] Julie Wuthnow points out that feminists have reason to fear the recreation of phallogocentrism around categories of the one: one source of desire (the lost breast), or one source of the male attraction to death (severance from the mother), or one site of pleasure (the penis), or one identity for women.[62] "The question of woman in general," Gayatri Spivak suggests, "is *their* question, not *ours*."[63]

Feminist ambivalence over language is at least as much political as it is epistemological. Those who share the suspicion of unified categories of understanding, as Elizabeth Spelman does in *Inessential Woman*, fear that such categories will lull the users into forgetting "the constant human effort it takes to create and maintain classificatory schemes, the continual human battles over which schemes are to prevail, and the purposes of such schemes." Spelman's argument reflects a decade's lessons about tendencies toward white solipsism in feminist theory, and a corresponding concern over the effects of such exclusion on feminist politics: "A description of the common world we share 'as women' may be simply a description of my world with you now as an honorary member." At one point Spelman goes so far as to claim that "unless I know something more about two women than the fact that they are women, I can't say anything about what they might have in common."[64] While in other places she modifies this claim to allow for some search for commonality, the force of her argument is to call into question this category *women*.

The fear of elitism and desire for theoretical and political acknowledgment of difference on the genealogical side is matched by a fear of impotence and a desire for theoretical and political unity in the interpretive domain. Sandra Harding reminds us that those who defend the status quo have few reservations about their unities: "Can we afford to give up the necessity of trying to provide "one, true, feminist story of reality" in the face of deep alliances between science and sexist, racist, classist and imperialist social projects?"[65] While Harding's answer to this question calls on a combination of suspicion of and struggle toward unified categories of understanding, she echoes many other feminist activists in her concern that to give up on, or even express doubt about, unities such as the shared position of women is to sabotage one of the few advantages the oppressed possess—the power of their numbers when they come together. Some feminists appeal to the possibility of coalitions that could maintain political efficacy "without obedience to a normative telos of definitional closure" as a way of negotiating specific solidarities without presuming prior unities.[66] While, as I argue in Chapter 6, coalition politics may offer a way to mediate the clashes between interpretive hopes and genealogical subversions, it does not erase the metatheoretical differences that produce these clashes.

Politically, the interpretive project allows its practitioners to criticize the current situation in light of future possibilities and to ground their recommended actions in their claims to knowledge. The critical knowledge made possible by looking underneath the appearances of things to their underlying reality allows for a full (or at least fuller) comprehension of the entire arena of inquiry and also makes way for a vision of a better alternative. The genealogical project sees the search for liberation as itself participatory in the will to truth, or the will to power over truth, and more modestly seeks to unsettle the settled contours of knowledge and power, to make way for disunities and misfits, to let difference be. Both postures are disruptive of established power but in different ways; interpretation subverts the status quo in the service of a different order, while genealogy aims to shake up the orderedness of things. "I think that to imagine another system is to extend our participation in the present system," states Foucault.[67] Interpretation requires of political theory that it offer a direct, perhaps a deductive, link between the way things are and the way things ought to be, between ontology, morality, and politics, while genealogy claims that such a link is unavailable, not because of some inadequacy in theory but because of the excessiveness and contingency of living and of knowing. The interpretivist envisions a more enabling alternative toward which we are invited to struggle, while the genealogist insists that those structures and processes that we take to be thoroughly liberating will also be constraining. The interpretivist holds up for us a powerful vision of how things should be, while the genealogist more cautiously reminds us that things could be other than they are.

Irigaray's feminism includes aspects of both theoretical projects. Her main emphasis is on the feminine as disruptive of phallocratic discourse, on its resistance to systematization. Yet she sometimes voices a vision akin to Hartsock's:

Exchanges without identifiable terms, without accounts, without end . . . without additions and accumulations, one plus one, woman after woman . . . without sequence or number. Without standard or yardstick . . . use and exchange would be indistinguishable. The greatest value would be at the same time the least kept in reserve. Nature's resources would be expended without depletion, exchanged without labor, freely given, exempt from masculine transaction: enjoyment without a fee, well-being without pain, pleasure without possession. As for all the strategies and savings, the appropriations tantamount to theft and rape, the laborious accumulation of capital, how ironic all that would be.[68]

This lyric and utopian invocation of a world based on the female imaginary is not quite the same as envisioning a different system, since it deliberately lacks the rigor that systems usually entail. But it does suggest an alternative worth seeking; not exactly a different order, but a particular and preferred kind of disorder.

Interpretation does its work by employing a hermeneutics of suspicion. It carefully analyzes historical structures and processes or individual identities or theoretical formations in order to see past the misleading surface to the reality beyond. The surface of things offers us the official definition of reality, that which serves the interests of power or perpetuates comfortable illusions. Interpretation is alert to the hand of power in packaging and distributing common understandings, and is often able to subvert power's claims by showing who actually benefits from them (the bourgeoisie, or the state, or white people, or men). That done, interpretation can proceed to erect a new field of meaning by putting the previously marginal at the center of the theoretical terrain, allowing the proletariat to speak, or listening to women's voice. Both Hegel and Marx, in different ways, exemplify an interpretive politics of inclusivity by seeking to establish arenas of fundamental agreement into which elements that do not seem to fit can nonetheless be assimilated as ever higher unities are established.[69] Hartsock continues this interpretive politics in her articulation of a feminist standpoint, which is both a theoretical and a political practice:

The ability to go beneath the surface of appearances to reveal the real but concealed social relations requires both theoretical and political activity. Feminist theorists must demand that feminist theorizing be grounded in women's material life activity and must as well be a part of the political struggle necessary to develop areas of social life modeled on this activity. The outcome . . . could raise for the first time the possibility of a fully human community, a community structured by its variety of direct relations among people, rather than their separation and opposition.[70]

This promise of eventual culmination of historic struggles in a stage of final completion contrasts sharply with genealogical suspicions that, as Donna Haraway suggests, "there is no single feminist standpoint because our maps require too many dimensions for that metaphor to ground our visions."[71] Genealogy does its political work less directly, and is often seen by the advocates of interpretation as not doing much work at all. The word *deconstruction* suggests an unfortunate architectural metaphor, implying that genealogy only tears down meaning, while interpretation builds it back up. Yet genealogy does more than serve as the wrecking crew of political theory, although that would be no small contribution; it calls our attention to that which has been omitted, suggesting, although not requiring, a politics of difference. By pursuing a relentless history of particulars, and giving examples of misfits and anomalies, genealogy is "compelling us either to find ways to draw these misfits into the fold or to acknowledge the element of dissonance or artificiality within unities themselves."[72] While genealogy requires no particular ethical commitment, there is an ethic that it makes possible: the genealogical project allows us to recognize the political claims of those marginalized by the prevailing categories. This is clearly at work in Kristeva's attention to all those at the margins of power who can work their disruptive influence upon it. Connolly develops out of Nietzsche an "ethic of difference" that "counsels us to come to terms with difference and to seek ways to enable difference to be. It is an ethic of letting be. It calls into question the project of perfecting mastery of the world on the grounds that, given resistances built into the order of things, the project would reduce everything to a straightjacket while pursuing an illusory goal."[73]

The struggle within feminism between a politics of inclusivity and a politics of difference is not a reformulation of older conflicts between liberal feminist efforts to integrate women into existing institutions and radical feminist efforts to transform those institutions. While this tension also continues to plague us, since we must both live in the world and change it, the dispute between interpretation and genealogy is a struggle between two different radical feminisms.[74] To make arguments against male rule, feminists need to take (some dimensions of) women's experience as a unified starting point and in a sense capture it, generalize from it. To make arguments against rule itself, against the rule of binary gender categories over sexual difference, feminists need to deconstruct gender. Both are radical projects in the traditional sense: they go to the root of (what each defines as) the problem, but the first proceeds in the name of a sought-for transformation of political conditions while the second seeks an ongoing subversion.

Genealogy typically employs disruptive and violent rhetorical devices to call our attention to the role that more docile tropes and narratives play in reassuring us of the stability and completeness of familiar interpretive accounts.[75] In her intimate juxtapositions of narratives from science and science fiction, for example, Donna Haraway calls attention to that which is implicitly privileged or silenced in each. By forcing contrasting genres into conversation, she "facilitate[s] revisionings of fundamental, persistent western narratives" about difference, reproduction, and survival.[76] By characterizing her own interpretive "triple filter of race, gender, and science" as a "trap," while continuing to use it skillfully for feminist ends, she calls attention to discursive practices as necessarily imposing themselves on the world rather than merely receiving it.[77] Derrida's deconstructive strategies are even more explosive with regard to the politics of enunciation: his metaphors slip and slide in many directions as he continually finds and claims space for the otherness within the text. By pointing out, for example, that the term *pharmakon* can translate as remedy, or poison, or recipe, or drug, Derrida draws attention to the violence involved in settling upon a single meaning.[78] By slipping among various associations of terms such as spur (prow of a ship, rocky point upon which waves break, trace, wake, indication, mark, spurn) or of *des voiles* (veils, sails) or of style/stylus (pen, sword, penis, thrust, inscribe, protect), he calls attention to the multiple possibilities that burst forth in texts, but gain no final stability (despite coercive interventions by authors and readers).[79] Derrida's "guerrilla warfare with Truth" may seem evasive to the interpretively inclined, but his point is that conventional logocentric writing conducts its own evasions when it ducks the fertile field of possibilities lying within it.[80] The history of the emergence of various interpretive codes is examined by genealogists to remind us of our history of constructing unities and pretending they are discoveries. The genealogist, in short, is a major inconvenience to deal with during and after the revolution, particularly for those who are convinced that there is no echo of their enemies in themselves.

Ironic Convergences and Common Front Politics

The advocates of these projects often speak as if the two were in total opposition, as if genealogy and interpretation had nothing in common. But the projects connect to one another in important ways. Genealogy, first of all, depends on interpretation to provide something to deconstruct. Beyond this, one follows the genealogical position to a return to interpretation. Because the world turns us no legible face, because nothing stands under the layers of constituted meaning except other layers of constituted meaning, one returns to interpretation with the fragile understanding that interpretation of various kinds is *all that there is*. The genealogist thus indirectly confesses her rootedness in interpretation, her "hermeneutic anchor."[81] Similarly, genealogy leads us back to the newly problematized subject, addressing us as embodied subjects and calling our attention to "the haunting sense of a lost potential of human being in the modern world . . . the voice of a subject deeply injured."[82] Seeking a place for the body in a world ruthlessly cognitive, and a place for spontaneity in a world overly organized, genealogy calls not so much for the end of the subject as for the end of the hegemony of the modern subject. One could still pursue (as I hope to do in later chapters) other forms of subjectivity that might be less colonized by and more resistant to the disciplinary strategies of modernity.

Interpretation's need for genealogy is less obvious, since one of the traits of interpretation is that it seeks a big picture that can stand alone in its comprehension of the world. Yet rebel interpretations often find themselves in need of genealogical strategies of investigation in order to push aside the hegemonic claims of dominant interpretations, such as those of racism or capitalism or patriarchy, to make discursive room for themselves. The deconstruction of the claims of power is always important to projects that attempt to dislodge and supplant such claims, and genealogy can open those doors effectively. Interpretation often scorns genealogy, attributing to it a lack of political commitment and an absence of moral sensibility. But the argument that history is in great part beyond our control, the outcome of strategies of power "without a subject," does not necessarily imply that changes are impossible; it is perhaps a more humble expectation for systemic change than many interpretivists prefer, but it does not eliminate hopes for change altogether. Rather, it warns us about the dangers inherent for the project of liberation itself in efforts to achieve it; this is a message of no small significance to those who want their struggles to lead to something other than the reconstitution of the old regime.

Neither does the argument that every form of life contains some constraining elements, and that these are often found in the places where liberation was most thoroughly anticipated, necessarily leave one to conclude that all forms of social life subjugate equally. Interpretation needs the constant interruption that genealogy can provide, that irritated, irritating interanimation of incompatible perspectives.[83] Genealogy tells us not that nothing is worth endorsing, but that claims of worthiness must themselves be scrutinized for their tendency to echo that which they oppose. One need not have a model of absolute liberation in order to identify forms of order imposing greater or lesser constraint or enablement. Connolly makes this point: "[Genealogy] is not an adversary of interpretation or of political affirmation as such but of those modes of interpretation and affirmation that insist on treating the subject or the community or something beyond them as a unified ground of human being. Genealogy alerts us to voices of otherness subdued by expressivist and rationalist modes of discursive practice."[84] Genealogy is incomplete because it directs our attention to the imposition of order on the world rather than to the losses and gains operating within particular orders.[85] But its incompleteness tells us something about the practice of theorizing: to expect one's understandings of the world clearly and neatly to specify values and actions, to expect some sort of deductive link between what is, what ought to be, and what must be done, is a kind of will to truth. It expects theory to be too clean, too whole, too all-of-a-piece.

Genealogy and interpretation can thus be seen as postures toward power and knowledge that need one another. Nevertheless they stand in irreducible tension and cannot be cordially joined. Neither is sufficient to a full feminist (or any other) political theory; each contains characteristic problems that the other is quick to address. Genealogy ruthlessly pursued tends to avoid the problem of political action, not because it is incapable of allowing for political distinctions and moral claims, but because the evocation of difference does not in itself tell us which differences are most worthy of our attention. On one level the call for the deconstruction of gender, the loosening of the identities and coherencies organized around male and female, is a radical project that strikes at the categories that enable sexism to exist. But if enormous inequalities between women and men are left intact, the deconstruction of gender may simply legitimate that inequality by disguising it, and rob women of the capacity for resistance and struggle that our own voice can provide. Interpretation ruthlessly pursued tends to avoid recognition of its own will to power over truth, subduing dissonances inconvenient to its unities. In one respect the articulation of a gynocentric perspective is a radical project that suggests an alternative to patriarchal arrangements and gives reasons to prefer it. However, the construction of a feminist standpoint can easily recreate the discursive practices of phallocentrism, disguising and forgetting its own participation in the imposition of order. In feminism the genealogical and interpretive projects need to listen to one another; genealogy keeps interpretation honest, and interpretation gives genealogy direction.

The lack of a smooth transition between the two projects, despite their need for one another, suggests that the practice of feminist theory is filled with tensions and stressed by opposing forms. One way of dealing with these opposing strategies of inquiry would be to outline their shortcomings in order to urge transcendence toward a position that draws the best points from both while going beyond their limitations.[86] Yet this call for transcendence, however comforting, is itself deeply implicated in the interpretive project, in that it assumes a narrative of progress toward higher unities. An alternative to rallying around the call for transcendence is to recruit the rhetorical and political resources of irony. "Irony," Donna Haraway argues, "is about contradictions that do not resolve into larger wholes, even dialectically, about the tension of holding incompatible things together because both or all are necessary and true. Irony is about humor and serious play."[87] Irony is a particularly appropriate strategy for feminism because it calls upon two virtues historically associated with women (who?): the recognition of limits and the struggle to continue. It also calls upon the laughter of women to serve as antidote to the longing for completion, recruiting humor in the form of an ironic shrug at the intransigence of being toward knowing. One can think about irony as a kind of doubleness that can take many forms.[88] It can appear as the slippage between what is said and what is meant, or between what is said and what can be understood, or between what is indicated and what is implied or evaded, or between stability and motion. Irony is not the same as sarcasm, although it can slide in that direction; sarcasm is the weapon and the excuse of the cynic, a way of distancing oneself and forestalling the need for political action. Cynicism can readily accompany despair, and express despair with a sharp tongue, while irony fends off despair by accepting its less fatal companion, ambiguity. Irony is a way to keep oneself within a situation that resists resolution in order to act politically without pretending that resolution has come. It is not a substitute for other forms of political struggle, but a vehicle for enabling political actions that resist the twin dangers of paralysis (nothing can be done because no final truth can be found) and totalization (there is one way to do things and it reflects the truth that has been found).

Irony is not without its own dangers, since as a political and epistemological strategy it requires participants who are attentive to doubleness. They must hear the gap between the spoken and the silent, between what is said and what is meant or can be heard.[89] They must tolerate, even appreciate, the back-and-forth between competing insinuations while they keep sight of the connections between them.[90] Irony is further complicated by its implicit relationship to some form of trust; without some reliable shared ground among speakers and listeners, irony turns into deceit and one risks being lied to or made a fool of. Irony's workings can nonetheless recruit humor to politically important ends. By using overstatement, irony makes otherwise ordinary events outrageous, problematizing them through farce. The film "Sammy and Rosie Get Laid," for example, uses overstatement to dramatize the power relations among the characters; in one scene a white woman walks unseeing and self-absorbed through a noisy urban riot; in another a young black man enacts a pantomine of servitude through the elaborate care he takes to move a television set to suit an older and more powerful Pakistani man, who participates in the parody by giving elaborate "commands" for a simple task. By exaggerating subservience and authority, they subvert them.

Understatement can also call on humor to problematize a situation, saying less than could be said while suggesting that there is much more to say. In "The 'Mechanics' of Fluids," an essay that brings together metaphors of science with metaphors of gender, Irigaray advises the reader in her first footnote "to consult some texts on solid and fluid mechanics."[91] The statement leaves much unsaid. *Some texts* is useless to the reader as a reference. It suggests the futility of referring to science's own self-understanding, and at the same time it mocks the practices of footnoting. By ironically disqualifying science's own accounts of the mechanics of fluids, Irigaray opens up a space for a different set of metaphors, those of gender, to do their work.

Although one can talk about what irony can do and give examples of it, one cannot capture it readily within a definition. There is no point in trying to set rules for irony. While it is usually thought of as a practice of reading or of writing, it can also be conceived more broadly as a temperament, a sensibility, a stance toward the status of meaning in life, an art.[92] Only so much can be indicated by words on a page, no matter what their antics; irony is also in bodies—their postures, expressions, presentations, decorations, omissions—and in kinds of gestures words alone cannot make: the collective political gestures of defying authority, for example, in massive civil disobedience. Without a lot of irony, public life becomes deadly, in many senses of the word.

To feminists and other activists, irony has often seemed an unacceptably apolitical practice, "an attitude of unending skepticism and eternal fatalism," a detached, noncommittal rhetorical technique to indicate uninvolvement.[93] Others find irony irrelevant to public life, arguing that its sabotage of secure foundations renders it irrevocably antagonistic to politics.[94] One anonymous feminist reader commented that irony might be a private vice but never a public virtue. She shared the fear of Aristotle and Hegel that irony is dangerous to political order, that it "takes something seriously only to promote its trivialization."[95] But I believe that irony offers resources untapped by such an apolitical stance. Following John Seery, I seek to take irony "in a positive direction, signifying an ethos, a mode of consciousness, a spirit, that tends toward politics and the political."[96] I view irony as a companion to feminisms' other political commitments, not as a substitute for them. Irony can be a public virtue for feminism when it enables political action that is both committed to its values and attentive to its incompleteness. Particular hermeneutic anchors become temporary resting points rather than fixed foundations; political goals and organizational arrangements become points of ongoing negotiation and contestation rather than permanent foundings. By giving doubt and partiality a place of honor within feminist theory, I want to bring them into conversation with hope and certainty, not drive them underground.

An ironic stance toward/within politics may seem like a practice entirely indebted to genealogy. But it makes an important contribution to facilitating feminist interpretations as well. It can invite us into perspectives not our own and give us access to standpoints not easily achieved more directly. This happens in Donna Haraway's "Teddy Bear Patriarchy."[97] A genealogical perspective is thoroughly manifested; yet Haraway also recruits the reader into the animals' point of view (and of course defines that point of view in the process). In her account of Carl Akeley's taxidermic constructions for the Africa exhibit at the American Museum of Natural History in New York City, Haraway makes available a perspective that might be called the gorilla's point of view—not directly, since it is difficult to assert with confidence that the human writer "knows what it is like" to be a gorilla (perhaps like being a human, only hairier?). A direct appeal for empathy with the animal does not offer a sufficient point of entry; empathy can readily be recruited into a gesture of appropriation (as in "I know just what you mean" when I really don't know at all). "Empathy," Haraway notes, "is part of the western scientific tool kit, kept in constant productive tension with its twin, objectivity."[98]

Empathy with the animals is made available indirectly in Haraway's account, in a way less dependent on denial of difference, through ironic strategies of juxtaposition, doubleness, and innuendo. Her constant and vivid references to Akeley's hunting and stuffing practices displace more familiar narratives about science and safaris to make a place for a consideration of the possible perspectives of the hunted. "From the dead body of the primate, Akeley crafted something finer than the living organism; he achieved its true end, a new genesis."[99] The "essence of their life" as Akeley constructed it (i.e., perfect specimens living nobly in families) is retained in "a spiritual vision made possible only by their death and literal re-presentation."[100] The exhibit in the African hall is referred to as "their sepulcher."[101] For those who remember the Vietnam War, it is a familiar logic: Akeley killed the gorilla in order to save him (for science). Haraway refers ironically to the "danger" to Akeley and his fellow hunters, implicitly contrasting their self-congratulatory "great white hunter" narrative with the actual deaths of gorilla after gorilla at their hands.[102] She notes the "healing gaze" offered to the living human viewer by the dead animals in the Africa exhibit, "the specular commerce between man and animal at the interface of two evolutionary ages," leaving no doubt as to who can be healed and who has paid.[103]

Akeley's longing to see the face of his prey, his alter ego in its natural state, matches his immediate desire to kill it, to make it a specimen. He resides vigorously and unthinkingly in his Akeley-centric world; the gorillas are *for him*. After a bit of filming of a small group of gorillas, Akeley notes: "So, finally, feeling that I had about all I could expect from that band, I picked out one that I thought to be an immature male. I shot and killed it and found, much to my regret, that it was a female. As it turned out, however, she was such a splendid large specimen that the feeling of regret was considerably lessened."[104] After killing one gorilla, he films the escape of the others: "The guns were put behind and the camera pushed forward and we had the extreme satisfaction of seeing the band of gorillas disappear over the crest of the opposite ridge none the worse for having met with white men that morning. It was a wonderful finish to a wonderful gorilla hunt."[105] He had "all that he could expect" so it was time for some killing; they were "none the worse for having met with white men," except that one of them was dead.

Akeley himself evades the bitter ironies of his quest by his earnest appeals to science; looking down on a kill, he remarks, "it took all one's scientific ardour to keep from feeling like a murderer."[106] He tells his story to himself, Haraway notes, as one of "a pure man whose danger in pursuit of a noble cause brings him into communion with nature through the beasts he kills."[107] Haraway makes this narrative escape unavailable to her readers, opening the way toward consideration of what might follow once the appellation *murderer* is taken seriously. The effect is of a truth both produced and discerned, thus inviting the reader into the realm of interpretive explanation where that feeling of recognition, of felt truth, offers itself for apprehension.[108] It is a leap of faith to get there. The bridge is not purely verbal, nor is it presented directly. Indeed, to make a direct claim for immediate access to the gorilla's point of view would imply that the otherness of the gorillas could be folded without difficulty into the contours of the human world. But there are indirect and imaginative ways to enter into such truth claims, and irony is one of them. Haraway's ironies offer the reader access to a different standpoint and reasons to embrace it. Her approach allows a move toward a politics of inclusivity, toward including the gorillas as participants in the available field of vision of the human reader, without denying or erasing the differences such inclusions encounter. Haraway's irony sidesteps the difficulties that cosmic feminism gets into when it tries for a one-to-one correspondence between human and other-than-human worlds, and at the same time accomplishes that connection. When one reads of the elaborate grave prepared for Akeley in the rainforests of Zaire, one cannot help asking, furiously, Why didn't they stuff *him*?

Interpretation produces the stories we tell about ourselves, and genealogy insists on interrogating those stories, on producing stories about the stories. This interrogation could go on forever: stories about stories about stories about . . . ; the infinite regress of metatheory. But that evasive maneuver need not dominate the field. One can insist on (unstable) bridges between interpretation and genealogy, ironically constructed, with a commitment to continue combined with a recognition of limits. This is a central virtue for coalition politics, where one must find common ground for collective action with people who may think, act, and live in unfamiliar or unattractive ways. In coalition politics acceptance of incompleteness is crucial. Many areas of disagreement must be allowed to continue while specific areas of agreement are hammered out. Persistence in the face of acknowledged limitations is well served by an ironic sensibility toward one's expectations.

An ironic stance allows us to hold together needed incompatibles, to stay honest and keep moving at the same time. Through the resources of irony we can think about how we do feminist theory and about what notions of reality and truth make our theories possible. From genealogy we learn that being will not be fully and completely known, that there is no single being waiting for our knowing to apprehend it. From interpretation we learn the necessity of putting things together as fully as we can from where we are. The tension between longing for and being wary of a secure ontological and epistemological home, if handled ironically, need not be a source of despair; it can instead produce an appropriate humility concerning theory and an ability to sustain the contrary pull of continuing to want what cannot be fully had. Rather than think of the tensions between the interpretive and genealogical impulses as contradictions that we must resolve, we might better approach them as riddles that we must engage, in which affirmations are always tied to ambiguity and resolutions to endless deferral.

Chapter Two

Male-Ordered Subjectivity

During the late middle ages and the Renaissance, representatives of the Catholic church debated the question "Are women human?"[1] This particularly blatant casting of the woman question might suggest to feminists an equally crude response. With regard to questions of subjectivity, the man question might prompt us to ask Are men human? Atrocities performed by male heads of governments, corporations, churches and families could be entered as evidence for a negative verdict, while protests about one's own sons, husbands, brothers, and friends might weigh toward a positive answer (assuming that one believes that *human* is a category one might aspire to).

Another reversal feminism might commit against patriarchy, this one against psychoanalytic rather than church fathers, suggests another question, What do men want? This question shifts the inquiry in the direction of desire and examines what men as a group seek rather than their status within the species. But it still suggests that men (and by implication women) can be taken as a group in which most or all are essentially the same. And it still has that whiff of crudeness to it, suggesting a certain low-minded revenge, a transparent effort to elevate the low and depose the high.

Is there a form of reversal that doesn't smack of simple reproduction of patriarchal strategies and practices, that doesn't simply threaten to do to men some version of what they have done to us? Well, no—and yes. No, in that most forms of feminist interpretation, most efforts to construct a worldview that privileges women, still play the female side of the male/female dyad. Thus the basic dualism that enables patriarchy to exist, the opposition of male/

masculine to female/feminine, is reproduced and maintained. But this is not the whole story, both because feminist reversals serve different political ends from those of their patriarchal predecessors, and because these reversals confront challenges from within feminism itself. Feminist reversals have their discontents, their troublesome genealogical comrades agitating for the explosion or disintegration of gender categories. Chapter 1 explored the relation between these two impulses at the level of metatheory; the remaining chapters look at some notions of subjectivity that these two strategies of inquiry both reflect and produce.

Despite a certain sly appeal, the questions, Are men human? and What do men want? are inadequate to the task of asking the man question in relation to subjectivity. The categories *men* and *human* reside too comfortably within these sentences, suggesting fixed arrangements with solid boundaries and readily available criteria for membership. Practices of desire and claims to humanness, however, are at least partly produced through complex discursive and institutional practices. They cannot be assessed without consideration of those practices. And practices that position themselves as oppositional (feminisms, for example) often find resources for their critiques in the positions they oppose, suggesting complex negotiations between interanimating views rather than simple and complete oppositions. A better way to engage the man question with regard to subjectivity might be to ask, What kinds of subjectivity, what vision of what it means to be a person, characterize the patriarchal world? What have men made out of personhood?

Even this question is too broad. It implies that patriarchal notions of subjectivity have been everywhere the same, when historical and geographic differences abound. But if one centers one's inquiry in the modern western world, the question takes a more coherent shape. One can then ask, What are the dominant notions of subjectivity in modern, western, patriarchal society? What has the modern, male-ordered world made of identity? Feminist responses to this question can articulate their disputes with the hegemonic formulations while still allowing inquiry into continuities and repetitions as well. Desire is still available as a point of entry into the arena of subjectivity, since desire ultimately takes us back to some version of the subject. Even when constituted as a force or energy operating agentless in the world, desire is always, ultimately, someone's (human or otherwise) desire. Desire is more useful as a verb than a noun in that it is something that is done, something that happens. The verb poses a question, allows us to ask what kind of person could do this sort of desiring, and what other kinds of desiring and other kinds of persons there might be.

Many feminist writers have noted a persistent tendency in western political thought to equate maleness with humanness. Susan Bordo sees in Descartes's early articulations of scientific method a "flight from the feminine" and a corresponding effort to assuage the pain of separation by aggressively converting it into rejection and conquest. Hannah Pitkin finds a similar desperation over autonomy that conceals a fear of engulfment by feminine forces in Machiavelli. In Hobbes's account of human nature and social order Christine Di Stefano reads a stress on differentiation and conflict in which fear and denial of the maternal goes hand in hand with a grim and instrumental politics.[2]

In her aptly titled essay "Any Theory of the 'Subject' Has Always Been Appropriated by the 'Masculine,' " Luce Irigaray echoes the suspicions of these and other feminists that the notions of subjectivity dominant in western life are relentlessly male.[3] The subjectivity claimed by men and denied to women typically constitutes the self as bounded agent in the world, the center of all things, active, reflective, coinciding neatly (immediately or eventually) with itself. This subject often designates itself "humanist" to establish that which is essentially the same for all humans and distinguishes the human from the other-than-human world. Women in male humanist discourse have generally been among those others, consigned to the world of the acted-upon, of otherness colonized in the service of maintaining the sameness of the subject. All male-ordered constructions of subjectivity do not necessarily figure women in the same terms; their commonality comes from their shared strategies of configuration. Like the orientalism Edward Said brilliantly portrays, phallocentrism "depends for its strategy on [a] flexible *positional* superiority, which puts the Westerner [/male] in a whole series of possible relationships with the Orient [/woman] without ever losing him the relative upper hand." As cultural apparatus, phallocentrism, like orientalism, is "all aggression, activity, judgement, will-to-truth, and knowledge."[4]

Paralleling the ways in which the orient appears to the west, women can be many different things to men so long as men name them. From a male-ordered perspective, a man can "really admire women" in the same way, for example, that Balfour admitted the greatness of Egypt while the English government decided Egypt's colonial fate. One can readily reconstitute Balfour's logic around the axis of gender: "Men know women; women are what men know; men know that women cannot be independent; men confirm that by denying women independence; for women, women are what men have taken over and control."[5] In the intertwining discursive formations of racial and gender dominance, parallel discursive strategies produce and maintain the privileges of men/whites/the west by constituting women/people of color/the east as other and lesser.

In the articulation of western discourses of subjectivity that privilege masculinity, Hegel is a pivotal figure. Like Hobbes, Descartes, and Machiavelli, Hegel's fingerprints are all over contemporary notions of selfhood and desire. His arguments figure prominently in the evolution of both interpretive strategies of inquiry and their genealogical counterparts. Indeed, Hegel could well be regarded as the master of the metanarrative, as well as one who is mastered by it. In relation to interpretation, he insists that we keep our metanarratives in order because they provide the secure historical foothold we need to ground political actions and moral commitments. In relation to genealogy, he suggests the possibility of asking metatheoretical questions of one's own metanarratives (because he is so skilled at asking them of others), thus risking that order and endangering that foundation. In both its interpretive and its genealogical formulations, feminism struggles sometimes to elude Hegel and sometimes to put him to work; either way, as Foucault notes, it is difficult entirely to escape from Hegel.[6]

Hegel does not stand out as intensely reactionary on the woman question; in fact, he grants women "certain significant legal rights" and takes care to mark the virtues attendant on women's familial domain.[7] Nor does he stand out as prescient for later feminisms, since the place he stakes out and praises for women is outside the dialectic of labor and struggle through which fully human consciousness arises. Nor, finally, is he particularly interesting as a child of his time. He declined to engage contemporary ferment on sexual matters.[8] Neither the best nor the worst of the male-ordered thinkers on the woman question, Hegel has significance for this project because of his rich, robust concentration on subjectivity and knowledge. He looked deeply into the intricacies of the emergence of the modern subject and the practices of knowing that can produce and sustain such a subject; and if he was more pleased with the outcome than feminists have any reason to be, he can nonetheless offer a map of its production that is fruitful in charting feminist disputes with, as well as recognizing feminist dependencies on, modernity's knowing subject.

The struggle of lordship and bondage in *The Phenomenology of Mind* has proved a potent metaphor for analyzing power and subjectivity for many subsequent theorists, including interpretivists, genealogists, and feminists.[9] Hegel is perhaps the primary theorist of otherness for the Enlightenment's reasoning subject, the completed, self-defining self, the self as walled city. He traces that subject's emergence and makes strong claims for its virtues. He has great confidence in modernity, seeing it as the culmination of a history of struggle. Neither ironic nor tragic, Hegel's modernity is the answer to earlier ironies and tragedies (with the exception, Hegel mused, of those necessary but inconvenient women). He thus frames the central issues of modern subjectivity with and against which feminism works. While very different from Hobbes in his teleology of development toward greater community, from Descartes in his approach to reflection, and from Machiavelli in his expectations of the state, Hegel shares with these and other figures in western thought an insistence on the primacy of separation and conflict over interconnection and affirmation and on the constitution of desire via domination.

Hegel is often taken to be a particularly difficult thinker, more often quoted than read. I believe he's worth the effort. Feminist interrogations of his views can reveal what is at stake in struggles over identity and desire. My considerations of Hegel are framed by the questions that contemporary feminisms implicitly put to him. Where many feminists valorize an intersubjectively constituted, relational subjectivity, Hegel portrays human consciousness as shaped primarily by domination, subordination, and death. Whereas a strong voice in contemporary feminism calls for an ecologically generous subjectivity, one that participates in rather than dominates the physical world, Hegel embraces modernity's project of mastering and utilizing nature. Whereas many feminists emphasize the opacities and contingencies marking both consciousness and history, Hegel strives for a mode of reason that can convey a fully transparent comprehension of life. And the privilege that many feminists accord to difference contrasts with Hegel's absorption of otherness into ever higher syntheses. In these ways Hegel has assisted in putting a decidedly masculine account of self and other into circulation as *the* human experience. Yet feminist efforts to critique this account and to offer alternative visions of identity often draw upon the resources that Hegel's investigations have made available. A consideration of Hegel's analysis of subjectivity and desire can provide a clearer picture of at least one take on the male-ordered notions of subjectivity that feminisms confront.[10]

Identity and Desire in Hegel

Hegel's famous analysis of the relation of lord and bondsman (or master and slave) is one moment in his account of the history of consciousness, which is also the history of the world. *The Phenomenology of Mind* is the autobiography both of the spirit of the world, as manifested in the most fundamental self-understandings of different epochs, and of the identity of individuals in that world. It is the story of a traveler journeying through the stages of the emergence of consciousness in both the individual and the species. As the traveler passes through the stages of sense certainty, conceptual understanding, stoicism, skepticism, and unhappy consciousness, he continually comes to know himself through a dialectical process of opposition and negation. Each stage of consciousness and history is subverted by what it generates but cannot contain, and it transcends this subversion through incorporation. Like the traveler, thought itself is also in motion, always involved in internal struggles in which different moments of experience clash and are *aufgehoben* (simultaneously maintained, negated and transcended). The Hegelian subject always has to go outside itself in order to know what is inside; by seeing itself reflected in the world it discovers relations constitutive of itself.

As Richard Bernstein has pointed out, the dialectic of master and slave "is only one brief moment in the realization of *Geist*," and its parameters describe a clash not just between individuals or between groups but also within the individual Unhappy Consciousness.[11] Charles Taylor argues against arresting Hegel's concept of the subject in the master/slave dialectic, since the rationality of the transformations Hegel charts lies in their processes of coming to be and passing away, and the unfolding logic that engineers and is revealed by these processes. For Taylor, no single external manifestation completely expresses this rationality: "Spirit never comes to one unchanging expression which says it all, but in the play of affirmation and denial it manifests what it is."[12] Granting these points, it is still the case that the master/slave relation sets the stage for interactions in other dialectical moments of Hegel's story; in it "the seeds of self-consciousness are sown."[13] In the encounter of lord and bondsman self-consciousness articulates its sociality; "it *is* only by being acknowledged or 'recognized.' "[14] This stage can be examined for its patterns of affirmation and denial, negation and transcendence. In the confrontation of lord and bondsman a particularly potent stage in the evolution of consciousness is articulated, and a decidedly male-ordered metaphor of identity and desire is put into circulation.

The setting for the story of lord and bondsman is the human quest for identity, for a unified subjectivity, wholeness, independence, autonomy, and self-sufficiency. This quest can only be fulfilled by recognition of an other who also possesses self-consciousness (that is, not a non-human animal or a plant). Because each person wants this acknowledgment, wants to command this recognition from the other, a struggle ensues. Each wants to be the essential, the primary one, and to render the other inessential so as to command his recognition. The one who wins the struggle does so not actually by killing the other (for that would leave no one to give recognition) but by being prepared to kill the other and to die in the fight. The one's willingness to kill and to die intimidates the other into submission. The first becomes the master/lord, the second the slave/bondsman.

The dialectical twists and turns of the master's journey are complex and ultimately self-defeating. The master seems to win; he holds the other in subordination; he commands the slave's acknowledgment and his labor. The master thus escapes the world of necessity. But his lordship proves self-subverting: his independence turns out to be dependency on another for acknowledgment and for material support. The more the master succeeds (at subordinating the other) the more he fails (at being independent). So lordship passes into its opposite; it becomes bondage.

The slave, on the other hand, seems to lose. The slave becomes the inessential, a thing, and labors in the world of things for the master. The slave internalizes the master's view of himself, learns to see himself as inferior, and lives in the shadow of the fear of "death, the sovereign master."[15] But the slave does real work; he is involved in shaping the world of things to meet human need and to create objects with permanence and utility. Through this he develops a sense of self, of his importance and of the master's dependence on him. The slave also has a handy opportunity to think over the dilemmas of life in the face of death, thus acquiring greater self-consciousness.[16] So bondsmanship passes into its opposite, becomes "real and true independence."[17] Hegel's hopes for liberation reside, ultimately, with the bondsman, or, more accurately, with what the bondsman has it in him to become.

In *Subjects of Desire* Judith Butler emphasizes that the scenes of lordship and bondage are "instructive fictions" for Hegel rather than literal portrayals of the human condition.[18] Granting this, one can still ask why these fictions rather than others are recruited to illuminate the development of subjectivity, and what possibilities are vanquished or silenced when such metaphors are deployed. As Butler goes on to note, "The dialectic of lord and bondsman is implicitly a struggle with the generalized problem of life."[19] What, then, from feminist perspectives, can we make of this portrayal of life?

There are at least four major points of entry into Hegel's argument for those with feminist concerns. The first involves the primacy of domination and death; the second, the subordination of nature; the third, the faith in language and self-reflection; the fourth, the absorption of difference.

The Primacy of Domination

For Hegel, the primary encounter with otherness is located in the fear of violent death and in the ensuing struggle. Self-consciousness and consciousness of the other are rooted in domination and inequality. Initially consciousness itself is rooted in death, since it is the awareness of the inevitability of death, the crisis of mortality, that makes man a conscious subject and distinguishes him from other animals. Then the life/death struggle between lord and bondsman ensues. Finally the circle of death is widened through war, the repetition of the master/slave struggle between groups and nations. Death is seen as the negation of life, as life's defeat in struggle. The metaphor of the traveler features and normalizes the sense of emptiness and rootlessness that characterizes his subject, preparing the reader for a dangerous solitary journey rather than some more secure and cooperative scene.[20]

Absent from Hegel's account is any other possibility of relationship, any other starting point for interaction, than one of conflict and domination. Speaking of the lord/bondsman struggle, Hegel says "each must aim at the death of the other, as it risks its own life thereby; for that other is to it of no more worth than itself; the other's reality is presented to the former as an external other, as outside itself; it must cancel that externality."[21] The freedom and the embodiedness of the other threaten the initial self. The other's freedom is a threat because the self thought freedom was his alone; corporeality threatens because it divides us from one another so completely that we can never be certain of one another.[22]

When read as a portrait of interactions between individuals, Hegel's account suggests a manly struggle for superiority between men otherwise bereft of self-constitutive relations. The self portrayed here is a kind of walled city, self-protective and combative. It is "independent, shut up within itself, and there is nothing in it which is not there through itself."[23] But why privilege so completely this ideology of isolation and conflict? Many human experiences are not adequately apprehended here: for example, the relations often found between mother and child, brothers and sisters, or friends. Why not privilege interconnection and mutuality, then account for their disruptions? Or name them as clashing possibilities, neither inherently prior to the other? It is not simply that Hegel's subject lacks relations; it is that the only relations Hegel can envision lack affirmation within themselves; they derive whatever reward they carry from their ever-increasing proximity to the culmination of Hegel's historical telos.

A second possible interpretation of the struggle between lord and bondsman roots it in history rather than in psychology, that is, locates it in Hegel's account of the emergence of early Greek society. When the story of master and slave is read not as a portrayal of individual consciousness so much as an imaginative historical reenactment of a battle between heroes from competing tribes, the contours of its portrayal of subjectivity shift somewhat. Now each "honored chieftain" represents his tribe, coming up against his opponent as a member of that tribe rather than as an individual.[24] Each struggles to win and to carry his tribe to dominance. Each brings his companions "as witnesses of his exploits, and his defenders in peril" and each seeks the immortality that poetic renditions of heroic battles can offer.[25] In this reading the fighters do not lack significant relations so much as they are sunk in them; each is so embedded in his collective tribal identity that he is able to act only as a member of the group, not as an individual. Lacking the capacity to reflect critically upon relations, the master and slave still operate as a kind of walled city, only this time the whole clan is inside the respective walls of each man. Connolly speculates on the possibilities offered by this reading: "Perhaps the early combatants in the struggle for supremacy which results are Greek warriors, each acknowledged to be noble in his own clan, and each seeking to wrest the recognition he needs from another noble being. But in leaving the dialectic unspecified Hegel reminds us that its echoes continue to reverberate within cultures which have transcended the objectivity of early Greek life."[26]

Although this reading, which follows Hegel's dialectic when it completes its story of the emergence of consciousness and starts over at the level of culture, seems very different from the first, the two configurations of the master/slave relation both issue from intersubjectively crippled selves. Neither interpretation describes a self that has the capacity to reflect upon the contours of relations, to attend selectively to mutually self-constitutive interactions based on concern or appreciation. Neither portrayal imagines subjects who can apprehend feeling as a form of knowing or who have access to a language that could make sense of, much less practice, love or care. Being completely stuck within a collective identity is not so different from being completely cut off from one: both positions disallow the articulation of a language or a politics capable of reflection on particular intersubjectivities or non-aggressive negotiations with otherness.

Several feminist writers have pointed to the traits of abstract masculinity written into Hegel's subject and its desires.[27] Caroline Whitback comments that "if a mother saw the emerging person

who is her child in the way that Hegel describes, human beings
would not exist." Kristeva argues that when identities and desires
are viewed as embodied rather than abstract, Hegel's subject becomes a problematic "paranoid" personality of the kind that capitalism requires. Jessica Benjamin suggests a psychoanalytic reading of Hegel, finding there a view of self-other relations that abrogates
the possibility of a constant tension-within-interaction in order to
declare a winner and a loser. Hélène Cixous notes that "unfortu-
nately, Hegel isn't inventing things." That is, she views Hegel's
account as accurately characterizing the dominant self-other relations of phallocentrism: "We are still living under the Empire of
the Selfsame." [28] Into this account women are either recruited as
supporting cast or written out of the script entirely.

Even the very generous reading of Hegel offered by Butler still
raises questions of gender with regard to his subject. Butler asks,
"Why did the journeying subject of the *Phenomenology* begin its
journey alone, and why was its confrontation with the sensuous and
perceptual world previous to its confrontation with an Other?" [29]
She sidesteps the simplest answer to this question—"Because it's
male!"—and answers that, for Hegel, the Other was there all along,
but was not yet thematized because it had not yet become an object of desire. Desire, she points out, develops in stages for Hegel's
subject: first the desire to consume, then the desire for the recognition of the other, then later the desire for the Other's desire.
Butler claims that Hegel knows throughout the *Phenomenology* that
"there can be no experience outside the context of intersubjectivity." [30]

While Butler's account of the emergence of desire is persuasive
and can be found in the pages of the *Phenomenology*, her argument
does not fully quiet feminist concerns. One can still ask why intersubjectivity is thematized so late in the subject's journey: why not
begin with recognition of interelatedness? And why always thematize encounters in terms of conflict? Granting that for Hegel
nothing ever appears ex nihilo, why not name the relation to the
other earlier and in more agreeable forms? [31]

Butler stresses the complexity of the initial self-conscious confrontation of self and other, perhaps in order to head off feminist
criticisms that she might consider simplistic. Recognizing that there
is conflict and anger in the initial self-other encounter, she also

reads ecstasy and reward therein. The self, she says, "comes out of itself when faced with the other" and this "coming out" entails "ecstasy as well as anger." The Self is "besieged by the Other," undergoing "a frightening and even angering experience."[32] However,

> in desiring the Other, self-consciousness discovers itself as ecstatic being, a being that has it in itself to become other to itself, which, through the self-surpassing principle of desire, gives itself up to the Other even as it charges that the Other has somehow appropriated it. The ambiguity of gift and appropriation characterizes the initial encounter with the Other, and transforms this meeting of two desires into a struggle (*Kampf*).[33]

But even in this generous reading of Hegel, gift is an afterthought to appropriation. Why not reverse their priority, making appropriation the secondary possibility and delightful completion the first?[34] Or refuse to order them at all? Why not thematize the possibilities of participation in life with others who are neither identical with the self nor inferior to it?

The Subordination of Nature

Like most other modern thinkers, Hegel continues Aristotle's hierarchy of nature with men preserved on its pinnacle. During the unfolding of the Hegelian telos, spirit breaks from nature, then eventually takes nature back into itself and transcends it. Like other apparent oppositions, that between humans and the other-than-human world is repeatedly established, explored, exploded, transcended—only to reappear in a higher form. Since man's natural existence continues to be necessary, and to reappear in multiple ways, nature and all that is associated with it must be continually reencountered and transcended: "nature is the object of a perpetual reconquest."[35] The passions must be subordinated to reason, to lift *man* above the level of the animal. The representations of nature in culture, such as blood ties, reproduction, and death, are inferior to and subordinated to the rational discursive community, the (male-ordered) state: "Because it is only as citizen that he is real and substantial, the individual, when not a citizen, and belonging to the family, is merely unreal insubstantial shadow."[36] Those aspects of culture associated with nature, such as other animals, women, and families, Hegel subsumes as "ironies" in the life of the spirit.[37] They cannot be dispensed with, so they must be controlled and absorbed into their proper place. Hegel grants the familial realm, and the women he locates there, its own virtues, but these are clearly of lesser value than the social and ethical world of universality and citizenship reserved for men.[38]

In the stage of nascent subjectivity that Hegel identifies as self-consciousness and that precedes the scenario of lordship and bondage, the human relationship to the natural world is articulated as one of consumption and mastery. Hegel's subject progresses, as always, through a complex process of assimilation (taking the outside in) and projection (externalizing itself). At the stage of self-consciousness, Hegel's subject literally eats its way through the world, consuming and destroying ("negating," in Hegelian terminology) the objects of the life world.[39] Lacking any substance within itself, the subject at the stage of self-consciousness fills its internal vacuum by consuming the life outside of it. It employs a strategy of mastery vis-à-vis the physical world, seeking to gain a monopoly on life by negating all living things. The destruction of living things allows the nascently self-conscious self to come to see itself as an agent of destruction. But with a familiar twist of the dialectic, Hegel shows that this strategy becomes self-defeating. The self that is munching its way through the world always needs more material to consume, so its success (in consuming and mastering nature) also spells its failure (to be able to go on consuming and mastering). Taking its identity from destruction, the self-conscious self needs what it destroys and destroys what it needs. The stage is set for the drama of lordship and bondage.

Eschewing any tendency to see the self as a talking head, Hegel's understanding of subjectivity pays close and particular attention to embodiedness. In fact, the form this attention takes suggests vividly why many contemporary feminists, at least until rather recently, have avoided talking much about bodies at all: such talk has been historically used against women to define women's bodies as conveniently suited for the kinds of work men find useful but unpalatable, in the places men are happy to romanticize but unlikely to stay for long. Not surprisingly, Hegel incorporates his reading of bodily differences into his historical dialectic: common differences in the bodies of men and women are taken to reveal distinct capacities for each gender and to suggest the different purposes each is to serve.

> He [the brother] passes from the divine law, within whose realm he lived, over to the human law. The sister, however, becomes, or the wife remains, director of the home and the preserver of the divine law. In this way both the sexes overcome their merely natural being, and become ethically significant, as diverse forms dividing between them the different aspects which the ethical substance assumes. . . . The husband is sent forth by the spirit of the family into the life of the community, and finds there his self-conscious reality.[40]

This set of assumptions allows Hegel to exempt women from the dialectic of self-consciousness that he attributes to other subordinates; since women's familial position is naturalized, Hegel need not worry that women's subordination and their subsequent reflections upon it will produce any rebellions inconvenient to his happy merger of family life, civil society, and the state.

Feminist encounters with the Hegelian view of nature have by and large been very critical of it, yet are not without their repetitions of Hegel's telos of bodies and spirits. Some early feminist analyses agree with Hegel in finding in women's bodies a limit on their activities; Shulamith Firestone and Simone de Beauvoir, for example, both saw women's participation in reproduction as endangering higher opportunities for transcendence and liberation. More recent feminist formulations have opposed the Hegelian account of nature in several different ways. One approach takes the form of a reversal that valorizes the practices of reproduction and kinship as vehicles for a more liberated vision of humanness; Nancy Hartsock and Sara Ruddick take versions of this path. A second moves, with Nietzsche, to question the separation, and subordination, of the animal from the human, the passions from reason. In her claims that emotions provide a kind of knowledge, Arlie Hochschild suggests this line of argument. A third and perhaps the most radical approach launches rescue operations for nature itself, seeking a nature less saturated with human agendas of conquest. Challenging the project of mastery with regard to the natural world, some feminists have developed a radical ecology/theology of nature, while others have called for a reinstatement of the female body and its pleasures, and still others have moved ironically to dislodge the hegemony of human interpretations of the other-than-human world. [41]

The hierarchical aspects of Hegel's philosophy of nature contain little appeal for most feminisms. However, there is an echo of the Hegelian telos of reconciliation in cosmic feminism's search for attunement. Hegel's scheme of dialectical conflict between "man" and "nature" aims toward an ultimate reconciliation of them, and accordingly construes nature as containing a telos that tends toward such a reconciliation. [42] Likewise, some feminists reach for an attunement with nature construed as receptive to such liasons. Others reject any telos of reconciliation in favor of more concrete political economies or less romantic construals of order. While feminist arguments about nature are often at war with each other on epistemological grounds, most challenge the contours of the Hegelian subject in favor of one whose bodily/natural boundaries are more porous and whose sites of meaning are more diverse.

Faith in Language and Self-Reflection

Hegel's subject is animated throughout its long, failure-laden but ultimately successful journey toward completion by the presumption of a coherent design in the structure of language, life, and desire. For Hegel, at least in his more ambitious moments, language is understood to be capable of full transparency; it can be penetrated completely by reason. Knowing is capable of apprehending being, and breakdowns or slippages are unnecessary. There is a correspondence between the knowing self and the world to be known. The ability to pose questions about security and completion indicates the possibility of "an answer, a satisfaction, an ultimate arrival." [43] Hegel assumes in this regard exactly what Nietzsche denies: that there is a shared ontological structure between the self and the world and that our desires disclose this structure; that our desire for a certain outcome indicates the availability of that outcome. Hegel employs what Derrida calls the metaphysics of presence, assuming that there is a structure to consciousness and that it is "preserved by the capacity of language to fix concepts." [44] Hegel takes for granted that the philosophical language he employs refers in a stable and coherent way to the world, that language is capable of mastering life.

There is reason to believe that Hegel does not always sustain his most ambitious hopes for transparency and completion. His stress on the continual, restless struggle between and within modes of consciousness and ways of life, and the centrality of contradiction in his account, suggest the possibility of a more tragic moment in Hegel. By this reading Hegel continually seeks a fully transparent resting place that continually eludes him.[45] Gaps surface and require mediation: between embodied particulars and the universals they are thought to carry; between identity and non-identity; between humanity and god. Following this line of argument, Michael Gillespie finds, in the midst of Hegel's claims for resolution, mystery: the ground of history remains "dark and elusive."[46] Hegel's own rhetorical strategies minimize the space available to entertain such doubts, since he often writes from a perspective that is above and beyond the story he is telling, employing a philosophic *we* that speaks from a consciousness uncaptured by any of the subject positions being described.[47] But what seems clear about Hegel's account of consciousness and history is that whether he actually believes he can arrive at absolute knowledge or only wishes he could do so, he yearns to end opacity and contingency and come finally to fully self-sufficient transparency.

Hegel's subject thus is always beckoned by the promise of renewal via the redemptive capacities of self-examination. The incompatibilities residing in any particular life or epoch can, through proper interrogation, offer themselves for reconciliation while simultaneously revealing the hidden telos they serve. The subject can employ language to scrutinize itself, to analyze and unearth latent truths disguised therein. Through self-reflection the Hegelian subject, and modern subjects generally, are invited to discover themselves. Our desires hold the key to our hidden secrets, and self-investigation opens the doors to the interior scenes of our most essential inner lives.

Feminist responses to this dimension of Hegel's portrait of the subject are complex and filled with internal tensions. From a genealogical perspective, many feminists critique language as a phallocentric vehicle organized around the presumed centrality of the phallus and the assumptions and practices of patriarchy. These feminists share Foucault's suspicion that the modern subject is produced rather than discovered by modernity's practices of self-examination and judgment; they go on to charge that these practices particularly disempower women and reinforce patriarchy, that it is disproportionately on women's bodies and women's lives that the constraints and seductions of self-discipline fall.[48] Further, a genealogically animated feminism moves with Nietzsche to embrace the discontinuity and incompleteness that Hegel seeks to transcend, seeing it as a source of creativity rather than simply of estrangement.

However, the more interpretive moment within feminism wants to hold onto the Hegelian promise of liberation through self-reflection, but to privilege women's self-understandings for a change.[49] Desires that could be attributed to women, such as the longing for affirmative connections with nature, for a primary interrelatedness with others, or for peace, can then be featured via a feminist hermeneutic of self-reflection. Women's desires thus attain a rationality denied to them in Hegelian terms, and women's subjectivity can claim an ontological solidity and a philosophical significance. Through this reversal it is men's desires and self-understandings that become the problem, and the philosophical and political potentials of women's desires—to desire a different world into being, or to desire differently and disrupt the world—promise solutions. Yet, like Hegel's, this feminism's hopes for liberation reside with the oppressed, or, better yet, with what the oppressed have it in us to become.

So the attempt to locate women's true desires, to say that women are fundamentally (essentially?) different from men in what they desire and thus in who they are, is a strategy that participates in and reinforces the Hegelian pattern of discourse; further, it is fully compatible with the dominant notion of the self-examining, self-disclosing subject of modernity. This raises difficult questions about feminism's relation to modernity. Feminism can marshal impressive resources to sustain a challenge to modernity, an opposing set of voices, a cluster of submerged discourses: the refusal of an instrumental stance toward nature, the critique of phallogocentrism, the affirmation of relatedness and the plea for difference can support this construal.

But in other ways feminism is part and parcel of modernity, its product as much as its foe. Feminism is "outside" modernity in the sense that it comes from modernity's "other": women. It is "inside" modernity in its participation in a long history of social and political criticism and commitment to liberation.[50] It is outside modernity in claiming equal or even higher subjectivity for women, and inside in the subject-centeredness that such a claim entails. The validation of women's inner lives, their hidden substance distorted but not destroyed by patriarchy, is both rebellious toward and complicitous with modernity. Montaigne's account of the pursuit of a deep hidden space could serve as well as a description of feminist consciousness-raising efforts as it does of an early modern thinker's encounter with the interiorization of the self: "I turn my gaze inward, I fix it there and keep it busy," Montaigne says. "I look inside myself; I continually observe myself, I take stock of myself, I taste myself. . . . I roll about in myself."[51] The increased articulation of the subject's inner life corresponds to the growing curtailment of emotional expression and the internalization of social control practices. This package is not one that feminisms can either fully applaud or confidently repudiate.[52]

Clearly, modernity is not a single entity, not a well-defined epoch or consistent set of practices. Rather, it is a "loosely bounded field" characterized generally by discursive and institutional practices that strive toward appropriation and mastery.[53] But these practices often create their own oppositions; for example, the claims to rights and to individuality in modern liberalism have been used by various outsiders—people of color (of all genders and classes), women (of all classes and colors) and workers (you get the idea)— to claim access for themselves to the opportunities liberalism denied them. Hegel himself played a significant role in construing subjectivity in such a way that it both excluded women and enabled them to demand inclusion. Connolly explains that Hegel's account of the modern world "introduces the principle of subjectivity into ethical life, civil society, politics, and intellectual life, and then informs women that they 'cannot attain to the ideal.' It creates its own internal enemy, giving it the principle of subjectivity as its goal and weapon in the battle."[54]

One of the great ironies of Hegel's treatment of women is that his account of modernity reproduces the same fatal flaw he found at the heart of Greek life; and in both cases the carriers of this subversion are women. In the case of the Greeks it is Antigone who reveals the fatal contradiction at the heart of her time. Lacking a vigorous notion of reflexive subjectivity, Antigone's community, and she herself, had no means to analyze and negotiate competing claims from the social order. Antigone's dilemma (bury her brother according to tribal law, or obey the king who forbids the burial, also in accordance with tribal law) impelled her toward a self-consciousness that was, in Hegel's eyes, a step forward for history but a defeat for Greek society: "*this* particular self has become self-sufficient and self-dependent (*Anund Fürsichseyenden*), but precisely thereby the ethical order has been overthrown and destroyed."[55] Connolly observes that, for Hegel, "this progress destroys the beautiful unity of Greek life."[56] Setting aside the question of just how beautiful (or for that matter, how unified) this unity was for its less privileged members, Hegel allows us to see Antigone's crucial role in exploding the hegemonic Greek self-understanding from within. Greek life, he argues, "creates its enemy for itself within its own gates, creates it in what it suppresses, and what is at the same time essential to it—womankind in general."[57]

Yet Hegel sets himself up for this same self-subversion: he introduces the principle of subjectivity into political and ethical life, holds it up as the ultimate attainment of history (when properly combined with the constraints of felicitous order), then denies full access to subjectivity for women. Hegel is confident that his world has achieved the subjectivity that enables full reflectiveness and independent moral judgment:

That very subjective Freedom which constitutes the principle and determines the peculiar form of Freedom in *our* world—which forms the absolute basis of our political and religious life, could not manifest itself in Greece otherwise than as a *destructive* element. Subjectivity was a grade not greatly in advance of that occupied by the Greek Spirit; that phase must of necessity soon be attained; but it plunged the Greek world into ruin, for the polity which that world embodied was not calculated for this side of humanity.[58]

Us here means only men, more specifically, the men positioned to achieve access to "the peculiar form of Freedom" modernity offers. Yet women have access to this same script, and Hegel has given us every reason to seek what he tells us we cannot have. The subjectivity Hegel reserves for men, in the act of reserving it, made it available to women in our struggle against such reservations.

It is in the interstices of such self-subversions that political and intellectual movements like feminism achieve their historic footholds. Feminisms' efforts to articulate and privilege women's subjectivity are both products of modernity and challenges to it, manifestations of the modern notion that identity is something one must pursue and protests against the prevailing discoveries claimed by those on modernity's quest. Feminist convictions that "the master's tools will never dismantle the master's house" must be weighed against the tendency of such tools to subvert the uses to which they are put.[59] Hegel's tools leak; ours may as well.

But where does this leave us politically? Does feminism primarily reinvigorate the dominant regimes of truth and power, or does it substantially challenge those regimes? How can we position ourselves so that we minimize our tendencies in the first direction, while further enabling the second? These questions will be taken up more fully in subsequent chapters; they are both addressed and echoed in the fourth and final concern that Hegel raises for feminism, the status of difference.

The Absorption of Difference

In her critique of essentialism in western feminist theory, Elizabeth Spelman explores what happens when white middle-class women take themselves to be the exemplars of womanhood for purposes of producing feminist theory: "How lovely: the many turn out to be one, and the one that they are is me."[60] This characterization could serve almost literally as an account of Hegel's approach to difference. The Hegelian subject, as Butler remarks, "wants to know itself, but wants to find within the confines of this self the entirety of the external world; indeed its desire is to discover the entire domain of alterity as a reflection of itself, not merely to incorporate the world but to externalize and enhance the borders of its very self."[61] Hegel "manhandles" life.[62] Every encounter with otherness offers an opportunity for expansion; the self grows by incorporating the other, discovering there "a more enhanced version of itself."[63] The self as walled city keeps expanding until everything is inside its walls.

Following Sartre, Butler characterizes this stance as "ontological optimism," but it is decidedly pessimistic from the standpoint of the other.[64] Marta Savigliano has characterized Hegel's traveler as an "imperialist cannibal" for whom every otherness constitutes so much raw material for consumption.[65] The imperialism of Hegel's stance is amplified by his conviction that the immediacy of pure life is less worthy than the project of transcendence; that is, the desire simply to live (as in, say, the practices of some aboriginal people, or women, or children) is inferior to, and a source of fodder for, practices of expansion, improvement and consolidation. "Mere absorption in the expanse of life," says Hegel, can't compete with "trial by death"; the opportunities presented by such trials enhance and confirm the self.[66] "The final satisfaction of desire," Butler writes, "is the discovery of substance as subject, the experience of the world as everywhere confirming that subject's sense of immanent metaphysical place."[67] The Hegelian subject's encounters with alterity always end up with the triumphant proclamation, "Everything is me!"

The drive for self-sufficiency animating Hegel's subject, so typical of modernity's quest for mastery and control, naturalizes conquest and renders it unproblematic. But why privilege self-sufficiency so completely? Why not posit as an essential drive the urge toward delightful recognition of difference, then require explanation for imperialism? Or why not name them as two possibilities for interaction, without giving either ontological primacy? When Hegel's unhappy consciousness finally arrives at a full awareness of its own contradictions (between unchanging universality and radically contingent particularity), it immediately sets about denying one side or the other of its dilemma or else absorbing both into a synthesis. But what's so terrible about living with paradox? Hegel takes his dialectic of longing and its interruptions as self-evident, his desire for "total integrity" as fundamental to the subject's self-consciousness.[68] But what kind of subject has this particular self-consciousness? Why not call it suffocation, or death, or simple boredom, this vision of fully coinciding with oneself?

Feminism's stance vis-à-vis the absorption of difference, like its stance toward modernity itself, is complex and creased by internal tensions. The inadequacy of most versions of the woman question stems from their strategy of absorption or control of women; taking male experience and male-ordered knowledge as the norm, the woman question assimilates women into discourses that reflect patriarchal design and serve patriarchal ends. Women, many feminist writers have insisted, cannot and will not be assimilated into the masculine orderings of the world; further, women's ways press against those orderings in potentially disruptive fashion, sabotaging the security of the male-ordered unities (and often intensifying the efforts at unification and assimilation). In many respects feminisms arose as a protest against the absorption of difference into pretentious and bloated unities. Yet some kinds of feminism perpetuate this sin against otherness by absorbing the variegated worlds of women, and on occasion of all oppressed peoples and beings, into a unified field called "woman," "women," "the feminine," or "feminism." While sometimes this move takes place out of ignorance or a disregard for particularities of time and place, often it reflects a desire not unlike Hegel's: to find something recognizable in that which is unlike the self so as to find solid grounds for understanding self and world, and to create a shared basis for political action.

So a confrontation with the Hegelian move against difference raises at least two difficult questions for feminist theory. One concerns the theoretical constitution of otherness: How can we thematize difference so as to encounter it without engulfing it? Butler offers two paths, both of which have been taken up within feminist circles. The first "deconstructs the illusions of a restorative ontological immanence and posits non-dialectical difference as irreducible." This strategy is reflected in much of what I am calling linguistic feminism, wherein the genealogical impulse to denaturalize claims to unity and feature particularity and contingency presides. The second "rejects the primacy of difference of any kind and offers a theory of primary metaphysical plenitude which eludes Hegelian categories and entails a defense of affirmation on nondialectical grounds."[69] This move characterizes much of what I here call cosmic feminism, in which the search for and assumption of wholeness and a solid metaphysical place provide the grounds for affirmations of connectedness with all sentient beings. Both approaches merit further consideration for the alternative visions of subjectivity they offer as well as for the stance toward otherness they entail. The second difficult question brings us back to the problems of political unity and action raised earlier. How can we change the world if we don't begin with a solid female subject who knows what she wants and can unite with others like herself to get it? One of the few advantages the oppressed and marginal have is that there are a lot of us; do strategies that feature and sharpen difference do so at the expense of political efficacy? Do we divide ourselves so that they can conquer us more effectively?

Feminist Alternatives to the Hegelian Subject

Faced with the hegemony of Hegelian and other patriarchal claims about identity and desire, feminisms have sought both to join that discourse and to generate alternatives to it. The most readily available move for nascent feminist discourse was (and is) to demand equal entry for women into the world of the human as the dominant discourse defines it. This amounts to shouting "Me too!" at Hegel and his fellow travelers; it is not really an alternative at all, but a demand for inclusion, a way of saying "I can be like that too, so include me." Humanist feminism, as Iris Young characterizes this position, "defines gender as accidental to humanity" and urges both women and men to "pursue self-development in those creative and intellectual activities that distinguish human beings from the rest of nature."[70] Much of de Beauvoir's argument in *The Second Sex* takes this approach. De Beauvoir's self is very like Hegel's, an empty ego traveling on a journey filled with conflict and danger from others. She sees human subjectivity as characterized by "the imperialism of the human consciousness," always needing to conquer as the only alternative to being conquered.[71] She then figures women into the picture, insisting that women should not be seen as the permanent other but should be recognized as being like men in viewing themselves as primary and others as inessential. Like men, women too seek or should seek fulfillment in the transcendence of the merely life-preserving activities toward the life-endangering and thereby life-enhancing ones.

The humanist subject, then, is a person who exists prior to the acquisition of attributes. Gender, race, or class are then introduced as qualifiers to the pre-existing person-unit. The noun *individual* is the stable point around which descriptors of various kinds can move. The socially imposed changes this subject undergoes (in a process often called "socialization") happen to the person who already is. Other kinds of changes are called "choices" and are given their claims to authenticity in relation to an allegedly pre-social arena of human freedom.[72]

Feminism's relation to the claims of a humanity prior to gender have been complex. Perhaps an example may be illustrative. During one of the semimonthly meetings of our feminist theory reading group, which is composed mostly of university faculty and students, a rather desultory discussion of the essay at hand was derailed by a complaint voiced by one of the faculty about her (predominantly male) department. The room quickly lit up with animated conversation. Many others had similar tales to tell about inequity, prejudice, and the denial of rights. One might interpret this event in a variety of ways: perhaps none of us had done the reading, and so we welcomed a change of subject; perhaps these women would rather gossip than attend to business; perhaps this group of predominantly white female persons slides readily into the discourse of rights because it is relatively available to them. But at least one other interpretation is possible: women who have substantial investments (material, psychological, intellectual, or other) in modern institutions like universities also have substantial investments in humanist discourses on subjectivity and rights. The most reliable way to cash in on those investments is first to be a person in the humanity pool, and only second to become sexed, classed, or colored.

Since there are often good political reasons to retreat to the familiar ground of humanist feminism (or, as Sandra Harding characterizes it, equity feminism), it is cavalier for those who offer more radical critiques to dismiss its claims altogether. Some willingness to inhabit the terrain of humanist feminism is necessary to protect oneself against the power of those distributing resources and opportunities, and is crucial for claiming access to those resources and opportunities. Nonetheless, this position is essentially a defensive posture: it contributes little to envisioning alternatives or bringing about structural or discursive change (although it may reposition individuals in relation to those structures in welcome ways). Humanist feminists have often turned to the law to claim the status of subjects, seeking the rights and opportunities that such status carries. The law is an appropriate vehicle for this project for two reasons: it can be a powerful tool in changing behavior; and more important, it rests heavily on the modern notion of subjectivity. Subjects are beings in possession of themselves and their property, and legal rights serve as property to be possessed. Rights are possessions of the subject, independent of where or who the subject is.

Humanist feminists point convincingly to the dangers of living in a society based on juridico-legal discourse and selves-as-subjects without possessing the same armor of rights. The laws and the courts do not oblige us by leaving us alone. Further, those who lack a sense of themselves as agents, as capable of acting and taking responsibility for their actions in the public world, are put at enormous disadvantage. In a world made by and for solid subjects, not to be one, or to be less than fully one, can be devastating. Many of the women in Carol Gilligan's abortion study and in Kim Chernin's interviews on body size suffer from a sense of paralysis, an inability to act, that leads easily to their victimization.[73] The women interviewed by the authors of *Women's Ways of Knowing* spoke consistently of a "quest for self and voice," indicating the psychic and material pain accompanying an ill-defined sense of self.[74]

Finally, it is very difficult to speak of liberation without some notion of a subject whose life will be improved in some way, or to envision political change without some idea of who will bring it about and why. As a philosophy of liberation, feminism has often appealed to the powers of agency and subjectivity as necessary components of struggle. Feminist projects for the betterment of women's lives have often been couched in terms of strengthening and validating the subjectivity of women.

But the question still remains, What kind of self do women want to claim, or does feminism want to claim for women?[75] What subject positions are discernible in women's articulated self-understandings, and what are the political consequences of embracing them? Granting that a coherent theory of political change requires some notion of the subject, the hegemonic claims of male-ordered subjectivity do not exhaust the available candidates. Beyond the defensive posture of "me too!" feminism lie the alternatives generated from feminist interpretive and genealogical practices. The interpretive move turns women's marginality in the hegemonic discourse to our advantage. "Gynocentric feminism," as Young presents it, "defines women's oppression as the devaluation and repression of women's experience by a masculinist culture that exalts violence and individualism. It argues for the superiority of values embodied in traditionally female experience, and rejects the values embodied in traditionally male dominated institutions."[76]

Conventionally female experience can be defined in many ways: by mothering and reproduction; by the political economy of the gendered division of labor; by the arrangements of the female body; by women's connections to non-human nature; by spirituality and contact with the divine. Arguments that focus on what women are said to *do,* that take women's practices, activities and events as the source of an alternative conception of subjectivity and desire, I refer to here as praxis feminism. This alternative notion of subjectivity focuses on persons-in-relations and on responding to needs, on taking care of relations. Arguments that focus more on what women are said to *be,* on women's participation in nature, divinity, or other higher unities, I have named cosmic feminism. Cosmic feminism offers a view of subjectivity that stresses the self-in-place with relation to a larger and higher natural/spiritual order of things. While genealogical moments run through both postures, they are primarily interpretive. They offer accounts of women's experiences or women's knowledge and claim center stage, politically and epistemologically, for those accounts.

The genealogical move contests the reversal that gynocentric feminism employs and seeks to explode the sexual dyad, to agitate into existence a space where identity might be constituted outside of the oppositions of sexual dualism. The modern subject, as Foucault and others remind us, is one who is *subjected,* brought to order by the disciplinary strategies of modernity. Modern subjects are constituted by a complex process of differentiation, fixation, interrogation; they are separated from the rest of nature, from the play of possibilities and pleasures in bodies and relations. The modern subject is a unity fabricated out of the diffuse flow of experiences and relationships, "an empty synthesis . . . a profusion of lost events."[77] Women's consignment to the outworld of otherness by the work and words of men has reserved the full force of modern subjectivity for the dominant male groups (although it does not attend with equal force, or appeal with similar strength, to all men). The subjugated and submerged discourses of those sharing the margins are ill-served by incorporation into the discourse of the same. Subjects keep their rights by force of the tyranny of sameness: one has rights by virtue of claiming to be the same as the rightful others, and one makes claims to difference at the expense of being assigned to the outskirts of the realm. To be equal is to be the same; to be different is to be inferior. Either way there is colonization, homogenization, and the erasure of diversity.

The position that I characterize as linguistic feminism carries the genealogical suspicions of the modern subject toward a discourse of semiotics/play and of bodies-and-pleasures. While elements of interpretive strategies run through this posture, it is more fully genealogical than the others in its stress on the denaturalization of meaning claims and on the contingencies at the heart of order. It also stresses the constitutive power of language to formulate, rather than simply describe, the values and practices of (any version of) subjectivity and desire.

Many of the arguments working within the loose configurations of praxis, cosmic, and linguistic feminisms are not unique to feminism; rather, they indicate feminism's obligations to and influence on other strategies of inquiry that position themselves as counterpoints to the hegemonic traditions of subjectivity in the west. Nor are these clear and distinct fractions within feminism. They resemble contrasting portraits, thematizations that share a great deal but nonetheless differ as to the kinds of knowledge claims they draw upon and the identities they make possible. Each is an effort to establish an identity for women not as lesser subjects than men, but as subjects differently.

Genealogy and interpretation are umbrella categories that take their coherence from the point of view of the other. Foucault's histories of particular practices and Barthes's textual moves to deconstruct meaning claims are dissimilar in many ways, but from an interpretive point of view, they share an ontology of disorder and an emphasis on producing rather than discovering meaning. Cosmic feminism's spirituality and praxis feminism's materiality are quite different, but, viewed genealogically, both can be seen as claims about an order discoverable in the world through proper attunement or investigation. It is indicative of the continued predominance of interpretation in political theory and feminist theory (despite poststructuralism's popularity in some circles) that the first set of generalizations may appear less problematic than the second.

Cosmic feminism invests heavily in assumptions about a discernible wholeness of things, while praxis feminism builds its arguments on claims about historically-gendered practices of production and reproduction. These are not reducible to one another, but located within disputes about the discovery of truth versus the imposition of meaning, they share substantial terrain.

In articulating these three categories of subjectivity within contemporary feminisms, other possible categorizations are likely to be silenced. This is not the only way to cut the pie. Although praxis, cosmic, and linguistic approaches to subjectivity call on readily available feminist self-understandings, they do not exhaust the field, and not all feminist writers fall comfortably within them. Each of these articulations of a feminist subjectivity corresponds more or less with one or more of the feminist responses to the Hegelian subject as outlined above (an approach to questions of subjectivity that was not articulated as a counterpoint to Hegelian formulations would probably map the terrain differently). The first criticism of Hegel, claiming his notions of relationship to be impoverished and overly invested in conflict and separation, arises largely (although not exclusively) from praxis feminism's stress on the female subject as constituted by connectedness and motivated by the need to take care, to respond to the needs of others. The second criticism of Hegel, pointing to his imperialistic account of nature, reflects (but is not limited to) cosmic feminism's insistence on locating the human subject within nature rather than on top of it. The third and fourth criticisms of Hegel, objecting to his faith in self-reflection and language and his obliteration of difference, call upon linguistic feminism's concern (shared to some degree by the others) with the constitutive power of language and the hegemonic tendencies of all totalizations in relation to that which refuses to fit. While this matching of feminist concerns about Hegel with feminist visions of subjectivity is overly neat, it nonetheless links the pulse of each alternative vision to the dimension of male-ordered subjectivity that each most heartily engages and disputes.

Given the context of the metatheoretical arguments of Chapter 1, which work to destabilize the (still necessary) categories of their own analysis, it is impossible to avoid a troubling question: What could the status of these categories be? And why call them by these names? Nietzsche reminds us of the power we claim when we seize "the lordly right of bestowing names": "The lordly right of bestowing names is such that one would almost be justified in seeing the origin of language itself as an expression of the rulers' power. They say 'This is this or that'; they seal off each thing or action with a sound and thereby take symbolic possession of it."[78] Cosmic feminism might also be referred to as ecofeminism; I prefer the former term because it stresses the cosmological dimensions of the position. One might also call it religious in the broadest sense of that term, but that name would suggest the inclusion of feminist theological and institutional arguments within Christianity, which are not my subject here. Praxis feminism might sound like an exclusively Marxist endeavor, given the historic deployment of the word "praxis"; I use it more broadly to include notions of subjectivity founded in (some version of) women's practices. As such it includes Marxist-inspired arguments but is not limited to them.

It may seem presumptuous to label any one approach as linguistic, given the attention to language that pervades all manner of feminisms; but this name designates formulations of subjectivity that stress the constitutive power of language to produce life. This perspective could be called postmodern or poststructuralist, but I am trying to avoid these terms because of their increasingly restrictive academic usage. Another name for this category could be subversive feminism, denoting its position of sabotage toward all fixed meaning claims, in contradistinction to the transformative goals of praxis and cosmic feminisms. However, in recognition that all three thematizations of subjectivity are subversive of at least some elements of male-ordered identities (while complicitous in others), I have selected linguistic as the shorthand appellation for this most subversive type.

These categories of feminist subjectivities disrupt other, more common, categories; they combine elements that are often seen to be at war with one another, and cut across mergers commonly accepted. For example, praxis feminism includes arguments common in socialist and radical feminism; cosmic feminism draws upon both secular and religious approaches to nature; linguistic feminism combines arguments that build upon psychoanalytic thought with arguments that reject or sidestep it. The division between praxis and cosmic cuts across what is sometimes called radical or cultural feminism; it insists upon a distinction between *kinds* of feminist interpretation, a distinction not readily visible from a purely genealogical perspective.[79] The distinction between praxis and linguistic cuts across the category of psychoanalytic feminism, distinguishing arguments that concentrate on the creation and maintenance of mothering as a relationship/practice/institution from those that feature it as metaphor or signifier.

Given these clashes between my proposed categories and others already in circulation, why irritate readers with yet another typology of feminisms? I am insisting on these categories because I am theorizing feminisms' complex fields rather tightly around the problematics of subjectivity. Following Foucault, I am inquiring into "the forms and modalities of the relation to self by which the individual constitutes and recognizes himself [*sic*] *qua* subject."[80] I found existing divisions inadequate to that task because they are not aimed primarily at visions of personhood, but at philosophical parentage (liberal feminism, Marxist feminism, anarchist feminism, psychoanalytic feminism, etc.) or at recommendations for political action (liberal, socialist, or radical feminisms, for example), or at some other feature of argument. My claim is not to have superseded the more familiar categories in all regards, but to make them come apart in useful ways. The economies implicitly established by my discourse on subjectivity put into circulation a certain set of questions about gender and identity. They enable investigation into the discursive and institutional practices that establish internal coherencies and continuities, as well as conflicting urges and energies, within and between persons over time. They do not fully thematize, or even recognize, all possible dimensions of the relation of the individual to herself and the social order (nor could any set of categories hope to do so). Again following Foucault, I regard analytic categories as sets of assets—"finite, limited, desirable, useful"—that can enable some inquiries at the expense of others.[81] Recognizing that there are predictable gaps in the problematic I am establishing—neither the practices of the unconscious nor the consequences of the economic and state apparatus are investigated—I hope nonetheless to sketch some significant semiotic and material practices by which identities and counter-identities are produced in three detectable feminist theorizations of self.

In articulating this typology of subjectivities, I hope to avoid some problems that such categorizations typically entail. Typologies, as Katie King and Donna Haraway have reminded us, tend to be used "to make one's own political tendencies appear to be the *telos* of the whole" and they usually take feminist theory to be a struggle among fixed and mutually exclusive positions.[82] I propose instead that these three positions be seen as discernible thematizations of subjectivity within contemporary feminist theory. There is no linear progression among them—that is, they do not range from least radical to most radical, or from inadequate to adequate—and no narrative of transcendence is available to reconcile their conflicts or to "go beyond" their limitations. While elements of each appear within the others, the borders between them being neither fixed nor impermeable, they nevertheless appear on the scene of feminist theory as detectable coherencies, recognizable portraits of what it means to be a person within the world each portrait names as real. Created, as Marilyn Frye recommends, by following "something like an aesthetic sense of pattern or theme," these categories often do not fully capture individual authors, but articulate contrasting coherencies in which different writers participate to different degrees.[83]

Many feminist authors who are not directly addressing questions of subjectivity still draw upon one or more of these thematizations, since most arguments in feminist theory stand explicitly or implicitly upon some notion of what it means to be a person. These categories allow me a way to get at the relation between visions of subjectivity and the ordering principles of knowledge and power they both inhabit and sustain. Feminist discourses, like all others, must delimit their field of objects, name the perspectives they consider legitimate, and establish their norms for the articulation of concepts and theories.[84] The utility of these characterizations depends on their ability to name recognizable portraits of subjectivity at work within feminist theory while retaining an understanding of their own partiality and fluidity, recognizing the "continual commerce between them," and resisting claims to have exhausted the possible field of meaning.[85]

As intellectual/political positions within feminism, these thematizations of subjectivity and desire are detectable both in academic debates on identity and desire and in extra-academic activities. They are, in other words, findable in texts (which are part of the world) *and* in the world (which requires interpretation as text). Feminist magazines, bookstores, rape crisis centers, battered women's shelters, women's health clinics, self-defense classes, lesbian community centers, women's studies classes, feminist therapy programs; women's enterprises for music, art, dance, theatre, and comedy; women's political organizations for reproductive freedom, against pornography, for environmental conservation, against militarism, for mothers' and children's health, against economic exploitation— all such organizations and activities mobilize some image of what it means to be a woman and of what women want. While there is usually no one-to-one correspondence between images of subjectivity and organizational expressions, different versions of these images make their appearances and do their work.

None of these portraits of subjectivity stands as unproblematic; each has limitations that the others are quick to address, including characteristic forms of kitsch, sentimentality, or self-indulgence toward which each tends to degenerate. Kitsch, as presented in Milan Kundera's novel *The Unbearable Lightness of Being,* is the aesthetic ideal of the categorical agreement with being. It is a basic faith that all is well in the world, or that all will be well once a different world is made. Kitsch can be generated out of whatever ground one gives to one's categorical agreement with being; kitsch comes in communist, democratic, feminist, European, and third-world varieties. "The identity of kitsch," Kundera tells us, "comes not from a political strategy but from images, metaphors, and vocabulary." Kitsch operates to "keep everyone in step . . . in proper agreement."[86] Kitsch allows one to belong too well to one's place; it ties up all the loose ends through its too-complete affirmations. While a certain amount of kitsch is probably unavoidable, especially in the struggle against larger powers that carry their own more dangerous varieties, an alertness to kitsch can warn feminists of the forms of sentimentality and self-delusion that our own formulations make possible.

Each of these thematizations of subjectivity undermines the unitary, armor-plated sense of self articulated by Hegel and central to modern western male-ordered thought, but they do so in distinct ways and toward somewhat different ends.[87] While there is considerable common ground among them, there are incompatibilities within and between them that sabotage any easy efforts at reconciliation or merger. They all make some contributions to the constitution of what I am calling mobile subjectivities, complex and partial articulations of identities that accept incompleteness while working toward connection. A consideration of the relations among praxis, cosmic, and linguistic feminisms suggests interpretive and genealogical strategies working together as ironic allies to create potent if unstable feminist discourses on subjectivity and desire.

Chapter Three

Praxis Feminism

The subjectivity thematized by praxis feminism focuses on affirmative intersubjective connections between persons rather than on autonomous or combative selves, stresses human need more strongly than rights, and privileges women's traditional activities as a source of self-understanding and social change. From this perspective women's experiences, their daily, practical, detailed activities in production and reproduction, as daughters, mothers, and workers, generate a psychology of connection with others and a relational morality. Seeing relationships as constitutive of identity, this view stresses persons-in-relations rather than autonomous and isolated selves. Praxis feminism is a subject-centered discourse that privileges the female speaking subject. It seeks a proper understanding of women's lives, and of the world women and men inhabit, in the words that women have to say. The possibilities for political change that it embraces are generated out of women's words and women's worlds.

As cosmic and linguistic feminists (among others) are quick to argue, praxis feminism carries certain characteristic weaknesses that are the underside of its strengths. Its exclusive focus on the intersubjective, on the ways women and men experience their relations to others and the world, can prevent praxis feminists from coming to terms with the prediscursive or nondiscursive, those aspects of life not reached or reachable with words. The world of intersubjectively constituted realities tends to give too much to the completeness and wholeness of our accounts of things, evading discrepancies between the nondiscursive and the discursive. That which does not fit into the web of communication " 'no longer seems to be' but

it still works its effects."[1] Also, a discourse of need and connection
may rest too readily on the authority of the (female) subject, whose
accounts of her own experiences (and those of men) are taken as
unique and privileged. But it is precisely the dominance of the
subject (at least, of certain kinds of subjects) that we were questioning in the first place. If to be a subject is to be subjected, if the
self-as-subject is the constituted outcome of the disciplinary strategies of modernity, then women's subjectivity and intersubjectivity are not exempt from this problematic.

This chapter charts a territory that appears when questions of
knowledge, politics and personhood are framed through the category of praxis feminism. I want to look at the strengths and weaknesses of praxis feminism, to indicate some significant questions
about essentialism that the category suggests, and to propose an
ironic intervention within it. To identify strengths and weaknesses
is itself a problematic approach to this analysis, both because it may
suggest an unfortunate accounting mentality, in which debits and
credits are totaled to ascertain a final score, and because it seems
to suggest some secure location, outside the perspective at hand,
from which the evaluation can take place. I intend neither of these
claims. Each of these thematizations of subjectivity offers some resources for self-critique; further, each produces critiques of the
others, calling attention to neglected fringes, silenced assumptions
or unintended consequences. I hope to end up not with a final
score but with an arena in which argumentative and appreciative
conversations between and among these portraits of personhood
can occur.

Creating Praxis Feminism

Praxis feminism as a thematization of subjectivity appears when
one ranges across the field of feminist theory, looking for approaches that draw conclusions about the kind of people we are by
attending to the productive power of what we do. The relationships
that this perspective privileges as key to women's practices can be
conceptualized both socially and historically. For example, Jessica
Benjamin draws upon Habermas, Winnicott, and the object-relations school of psychoanalysis to offer a perspective on the self that
she calls "intersubjective." This view "maintains that the individ-

ual grows in and through the relationship to other subjects." The need for mutual recognition stimulates the relational orientation that produces the capacity to empathize. The opposition of otherness and sameness can be transcended through interaction to the feeling of "being with": "It ['being with'] forms the basis of compassion, what Milan Kundera calls 'co-feeling,' the ability to share feelings and intentions without demanding control, to experience sameness without obliterating difference."[2] Women's greater access to the circumstances and practices that produce co-feeling, and men's struggle to escape them, produce a gender-polarized psyche and society: what passes for human subjectivity and genderless rationality in the hegemonic discourse (Hegel, for example) is in fact quite male. "The psychic repudiation of femininity, which includes the negation of dependency and mutual recognition, is homologous with the social banishment of nurturance and intersubjective relatedness to the private domestic world of women and children."[3]

Benjamin's plea for a subjectivity that can sustain contradiction and live with tension (a genealogical gesture) offers a persuasive contrast to Hegel's tiresome pursuit of resolutions; but it is undercut by her reassuring language of wholeness and balance (a move into interpretation). Her hope, like Gilligan's, is that a feminist critique of male-ordered subjectivity and rationality can valorize a neglected, female dimension of human activity and thus provide "for a more balanced differentiation of self and world."[4] Appeals to a wholeness thought to be available to properly balanced subjects tend to smuggle back into the account the assumptions of resolution that an emphasis on contradiction was meant to disrupt.

While Benjamin's psychoanalytic account emphasizes the intersubjective emergence of the self from infancy to adulthood, Aihwa Ong's ethnography of Malaysian factory women stresses the long history of familial and class relations as shaped by colonialism. Her analysis looks at "women as historical subjects." To counter the colonial accounts of the "natives," she proposes "to seek out local practices buried within the imposed coherence of colonial records."[5] She finds that in the agrarian economy, women's labor in the fruit and spice trees provided the margin of survival for rubber-producing peasant families when rubber prices fell. Women's work in fishing, in organizing market production and sales of eggs, to-

bacco, poultry, and home-cooked foods also helped insulate families from the vagaries of world commodity prices. Women recruited from peasant families into the electronics industries in the
free-trade zones provide crucial income and challenge traditional
male authority in the family: "The changing content of daughter-
parent, sister-brother relationships is displayed in refusal of money
to parents who remarry, criticism of brothers, more daring enjoyment of premarital sex, power over younger siblings who ask for
money, and decisions to hand earnings over to the mother."[6]

Women's traditional work in rural Malay society is self-orga-
nized and patterned to the rhythms of village and household life;
in contrast to factory labor, it is done largely without male supervision. When these women go into the factories they are "confronting capitalist time": the ruthless industrial clock, continual male
supervision, repetitive and meaningless labor, and a radical separation of work and leisure. Such wrenching changes produce
changing self-identities as well, which in turn alter personal practices in courtships, marriages and family life. Factory jobs for rural
women in transnational companies "have reconstituted their very
sense of self as women and as a nascent proleteriat."[7] Ong ends
her discussion of resistance with a quasi-Marxist appeal for transcendence through a new and improved collective consciousness,
combined with a dubious gesture backward in time toward the virtues of an ungendered precolonial humanity (despite the prior discussion of male authority in pre-colonized Malay society). At this
point the interpretive thread of the argument tightens, highlighting the promises of transcendence and return.

Praxis feminism can also perform as a reading strategy, enabling
a feminist re-reading of texts (such as, in part, my re-reading of
Hegel). Commentary on texts in "the tradition" (or elsewhere) is
one way to enter conversations about/within political theory, and
to put a feminist perspective into circulation. Further, the feminist
practices that enable us to comment critically on texts-in-books can
also enable us to position ourselves critically toward the texts-in-
the-world. The metaphor of the world as text, or of reading as a
stance toward the world, does not entail the simple claim that life
is a book but rather the political claim that life requires interpretation; its categories and meanings are contestable.[8]

A good example of the promise of praxis feminism as a reading strategy is Hannah Pitkin's discussion of Machiavelli in *Fortune Is a Woman*. Although it calls on the (scant) information available about Machiavelli's life, the book is not a psychobiography or psychohistory; rather, it is an investigation of "the relationship—in Machiavelli's thought and in our own—between inner and outer reality, private and public life, 'the personal' and 'the political.' And that investigation will seek not causal links of dependent and independent variables, but interrelationships of meaning." Pitkin argues that autonomy is "Machiavelli's central preoccupation, the thread that unifies the contradictions and tensions in his works, enlarging the seemingly personal issue of machismo and tying it to his meditations on political themes." She places Machiavelli in his time and place, in early modern Europe as it broke away from the medieval acceptance of dependence and interconnectedness toward a self-understanding in which "dependence had now become both contemptible and dangerous; autonomy was the goal."[9]

This autonomy was problematic both because it was not readily available—because of the vagaries of the market and the destructiveness of war—and because it was not for everyone. For Machiavelli, "autonomy is intertwined with manhood. Dependence is characteristic of women, children, and animals; for men it is despicable and fatally dangerous." But Machiavelli's texts present conflicting images of what autonomy might mean. Pitkin identifies three core images of manly autonomy: the fox, the founder, and the citizen. She pilots the reader through an inspired reading of Machiavelli's texts and of his time, demonstrating the internal tensions within and between the three images and the circles in Machiavelli's thinking as he moves among them. "What is it that traps Machiavelli," she asks, "that so divides and confounds his understanding of manhood?" The answer, in brief, is given in the title of the following section: women. "The feminine constitutes 'the other' for Machiavelli, opposed to manhood and autonomy in all their senses: to maleness, to adulthood, to humanness, and to politics." But the image of the other is not simple because women are not all the same: young women are dangerous for their seductiveness, mature women for their power. "The virago, one might suggest, is not merely woman experienced by adult men as the resentful wife, but also woman experienced by small children as the dangerous mother, who feeds but also dominates and threatens to engulf." And fortune herself is a woman, the opposite of manly *virtu*, who can be wooed, or conquered sexually, but never completely controlled. Machiavelli's belief in fortune, according to Pitkin, resembles a child's relation to its mother, "understanding the world as if, feeling about it as if, acting as if it were mostly run by a large senior, female person, who holds men in her power to a greater or lesser extent depending on their conduct and specifically on their manliness."[10]

Pitkin finds what one might call a feminist moment in Machiavelli: "mutuality within difference . . . the tolerance for ambiguity and uncertainty, the capacity to trust fallible others and be oneself trustworthy." Machiavelli at his best articulates a vision of citizenship as mutual participation among equals, but he cannot sustain that vision because the "family drama" enacted in his writings continues to reintroduce fear of and struggle against the mother as the grounds of autonomy. Autonomy, burdened with the weight of infantile fears and fantasies, becomes synonymous with masculinity on the run. When men who are fleeing from this family drama create public life, it is likely to resemble an army: it reflects "their fear of the feminine, their need to prove manliness, and as a consequence, violence, hero worship, relations of command and obedience."[11] There is a struggle between citizenship and masculinity in Machiavelli's writing, and citizenship loses:

> Machiavelli undermines the very teaching he wants to convey by appealing to his audience's desire for manliness and thereby also summoning up childishness: fantasies of huge engulfing mothers and rescuing fathers, relationships of domination and submission, an unstable combination of cynicism and exhortation, and misleading conceptions of action, membership, judgment, and autonomy. The appeal to machismo can move men all right, particularly men troubled about their manliness, but it cannot make them free.[12]

Pitkin's work exemplifies the explanatory power of praxis feminism. She applies the arguments of Nancy Chodorow and others to Machiavelli's particular time and place, setting up a dialogue between Machiavelli's texts and the life that was available to the men and women of early modern Florence. Machiavelli's notion of hu-

manness as maleness is problematized and seen as needing explanation. Machiavelli's quest for autonomy is placed within the context of the relationships he and his audience were likely to have
experienced. The way is opened for more robust conceptualizations of citizenship and autonomy that include gender without being
confined to it. The cost of the tightly knit narrative that Pitkin
weaves, as Carolyn DiPalma and Julie Wuthnow have noted, is
also characteristic of the genre: there is a place for everything, and
everything is in its place.[13] The charm, for the interpretivist, of a
rich and dense hermeneutic is opposed, for the genealogist, by the
suspicion that not everything could have fit so conveniently into
the story. Interpretively, this could indicate the truth of the story:
it can account for all of its material. Genealogically, it is the drive
to account for everything that breaks down under scrutiny.

A particularly potent version of relational subjectivities is developed in praxis feminism through appeals to and interpretations of
mothering. Sara Ruddick, for example, examines the perspective
on self and world that maternal work makes available to construct
a political/psychological category of "maternal thinking." Her analysis
gives philosophical significance to the experiences of mothers, and
also suggests the political possibilities that reside in those experiences. Maternal thinking, at its best, has certain central qualities:
it is ongoing, processual ("though we desperately needed to act, it
was abundantly clear that our nighttime conclusions simply yielded
the next afternoon's questions"); it is practical ("We were not reflecting for the sake of reflection; we needed answers").[14] It requires a kind of control that limits itself and strives to make itself
unnecessary. It calls for a scrutinizing of the world that looks un-
obtrusively for danger without unduly limiting exploration. It requires the muting of narcissism and the appreciation of "alternative
excellences and virtues." It births an attentive love that Ruddick
calls holding, a connection like empathy but not so self-oriented:
"knowing another *without* finding yourself in her." It relies on feelings, properly assessed, to direct and explain acting and thus establishes feeling as a form of knowing:

Rather than separating reason from feeling, mothering makes reflective
feeling one of the most difficult attainments of reason. In protective work,
feeling, thinking, and action are conceptually linked; feelings demand re-

flection, which is in turn tested by action, which is in turn tested by the feelings it provokes. Thoughtful feeling, passionate thought, and protective acts together test, even as they reveal, the effectiveness of preservative love.[15]

Ruddick's "thoughtful feeling" undermines the male-ordered dualism of reason and passion; the practices of mothering make available the constitution of a self-in-relation that thinks her feelings and feels her thoughts.[16]

The particular relations that Ruddick most closely examines are with children. Ruddick, like Benjamin, emphasizes the child as actor, not as raw material to be managed. Ruddick speaks of the "child's body, from its birth" as "enspirited." In granting subjectivity to those beings usually excluded from political theory except as the recipients of authority, victims of power, or carriers of the next generation's responsibilities, these feminists name a site for the production of powerful intersubjectivities and also bring into view a perpetually silenced other—children.[17]

Ruddick's connection of mothering to peace is delicately drawn. Mothers are not seen as inherently peaceful, but as beings whose work requires them to make *efforts* toward being peaceful. She emphasizes that mothering is a struggle; mothers struggle toward their own commitments, with their failures and temptations, with or against the demands of others upon them. The skills and practices of mothering offer "resources for creating a less violent world," not guarantees.[18]

Like most feminists who adopt a praxis approach to subjectivity, Ruddick grapples with the differences among women that her analysis might obscure. "One does not become a 'woman' in some general sense but, for example, a French or Mexican or Japanese woman, living in a particular decade as a member of a particular class." Recognizing that every mother speaks from some location, she notes that "conceptions of 'maternal thinking' are as various as the practices of mothering from which they derive."[19] Then, like Hartsock, Chodorow, and others, she switches her emphasis to that which can be held to be common across such differences: "But I do expect sufficient commonality in the demands made by our children to enable us to compare, which also means to contrast, the requirements of our work." She elaborates this claim in a footnote: noting the pitched debates about the deployment of such terms as women, she takes up a position with Nel Noddings, whom she quotes approvingly as follows: "Writing as a woman, one can be careful to choose experiences that cut broadly across the lives of most women; note situations, opinions, or problems that are affected by membership in other groups; couch one's conclusions in language that is moderate and makes claims only to a contribution toward a cumulative universality—not for a universality itself."[20]

This is precisely the epistemological gesture central to praxis feminism and thoroughly contested in its linguistic counterpart. Praxis feminism asks: "We've got lots of different kinds of women; now, what do they share?" From the linguistic perspective, this sidesteps a prior question: "How do we come to have women?" Ruddick's nod to the significance of particular locations is necessarily elided through her interpretive gesture, which assumes a common "woman space" that can serve as a foundational space for rendering lucid the experiences of those who inhabit it. But such spaces are not merely discerned; they must be constituted, their various habitations marked with significance through discourse. Ruddick's "spatial strategies" depend on some prior constitution of certain boundary practices (for example, the separation of public from private domains) or temporal markings (for example, the distinction between preindustrial and industrial societies) that become so familiar through continuous occupation that their traces are not readily articulated.[21] Similarly, to contribute to a "cumulative universality" presupposes both the possibility and the desirability of such a thing as universality at all. It is Ruddick's interpretive move, following the "promising political consequences of maternal identification" that gives her argument its power and marks its limits.[22]

A few further examples of praxis feminist arguments can help to mark the category's constitutive components and to flag its appearances on feminist horizons. Sandra Harding outlines several feminist approaches to science that express different formulations of praxis feminism (or what she calls feminist standpoints): those that stress the craft labor typically done by women scientists, which unifies the manual, mental, and emotional dimensions of the work; those that emphasize women's subjugated activity in attending to concrete and bodily needs and in maintaining relationships; those that problematize men's tendency to project their own early traumas of separation and individuation into philosophy, thus obscuring the more robust relational field inhabited by women and children; those that feature women's labor in taking care of men's bodies and places of living, enabling men to create and live in a world of abstract concepts that mystifies women's lives. Each of these versions of feminist standpoint theory can be generalized from its analysis of science to an application to society; each looks to what women and men *do* to understand the notions of self and other that activities produce.[23] Standpoint theory is a particularly potent expression of praxis feminism's politics. It combines insistence on the productive power of practices in forming consciousness with attention to the intellectual and political struggles through which traditional practices are criticized and conventional consciousness is radicalized.

Hartsock is a key contributor to standpoint theory. She calls upon women's life activity to construct a political economy of gender, one that builds from women's experiences of eros, community, and power. She explores women's writings on power that emphasize energy, capacity, and potential rather than domination and exclusion. The material circumstances of women's lives produce in women an experience of self in relation to others, an opposition to dualisms, a valuation of the concrete, and "a sense of variety of connectedness and continuities both with other persons and with the natural world." Feminist theory, Hartsock argues, should be grounded in women's material activities and directed toward the political struggle necessary to create "areas of social life modeled on this activity."[24]

To cite another example, Haunani-Kay Trask draws on Herbert Marcuse and on a number of feminist writers, including Adrienne Rich, Cherríe Moraga, and Jill Johnston, to advocate a feminist eros "developed out of the culture of women's everyday lives: the texture and substance of women's reality as mothers, wives, and sexual object/victims."[25] Like Hartsock's, Trask's argument is exemplary of one of praxis feminism's central tensions. It combines a valorization of the distinct practices in women's lives under patriarchy with a critique of patriarchy's modes of domination. This tension is central for the female subjectivities that praxis feminism articulates because the perspective sees both value in women's traditional activities and domination within the society whose traditions they are. Untangling the valued practices from the oppressive conditions of their performance requires a hermeneutic rich enough to distinguish them from one another, to account for both, and to valorize a critical consciousness that both emerges from and struggles against the conditions of its production.

Many versions of praxis feminism, including Benjamin's, Hartsock's, and Trask's, invoke the influential writings of Carol Gilligan and Nancy Chodorow to make their arguments. Gilligan argues that women are more likely than men to attend to the concrete needs of particular others, more likely to judge themselves and others by the moral injunction to take care, to respond. More often than men, women define themselves in terms of their relationships with others, experiencing connection and empathy at the heart of identity. Men are able to sustain an identity of separation and independence, and a morality that stresses autonomy and rights, in part because women are weaving the web of sociality on which men depend even as they devalue it in their theories and in their institutions. The strategies that women bring to moral problems focus on conflicting responsibilities rather than competing rights, and employ a mode of reasoning that is contextual and narrative rather than abstract and rule-governed.

While men tend to worry about the problems of ranking and/or respecting individual rights, women tend to worry about the dangers of disregarding the needs of others. Gilligan's project in relation to women's voice is twofold: to rescue it from the devaluation it suffers when judged only from the male point of view; and to balance it by sketching a vision of adult maturity that combines the male concern for rights with the female attention to needs. Women, she argues, need to attend to the rights perspective in order to better include themselves in the injunction to take care, to respond; men need to cultivate a greater relational sense in order to overcome their problems with intimacy. Careful to differentiate moral themes rather than the sexes per se, she locates the differences she finds in "the interaction of experience and thought, in different voices and the dialogues to which they give rise, in the way we listen to ourselves and to others, in the stories we tell about our lives."[26]

For an explanation of how these patterns came to be, Gilligan, like many other feminist theorists, turns to Chodorow. "Women mother," Chodorow tells us. "Women's mothering is one of the

few universal and enduring elements of the sexual division of labor." She acknowledges that the particular organization of mothering varies across cultures: "[Cross-cultural evidence] suggests that
there can be a variety of other participants in child care. Children
of both sexes, though more often girls, often perform caretaking
functions in addition to women." Nonetheless, she claims that the
practices of mothering are sufficiently fundamental to women's lives
to merit the claim "universal." Finding biological and evolutionary
explanations inadequate, she offers a social/psychological account
of the reproduction of mothering: "Women's mothering reproduces itself cyclically." Daughters are mothered by women who
see the daughter as like themselves, an extension of themselves;
thus the girl's primary sense of herself is formed within a context
of fusion with another. Sons, in contrast, are experienced "as a
male opposite" by the mother; boys come to think of themselves as
separate from the mother, as not-mother. "Girls emerge from this
period with a basis for 'empathy' built into their primary definition
of self in a way that boys do not."[27] Women's mothering, and men's
lack of it, produce girls who are prepared to mother and boys who
are not.

One of the most common criticisms of Gilligan and Chodorow,
of praxis feminism generally, and beyond that of nearly any face of
feminism is the accusation of essentialism. Nancy Fraser and Linda
Nicholson find "a problematic essentialism" in Chodorow and Gilligan. Young finds essentialism throughout gynocentric feminism,
which "theorizes women as a category with a set of essential attributes." Alcoff identifies cultural feminism as "the ideology of a female nature or female essence." Haraway criticizes both socialist
feminism and radical feminism for the "essentializing move" that
tends to "erase or police difference." Bordo finds in Gilligan, Chodorow, and Ruddick claims for "a natural foundation for knowledge." Harding asks if the feminist standpoint theories are "too
firmly rooted in a problematic politics of essentialized identities?"
Jeffrey Weeks finds in Adrienne Rich's praise of lesbianism an "essentialism about femininity." Spelman takes most of feminist theory to task for producing a "story of woman" that substitutes a few
women for all: "essentialism invites me to take what I understand
to be true of me 'as a woman' for some golden nugget of womanness
all women have as women; and it makes the participation of other

women inessential to the production of the story." Moi accuses both Irigaray and Cixous of falling into the same "essentialist trap" they set out to avoid.[28]

And so on. Feminists love to hate essentialism, to track it down in its various hiding places, to identify its disguised reproductions, to ferret it out in fellow feminists, and to assure ourselves that we are not committing its sins. Exactly what is at stake here? What slippages can we find if we look into the various deployments of the term, and what can they tell us about our own dependency on that with which we do battle?

Essentialism?

It is time to unpack the term *essentialism* and the charges that accompany it. I find at least three different accusations that go under the heading of essentialism. One is largely a straw argument; a second raises serious political and epistemological questions; a third reflects back onto our own practices in ways we would do well to examine.

One meaning of the term is what I call essentialism per se. It attributes women's psychological and social experiences to fixed and unchanging traits resident in women's physiology or in some larger order of things. The experiences women have and the meaning of their experiences are determined by this underlying essence of womanness, an essence contained in bodies and expressed in culture. Because this position clearly echoes Aristotelian and Hegelian arguments, Judeo-Christianity, and other male-ordered notions of women, it is not surprising that most feminists eschew it. In fact, we have been so determined not to participate in this discourse that we have difficulty talking coherently about bodies at all. Essentialism per se is sometimes detected in the writings of cosmic feminism, although it is also contested there; at any rate, the cosmic side of feminism carries so little academic legitimacy that it is accorded scant attention within feminist theory.[29] Within current debates in feminist theory, accusations of this form of essentialism do battle with an argument made largely out of straw. Few theorists make such claims, and certainly Gilligan and Chodorow do not.

A second meaning of essentialism refers to a universalizing move that takes the patterns visible in one's own time and place to be accurate for all. Many feminists share this problem of overgeneralization with Hegel; it's a way of saying that, ultimately, "everything is me." Praxis feminism's focus on women's practices strives to articulate the concrete activities and events of women's lives, but when one set of practices, or one account of their meaning, takes precedence over all others, it prevents further appeal to the concrete and the particular. Some of the practices of some of the women then come to stand for all; through this metynomic move, one part becomes the whole. As Jane Flax reminds us, such "reductive moves" make our practices into overly docile metaphors: "each of our conceptions of a practice (e.g., mothering) may capture an aspect of a very complex and contradictory set of social relations. Confronted with complex and changing relations, we try to reduce these to simple, unified, and undifferentiated wholes."[30]

Such conceptualizations of women's daily practices disqualify unlike women and also unduly exclude men from the world of concrete and daily knowledge. Both Benjamin and Chernin, in her influential work on body size, make assumptions about mothers who lack a sense of self and fathers who possess one, assumptions that irritate the reader into protesting, "But what if it wasn't like that?!" What if our mothers did not fail "to synthesize subjectivity and femininity"?[31] Haraway points to the inability of women to claim a monopoly on dailiness when she asks, "What about men's access to daily competence, to knowing how to build things, to take them apart, to play?"[32] So this second meaning of essentialism is more properly called universalizing: it assumes a sameness across places and times for one's categories and interpretations.

A third notion sometimes included in the charge of essentialism entails any constitution of a unified set of categories around the terms *woman* and *man*. To constitute a coherent category, some phenomenon, say *women*, is pulled out of its infinitely complex context and made to stand on its own. Some connections of that phenomenon to others (for example, of women to children) are featured, while other connections (say, of women to violence) are silenced. Any analysis requires the naming of such coherencies; it is fundamental to the use of language to employ some set of categories about which generalizations can be made. There are ways to assert one's categories that contain periodic reminders of their partiality, and ways that do not, but the need to operate with some set of unified categories is unavoidable. Feminists who deplore this as essentialist or universalist are overlooking their own necessary participation in this linguistic practice.[33]

Examples of the slippage among different meanings of essentialism can be found in two recent analyses: one of Gilligan and Chodorow in particular, the other of western feminist theory more generally. In "Social Criticism Without Philosophy: An Encounter Between Feminism and Postmodernism," Nancy Fraser and Linda Nicholson make a persuasive plea for more historical and comparative analysis within feminist theory, for recognition that no single political or epistemological approach is adequate to the situation of all women. They reach this sensible conclusion, however, through a discussion in which the various connotations of the term essentialism are elided and the authors' own participation in aspects of the practice they decry goes unremarked. The first use of essentialism comes in the form of a criticism of Shulamith Firestone, who "invoked biological differences between women and men to explain sexism." Arguments like Firestone's are found to be essentialist because "they project onto all women and men qualities which develop under historically specific social conditions." This is essentialism per se, an argument from (some aspects of) biology to (all of) society.

The second use of essentialism is in connection with Chodorow's discussion of mothering; Fraser and Nicholson claim that Chodorow "posits the existence of a single activity, 'mothering,' which, while differing in specifics in different societies, nevertheless constitutes enough of a natural kind to warrant one label." Along with Hartsock, Catharine MacKinnon and others, Chodorow "claims to have identified a basic kind of human practice found in all societies which has cross-cultural explanatory power. . . . It is not the sort of thing, then, whose historical origins need to be investigated."

This take on essentialism refers to what I am calling universalism; it criticizes the sort of overgeneralization that allows historical and geographic differences to disappear and substitutes claims to universality for investigation of how things come to be. The third way in which essentialism is used to criticize Chodorow and Gilligan involves the constitution of unified categories:

The difficulty here is that categories like sexuality, mothering, reproduction and sex-affective production, group together phenomena which are not necessarily conjoined in all societies, while separating off from one another phenomena which are not necessarily separated. . . . for a theorist to use such categories to construct a universalistic social theory is to risk projecting the socially dominant conjunctions and dispersions of her own society onto others, thereby distorting important features of both.[34]

Fraser and Nicholson are on solid ground in their criticism of Firestone for essentialism per se, although it is telling that they had to go back to a very early contribution to feminist theory to find a culprit. Their footing remains solid when they tackle the problems of universalizing in Chodorow and elsewhere. Chodorow's adaptation of psychoanalytic thought retains ideas about a deep self formed through processes of separation and individuation that are arguably quite modern and western. But their shift into the third meaning of essentialism, in which the constitution of categories is itself the problem, misrepresents Gilligan's argument to some extent and also overlooks their own participation in the constitutive process. "Gilligan's disclaimers notwithstanding," Fraser and Nicholson argue, "to the extent that she described women's moral development in terms of *a* different voice; to the extent that she did not specify which women, under which specific historical circumstances, have spoken with the voice in question; and to the extent that she grounded her analysis in the explicitly cross-cultural framework of Nancy Chodorow, her model remained essentialist."[35]

Meanwhile, Gilligan explicitly disavows any historical or cross-cultural application of her analysis, and is reasonably specific about the populations from which her generalizations are drawn.[36] Her use of Chodorow's arguments is brief and serves primarily to contrast feminist readings of psychoanalytic material with male-ordered ones. She frequently qualifies her generalizations, stating, for example, that men "more often" fear personal affiliation than women, that concern about not hurting others is a "major theme" for women, that women's moral judgments differ from men's "in the greater extent" to which they are tied to compassion, that women have a "proclivity" to stress the concrete over the abstract, and so forth.[37] But having made those qualifications, Gilligan, like Chodorow, Hartsock and most praxis feminists, goes on to speak of women and men as coherent categories with stable boundaries. This move is not an oversight or an expression of insensitivity. It is a requirement of the kind of theorizing that contrasts men-as-a-group with women-as-a-group. In order to make generalizations about women, these theorists set up contrasts not with other women but with men. The search for a systematicity within women's psychosocial development or women's labor incites a unification within these categories, sacrificing differences to achieve a coherent analytic unit. Fraser and Nicholson are correct when they observe that to do this, one must "group together phenomena which are not necessarily conjoined in all societies, while separating off from one another phenomena which are not necessarily separated." [38] But all feminist analyses, indeed all analyses, have to make some such move, have to stand at least temporarily on some stable territory in order to bring other phenomena under scrutiny. Fraser and Nicholson themselves have recourse to posited unities such as "feminism," "postmodernism," and "the oppression of women."

One might, then, ask Gilligan to remind herself and her readers more forcefully of the tentativeness of her generalizations and the partiality of her categories. There is a disturbing completeness to her analysis. Does everything fit so neatly into her narrative? Were there no responses in her interviews that confounded rather than affirmed her interpretations? Praxis feminism strives to articulate a coherent women's experience that can pose an alternative to existing coherencies. When the coherencies are overly tight and work to disqualify that which resides upon their own margins, a move toward universalism is afoot. But to call this essentialism is unhelpful. All categories are vulnerable to the charge of arbitrariness, and all language operates metaphorically, allowing parts to come to stand for wholes. So to label such moves as Gilligan's essentialist is too easy. It lumps them too readily with dissimilar practices and claims an innocence for one's own categories and generalizations that does not withstand scrutiny.

A second interesting treatment of questions concerning essentialism comes from Chandra Mohanty in "Under Western Eyes: Feminist Scholarship and Colonial Discourses." Although Mohanty does not use the word essentialist, her concern is with the problem of universalizing in western feminist theory. She does not criticize what I have called essentialism per se, since she sees it infrequently at work. But she sees as problematic analyses that employ an "ethnocentric universalism" by which they "discursively colonize the material and historical heterogeneities of the lives of women in the third world, thereby producing/representing a composite, singular 'third-world woman.' " This universalizing move occurs when western feminists (whom Mohanty recognizes are not all the same) take themselves as the norm or referent for defining the category *women* and assume that third-world women can be fitted into that category. Mohanty's argument is an eloquent call for contextualization, for replacing assumptions about women as "an always-already constituted group" with specific historical and geographic analyses of "the production of women as socio-economic political groups within particular local contexts."[39]

Her call for attention to the complex contexts through which the meaning of being a woman is produced in different racial, ethnic and class circumstances is similar to Fraser and Nicholson's argument for greater historically- and culturally-specific analysis. Both essays rightly argue for more tentative and multidimensional conceptualizations. Fraser and Nicholson call for replacing "unitary notions of 'woman' and 'feminine gender identity' with plural and complexly constructed conceptions of social identity, treating gender as one relevant strand among others, attending also to class, race, ethnicity, age and sexual orientation."[40] Mohanty is even more cautious in suggesting that "it is the *common context* of political struggle against class, race, gender and imperialist hierarchies that may constitute third-world women as a strategic group at this historical juncture."[41] My quarrel is not with their solutions to the problem of universalizing in feminist theory, solutions with which I agree. Rather, I take issue with their formulation of the problem: they make too simple a distinction between bad feminist theory (universalizing, essentializing) and good.

All of us are implicated in the difficult process of constituting serviceable categories, learning to remember what we overlooked in order to do so, reminding ourselves to come back to our omissions and erasures with an open mind and heart toward that which does not fit. Mohanty's own language brings back into circulation some of the unities she rejects. "By women as a category of analysis," she observes, "I am referring to the crucial presupposition that all of us of the same gender, across classes and cultures, are somehow socially constituted as a homogenous group identifiable prior to the process of analysis." What could *of the same gender* mean here? For that matter, who could *us* be? At another point she contrasts "(usually white) Western feminists" with "working-class and feminist women of colour around the world."[42] The unstated assumption here is that all western feminists are middle-class or elite. White women who identify themselves both as working-class and as feminist disappear from the scene.

Mohanty finds it necessary to employ the same kinds of categories she rightly suspects. She tries to get around the problem by distinguishing between purely descriptive uses of gender categories and explanatory uses, but her own arguments suggest that description cannot be so easily uncoupled from analysis: the realm of empirical facts never makes an appearance outside of some analytic framework by which facts are qualified or disqualified for recognition. Greater awareness of the difficulty of avoiding a reinscription of unities into a discourse critical of unities would perhaps mitigate a certain tendency toward self-righteousness in her argument; self-righteousness follows less readily when one recognizes the problematic constitution of unified categories as a common dilemma rather than as something that wrong-headed people do.

In summary: I have considered the arguments of Fraser and Nicholson and of Mohanty extensively here because they illustrate a common slippage in arguments against essentialism and universalism. Beginning with the easy target of essentialism per se, the argument slides through a criticism of universalism into an untenable rejection of unified coherencies themselves. In the process, a comforting but overly simple distinction emerges between virtuous theories that do not employ unified categories of analysis and offensive theories that do. I do not mean to say that there are no offensive theories. Far from it; the disturbing tendency of much of western feminist theory to go right on universalizing despite cogent arguments to the contrary suggests that some of us are very slow learners. (Or that something less innocent than misunderstanding is going on.) My point is that important critics of universalizing weaken their case by neglecting their own participation in the linguistic/political practices they deplore.

The difference between universalizing, with its absorption of difference into sameness, and any constitution of analytic categories is largely in the care with which one approaches one's material. When you take some more-or-less stable category as your unity, the point of reference from which your analysis can proceed, at what point do you remind yourself of what you have disregarded in order to do so? What signposts do you build into your accounts to serve as reminders? What posture do you take toward that which does not or will not fit into even the most liberation-bound of categories? The taking of the unity is an interpretive strategy of argument, and allows, among other things, for praxis feminism to criticize male power and to identify and valorize (some version of) women's experiences. The reminder that the unity was imposed rather than discovered is a genealogical move, an effort to be alert to the limitations of strategies of analysis that one must nonetheless use in some form. Living with the tension between these two impulses takes ironic humor and persistence.

The epistemological codes that an argument employs are key factors in pressing the argument toward or away from a universalizing posture. Praxis feminisms strongly indebted, for example, to Freud, Marx, Hegel, Darwin, or Kohlberg, tend to employ narrative epistemologies to order their accounts of things.[43] These are often stage theories that provide an ordering grid by which changes through time and across space can be arranged sequentially. Narrative epistemologies provide a beginning, middle and end to the stories they tell. History (or personality, or the species) can be said to be "going somewhere." Feminist writers usually differ radically with their male predecessors over the content or import of the stages, but they hold onto the basic conviction of such an ordering. Narrative epistemologies often accompany, and are disguised by, empirical codes of knowing. Echoing Joe Friday's demand for "just the facts, ma'am," empirical codes of knowledge may seem more reliable because of their greater closeness to their evidence. One interviews X number of women, or observes them at work, or participates with them in their rituals, or studies their society, and then offers an analysis and account of their words and deeds, their experiences. In this sense praxis feminism, compared to its cosmic and linguistic cousins, is the most firmly rooted in the standard claims to knowledge of the social sciences, even in modernity itself. This is not to say that praxis feminism is crudely positivist; usually it is not; but it generally relies upon an interpretive strategy that dips into an established hermeneutic to make sense out of the particulars of the analysis.

The problem here is not that praxis feminists make reference to some reality standing outside their accounts of it—all of us do that in some way. The problem is rather that the language of observation and report disguises the move while making it. Empirical codes function as show-stoppers, relieving a theorist of the need to probe further into the connection between her material and her own activities as a knower. Such codes thus allow one to underestimate the potency of one's conceptual interventions, even to avoid recognition of them at all. Can the interviewer be so sure, for example, that she interviewed X number of women? She may have interviewed some white people who happened to be female, or some heterosexuals, or urban-dwellers, or English speakers. Praxis feminism can slide toward positivism by being so embedded in its narratives that certain claims become self-evident. The fringes of one's own argument tend to disappear, and the very possibility of a fringe as well; we forget, then we forget that we forgot. Crucial categories can acquire an almost metaphysical solidity, becoming the "first premise rather than the first question" of the argument.[44] Words like *objective, real,* or *true* can then be used without even a raised eyebrow. A closed hermeneutic produces the dangerous, often unarticulated, assumption that experiences have lodged within them a meaning that is revealed in the light of theory.[45] In this moment praxis feminism, from a genealogical perspective, is in bed with conventional social science and the law.

Praxis feminism's conviction that doing produces knowing, that what we do makes us who we are, leads to an investigative stance toward the conditions and substance of the doing. Such investigations are among praxis feminism's outstanding contributions. But there are different ways to position oneself in relation to the activity of investigating, and empirical knowledge codes tend to treat data as self-evident and thus to disguise the positioning that is going on. This move takes place even within investigations that are aware of such dilemmas and reflective about participating in them. Two examples illustrate the problem. The first comes from Jane Flax's negotiations among postmodernism, psychoanalysis, and feminism, which are both attentive to and selectively forgetful of the dilemmas of the empirical code. Flax expresses her suspicions about claims to have uncovered a reality that waits to be investigated, yet when she discusses Benjamin Winnicott's contributions to object-relations theory, notions of the "true self" are referenced and deployed unproblematically, no longer marked as suspicious with quotation marks or other flags.[46] Claims about an "external reality" and "internal reality" somehow get sufficiently firmed up that they serve to fend off previously stated reservations.[47] The categories and convictions of psychoanalysis come to be taken as foundational: "For all its shortcomings psychoanalysis presents the best and most promising theories of how a self that is simultaneously embodied, social, 'fictional' and real comes to be, changes, and persists over time."

But no argument is mounted about the comparative deficiencies of contending theories of the self (developmental, social psychological, behavioral, and so forth). Such confident residence in the narrative structures of psychoanalysis allows the empirical code to operate unhindered. Discussing sources of domination, Flax comments that "because so much remains unknown about the constitution and effects of gender relations, we should first assume that such relations are social, that is, not the result of the differentiated possession of natural or unequal properties among persons, until evidence to the contrary is amassed."[48] But what could count, prima facie, as evidence, unless some set of ontological and epistemological presuppositions, "bound together by insistence," has already been maneuvered silently and potently into position?[49] Flax's arguments for an "unstable, complex and disorderly" reality do not comply readily with her firm residence in object-relations theory.[50]

A second example of disguised positioning comes from Rosemary Hennessy and Rajeswari Mohan's "The Construction of Woman in Three Popular Texts of Empire: Toward a Critique of Materialist Feminism," which also both critiques and relies on an empirical code. Rejecting "an empiricist notion of history as data," the authors eschew an "empiricist emphasis on the visible as self-explanatory" because it mystifies and naturalizes conventional social arrangements. Yet their analysis of three empire-sustaining texts confidently tells of "the immediate context" of their stories as if there were only one context that mattered. Claims to have found "the objective links" between women in Britain and in the empire assert, rather than establish, one set of connections as primary and dismiss others as inconsequential.[51] The women who participated in or supported the Married Women's Reform Law in Britain (which helped middle-class women in Britain at the expense of the colonies) or the Age of Consent Act in India (which helped impose British legal codes on Indian society) are revealed in this argument to have cooperated in tightening class and colonial controls. But this is not the whole story. Because the British women reformers are not present as players in this account, but instead occupy part of the field against which the account becomes intelligible, other possible stories cannot appear or even suggest their existence. Hennessy and Mohan are persuasive, even brilliant, in their shift of class perspective away from privileged women to economically exploited women, but less so in their positioning of themselves in relation to that shift.

Ironic Interventions

Praxis feminism's shift from rights to needs and from separation to connection offers many possibilities for developing feminist discourses. By putting reflexively constituted intersubjectivity at the heart of identity and desire, praxis feminism problematizes the Hegelian subject (and others like him); when praxis feminism gives value to the affirmation interconnectedness implies, hostility toward others and anxiety over relationships require explanation. Despite problems of universalizing, praxis feminism possesses tools to resist universalizations in its focus upon lived structures, concrete practices, daily experiences, and particular events. The approach is in principle open to history and geography and thus to recognizing diversity among women and men. The claim that "these women in this place do certain things and think of themselves in certain ways" can too easily become "women do this and think that," but the resources to call attention to and resist this move come partly out of the perspective that produces it. The emphasis on human need and on political economy connects feminism to socialism and class analysis, a welcome affirmation in light of the rejection of the material by other contemporary feminists. Because they interpret women's experience as revealing positive virtues rather than unrelenting victimization, praxis feminists can articulate women's ways as models for a reconstituted individual and collective life. Their focus on needs and persons-in-relations is also compatible with some version of rights—people can be seen as having a right to their needs as well as a need for their rights—and such a focus could thus connect to and expand the dominant discourse.

Praxis feminism looks to the traditional and typical experiences and activities of women for both an explanation of the world and a model of a different and better world. But the traditional and typical experiences of women are precisely those that patriarchy has assigned us. So this form of feminist argument risks collaboration with the very discourse it set out to combat. After all, (some version of) mothering is lauded by *Reader's Digest* and Hallmark as well as by some feminist theorists. Mothering as a hermeneutic anchor can easily give rise to a sentimentalization rather than a radicalization of women's lives.[52] It could become the basis for a feminist categorical agreement with being. Ruddick and others who valorize mothering are often careful to distinguish their approaches from those producing the kitsch of the hegemonic order; Ruddick anticipates the kitsch of the woman peacemaker when she comments that "the 'peacefulness' with which mothers are credited is usually a sweet, appeasing gentleness that gives peace a bad name while alienating almost anyone who had a mother or is one. Maternal peacefulness is a way of fighting as well as of loving, as angry as it is gentle."[53]

Nevertheless, it is difficult to talk about mothering at all without some association with the enthusiastic sentimentalization of mothering already in circulation. Although it is not completely captured by power, the official interpretation of mothering holds a place of dubious honor in dominant discourses and institutions, as a trip to the parenting section of the bookstore or to a florist's shop on Mother's Day will attest. This form of kitsch is readily available in a society that easily becomes maudlin about mothers but legitimates little power for women. Similarly, the valorization of care can, depending upon the context and direction of argument, either work toward an alternative ethical theory or degenerate into a homily of self-sacrifice.[54] Audre Lorde reminds us that women are not all equally situated in relation to patriarchy's care-taking demands: "In this country, Black women traditionally have had compassion for everybody else except ourselves. We have cared for whites because we had to for pay or survival; we have cared for our children and our fathers and our brothers and our lovers."[55] Exhortations toward care and responsibility have to be coupled with radical critique of the current institutional and discursive circumstances in which caring and responding are embedded. Most praxis feminists evince an awareness of this dilemma but are not always able to negotiate it successfully.

Irony could be marshaled as a resource to combat kitsch. Mothering itself could be viewed ironically for its constant slips between confidence and befuddlement, between fearing the danger in the world and acting as though the life of the child is secure. The "double focus on small and great, near and eternal," that Ruddick finds in mothering could, with a bit of urging, become an ironic doubleness, a desperately casual commitment to continue in the face of uncertainty.[56] There is a lot of serious play in mothering. Mothering's humility ("In a world beyond one's control, to be humble is to have a profound sense of the limits of one's actions and of the unpredictability of the consequences of one's work") and cheerfulness ("To be cheerful means to respect chance, limit, and imperfection and still act as if it is possible to keep children safe") lend themselves to (without requiring) an ironic stance. Mothering demands that we live with ambivalence and tension, with competing urgencies that can never be once and for all resolved but must be negotiated and renegotiated daily: "A mother can never stop looking, but she must not look too much."[57]

Turning mothering toward irony both moves it away from kitsch and suggests a particularly praxis feminist twist on irony. Valorization of the self-in-relation, of subjectivity made meaningful through connectedness, makes the configuration of elements in Seery's irony begin to look particularly male. Seery's irony issues from the meaninglessness of life in the face of death, the pretense that "caring about another human being matters at all (rather than not) in view of human finality." This construal of an ironic dilemma is the construal of the self as walled city, the isolated individual besieged by others and prepared to fight. Death is equated with futility, life in common doomed by "the inescapable facts of mortality and separation."[58] Hegel, again. Seery assumes a "radical separateness" between subjects. His ironic path yields the conclusion "that life with others might be thought meaningful after all, not because of an ultimate, essentialist purpose but thanks rather to certain temporary postures of pretense."[59]

But these are not the only two choices. Between blind essentialism and total pretense is the joy in connection, the self-reflective affirmation of relationships, that constitute the subjectivities of selves-in-relation. Out of the lived dailiness of women's work, praxis feminism offers the resources to see the hidden genderedness of Seery's stance. Praxis feminism provides a language for valuing community without sinking people unreflexively into it. Praxis feminism cannot afford uncritically to valorize the relational experiences of women, for those experiences are also deeply marked by subordination; neither can it afford blithely to dismiss them in the name of unfettered individuality, since such individuality comes at the expense of denying worth to women's lives unless they are like men. Praxis feminism offers a language for critical reflection on relations without either abandoning them or disappearing into them. It points toward a kind of knowing that acknowledges the validity of feeling as a form of knowledge while enabling critical reflection on the kinds of knowing that feeling can deliver.

My point is not that women necessarily fear death (their own or another's) less than men do; in fact, a greater appreciation of relational identities can lead to an even greater sense of bereavement when cherished others die. But there is a way to mediate the tensions between the continuity of life and the finality of death other than unreflective faith in a higher purpose ("Things were meant to be this way") or temporary pretense with regard to meaning ("Let's pretend life together is meaningful, even though we know it really is not"). One can agree with Seery that "political order must be understood as a rare achievement given the chaos and flux of life," but this insight into the fragility of community (not to mention its contraints) does not require an a priori separation of selves.[60] One can also agree with his claims for the perpetual incompleteness of politics, its partialities and ambivalences. You don't have to be a walled city to recognize fluidity and to need some slack in the social order. The doubleness of Seery's irony moves, ultimately, between affirmation and skepticism, between belief and disbelief. I am seeking an ironic posture between interpretation and genealogy that stands between two contrary beliefs. Holding together needed incompatibles is not quite the same as holding commitment in the face of doubt. Disbelief is the erasure of belief, but genealogy is not simply the erasure of interpretation: it is interpretation's uncooperative partner. Seery's irony allows the ordering of collective life in the face of "natural" separation and death. Mine enables the self-undermining/affirming ability to take apart what you put together and to put back together what you take apart.

Praxis feminism could also generate irony through a playful approach to crossing boundaries and naming differences. Ethnographic, historical, and comparative inquiries within this perspective especially suggest such a move. They require frequent crossing of borders between subjects and audiences, or between past and present, or between the theorist and her subject matter. An example of this sort of irony might be found in Ong's analysis of Malaysian factory women. The first sentence of the preface, and of the blurb on the back cover of the book, asks, "Why are Malay women workers periodically seized by spirit possession on the shopfloor of modern factories?"[61] There is very little in this book about spirit possession; it is primarily a complex and rewarding analysis of the intersecting political economies of patriarchy and imperialism, with thoughtful reflections on the perils of the ethnographic practices that allowed the production of the analysis.

So why the false advertising? Is it merely a marketing strategy, a way to seduce the reader with the promise of exotic/erotic adventures in third-world otherness?[62] Perhaps. But I prefer an interpretation more generous to the author and to the argument. The briefness of the discussion of spirit possession can be taken ironically, as marking the perils of addressing an English-speaking audience about third-world themes, especially those involving women's bodies and religious possession. Before getting to the brief chapter on spirit possession, the reader must acquire an education about the configurations of traditional Kampung society, the evolution of the class structure, the organization of kin relations and domestic life, and the effects of colonialism on all these processes. Further, Ong explores the relation of the expanding state bureaucracy to global corporate strategies and the organization of gender, sexuality, and families. Only then does she offer her arguments that "spirit imageries reveal not only a mode of unconscious retaliation against male authority but fundamentally a sense of dislocation in human relations and a need for greater spiritual vigilance in domains reconstituted by capitalist relations of production."[63]

The ironic gesture here could serve to gently mock the predictable handicaps of western readers while nonetheless continuing to address us. The prominent mention of spirit possession can be expected to hook a western audience; who could resist an opportunity to view vicariously this mysterious world? But once immersed in the text, the western reader eager for cheap thrills finds out that a thorough education in the political economy of colonialism and male dominance is a prerequisite. The unspoken warning: "Don't think you can just peep into my culture here and there, shopping for some access to the third-world exotic/erotic, pulling it out of its geographic and historical context. Learn something about Malaysia and its exploitation by western capitalists first. Pay your dues." As a political strategy to resist appropriation and exoticization while still addressing the audience that might be inclined toward those practices, this ironic gesture serves well. Praxis feminism might find some resources to survive its tensions and sustain its needed incompatibilities in the political opportunities of irony.

Chapter Four

Cosmic Feminism

Cosmic feminism offers an alternative vision of subjectivity stressing the self-in-place in relation to a larger natural or spiritual order
of things. There are many versions of this perspective, as there are
of the other feminisms as well. Some authors appeal to the (selected) heritage of Native Americans, stressing women's ancient
wisdom that men have suppressed but not completely obliterated.[1]
Others invoke the traditions of ancient goddess religions and the
heritage of witchcraft as sources of personal strength and creative
power for women, and as validation of nurturance for women and
men.[2] Still others speak of a poetic bonding between women, other
animals, and the earth, a bonding constituted partly by what men
have made of us but not reducible to a residue of male power.[3]

This chapter marks the terrain that comes into focus when claims
about subjectivity and knowledge are examined through the lens
made available by cosmic feminism. Cosmic feminism is usually
accorded scant attention within the academy. Perhaps this is because its metatheoretical operations are somewhat unsophisticated;
perhaps because its productions and circulations go on largely outside academic environs; or perhaps because it lends itself readily
to kitsch. Yet each of these traits can be reformulated to stimulate
theoretical interest rather than to discourage it. Cosmic feminism's
metheoretical apparatus, its strategies for making truth claims and
framing inquiries, are situated within a set of discursive claims about
origins, ends, and depths that are well worth serious inquiry. The
widespread interest in cosmic feminism outside the university suggests its significance for feminism's more popular, often more explicitly political, manifestations. Its frequent slides into kitsch may

signal both tendencies toward sentimentalization and possibilities for ironic mediations.

Like other kinds of feminisms, cosmic feminism offers resources within itself from which to address its limitations. Further, the perspectives made available by its praxis and linguistic companions can work on cosmic feminism to bring both significant differences and unexpected similarities to light. Cosmic feminism's robust political activism, its widespread availability outside the university, and its theoretical construals of nature, culture, and gender all suggest its importance for feminist meditations on subjectivity.

Creating Cosmic Feminism

Cosmic feminists typically invoke the political and epistemological possibilities of transcendence and return. While some look to accounts of pre-Enlightenment Europe, others go back to various pre-Christian paganisms and/or to hunting and gathering societies. Susan Griffin, for example, makes her arguments against both modern science and mainstream Christianity in part by invoking the worldview of medieval Europe. This worldview has been characterized by Jane Bennett as "robust faith," "an enchanted view of the world, where nature is filled with mystery and meaning and where each thing in nature is interconnected with every other. . . . Nature speaks and says that it coheres through relations of resemblance."[4] The world is presumed to be a creation, thus positing the existence of a creator. The assumption of such a creator allows cosmic feminists to posit, or at least to assume, "an authority responsible for guaranteeing the truth as well as the reality of the world."[5] The cosmos is thought to have a binding character, to manifest an order not completely at human disposal. Knowledge consists in listening for the world's whisper, recovering "divine intentions embodied in the natural world and revealed in signs."[6] The sensuous and the supersenuous are united through rituals and practices that seek to participate in rather than to master the world.

The cosmological order in which cosmic feminists invest has a significantly gendered dimension. They often appeal to historical or anthropological analyses of the strength of female symbols or practices in pre-Enlightenment modes of consciousness. Hans Peter Duerr, for example, charts in the emergence of modernity the gradual attack on and erosion of the boundary between wilderness and civilization. Those who had knowledge of that boundary, of "the time between the times," were women: "Initially, this displacement process especially involved those who were situated in a particular manner 'on the boundary,' and who since ancient times were in some uncontrollable way open to the other world. These were women, and among them principally those who had specifically developed their ability to cross over that line at one time or another."[7]

The subduing of boundary-crossing consciousness, according to Duerr, simultaneously entailed the intensification of male power over women. Marija Gimbutas's work on the divinities of Old Europe and Gerda Lerner's history of patriarchy are other examples of writings that, although they cannot themselves be characterized as cosmic feminism, provide historical material for cosmic constructions.[8] Cosmic feminists recruit such insights and arguments to construe early societies in ways that supply congenial origin stories for an anti-patriarchal quest.

Cosmic feminists who claim the title of witch are often invoking the traditions of premodern societies. Some trace this tradition to residues of pre-Christian goddess religions (as Duerr does) and/or to hunting and gathering societies. Charlene Spretnak, for example, praises "the sacred link of the Goddess in her many guises with totemic animals and plants, sacred groves, womblike caves, the moon-rhythm blood of menses, the ecstatic dance" as central to ecofeminism.[9] Paula Gunn Allen looks to her own Native American traditions for "the roots of American feminism." Further, she contends that "the gynocratic tribes of the American continent provided the basis for all the dreams of liberation that characterize the modern world."[10] Written in what Renato Rosaldo has called, in a different context, "a nostalgic mode," cosmic feminist appeals to a premodern order are sometimes quite literal and other times "more tropological than anthropological."[11] Although Ynestra King claims that "ecofeminism is not an argument for a return to prehistory," a selective reading of primal peoples provides its inspiration, if not its model, for social change.[12]

To call these sources of inspiration *premodern* entails some difficulties. I am using this term as an umbrella category for cultural orderings that, while perhaps having little else in common, pre-

date the western Enlightenment (although their remnants and leg-
acies may also survive it) and serve as sources for cosmic feminism's
struggles against modernity. They can generally be characterized
by what Peggy Sanday calls an "inner orientation": they are likely
to have feminine rather than masculine deities, and to be relatively
less violent and more egalitarian than modern societies.[13] To call
them premodern is to privilege modernity; it makes the modern
serve as ballast by which what came before is stabilized. *Premodern* is certainly not a term most such cultures would apply to themselves, at least not until after their demise following the assaults of
modernity. But the term is helpful in inquiring into cosmic feminism's ontologies precisely because cosmic feminism is a modern
(and perhaps also a postmodern) phenomenon, a quest for return
thoroughly located in exile. Any vision of early societies available
to the residents of modernity, no matter what their political and
spiritual sympathies, is a version filtered through modernity's categories and affected by its conquests.

Cosmic feminism employs a heavily interpretive approach to
questions of meaning. It partakes of cosmological thinking in which
ultimate questions of meaning are asked, origins are sought, and
an order able to provide those meanings and establish those origins
is presumed. The dominant notion of subjectivity within this feminist territory is less one of a self than of a soul, a spiritual or natural
dimension of a person that participates in some larger and higher
scheme of things. The soul sketched in cosmic feminism is not necessarily unitary; it might feel the contrary pull of conflicting urges;
but there is usually some promise of resolution through participation in a higher order. Cosmic feminists believe that they can approach this transcendent realm through appropriate attitudes,
practices, or events; it is not just an inspirational fiction, but a place
of completion that beckons its adherents.

A soul-oriented subjectivity can provide an appeal against the
pull of self-interest enshrined in modernity. Connolly notes that
"the disappearance of the world of divine signs and the accentua-
tion of self-interest go together. When the self is not enclosed in a
cosmic world of divine meanings it tends to invest more significance in the microcosmic world of the self. And if the self then
confines its love to itself, the demands of order intensify while the
means of attaining it are reduced to force and the manipulation of

self-interest." Further, the rise of self-interest ushers in the fall of nature; when the world ceases to be a site for the (mysterious) inscription of divine truths, nature is demoted from enchanted to inert. While some cosmic feminists seek a literal return to (some version of) the premodern, others strive for "a rhetoric of divinized nature" that can speak to people embedded in modernity. [14] Either way, the longing for a consciousness that can participate in rather than dominate the world of trees and grass, ocean, mountain and sky, is pervasive.

When cosmic feminists speak of knowledge, depth metaphors prevail. For example, one writer speaks of that which can "touch the deep places"; another speaks of discovering "the wisdom of [women's] bodies" in a place of "deep knowing and assured teaching"; yet another calls upon "the deep drives in us to experience and share pleasure, to connect, to create, to see our impact on others and on the world." [15] Relations within and among women, other animals, and the planet are conceptualized organically: much stress is placed on wholeness; change is equated with healing; the uncovering and restoration of balance and harmony are valorized. Starhawk, for instance, calls upon agricultural metaphors to make her case for magic: "I am on the side of the power that emerges from within, that is inherent in us as the power to grow is inherent in seed. As a shaper, as one who practices magic, my work is to find that power, to call it forth, to coax it out of hiding, tend it, and free it of constrictions . . . we cannot bear our own true fruit when we are under another's control." [16] Women are often held to have natural qualities inclining them toward the spiritual; for example, one woman profiled as a contemporary shaman claims that "women had, amongst other qualities, an ability to heal, to have direct insight into situation, and to give support without judging." [17] Metaphors of darkness and endarkenment are employed to claim that which is inner and of the earth from the tyranny of light and enlightenment. [18]

While akin to linguistic feminism in the power it attributes to language, cosmic feminism usually discerns a prediscursive or nondiscursive order prior to and unproduced by discourse. Like praxis feminism, cosmic feminism sees in women's daily labor the grounds for a different and better perspective; but for cosmic feminism this

labor is buried deep within the rhythms of the natural and/or sacred:

We dealt with hunger. We dealt with cold. We were the ones who held
things together. Knit one, purl two. *We were the ones who, after working*
all day, made the meals. And the beginning. *We made sure everybody*
ate. And the end. *We were the ones who, if the cupboard was bare, faced*
the open mouths of our children. And the way we thought grew from
what we did.[19]

In Susan Griffin's poetic imagery the evocation of concrete activities is contained within cosmological metaphors of sacredness and
unity. Speaking in "women's voice," Griffin writes:

We say if you change the course of this river you change the shape of the
whole place. . . . And that one act cannot be separated from another.
. . . We say look how the water flows from this place and returns as
rainfall, everything returns, we say, and one thing follows another, there
are limits, on what can be done and everything moves. We are all a part
of this motion, we say, and the way of the river is sacred, and this grove
of trees is sacred, and we ourselves, we tell you, are sacred.[20]

The *we* here is women. Cosmic feminism's version of women's
subjectivity invokes ancient connections of women to nature, bodies, and the divine. Like praxis feminism, cosmic feminism emphasizes relations; but they are relations that go beyond the intersubjective and contest the boundaries between human and animal,
human and nature, human and divine. Strongly anti-dualistic and
anti-hierarchical, cosmic feminists "strive toward a new way of living in the world as co-members of the ecological community."[21] In
Woman of Power: A Magazine of Feminism, Spirituality and Poli-
tics, editor Pia M. Godavitarne talks about a self in relation to "animal and plant spirit realms."[22] Another essayist invokes "psychic
arts [astrology, tarot, trance, etc.], the psychology of dreams and
the unconscious, knowledge of reincarnation, Goddess religion, and
women's blood mysteries."[23] In Griffin's *Women and Nature* common ground is forged between women and various other animals—
show horses, cows, and mules—and between women and natural
elements—wind, forests, land, and matter. In his explorations of
Gaia, Chris Jones finds that "women's spirituality and the emerging 'theology of ecology' are laying the foundation for a religious
movement whose Goddess is the Earth."[24] Cosmic feminists share

with genealogical thinkers an attention to mystery, to excess, to that which exceeds conventional understandings; but while the genealogist attributes excess to the inherent inability of any conceptual apparatus to order completely the recalcitrant material upon which it works, cosmic feminists find their mysteries in that which has not yet been charted, or was known once and then lost.[25]

Likewise, cosmic feminism shares its "pleasure in the confusion of boundaries" with more genealogically oriented feminisms.[26] Donna Haraway, for example, both invokes ecofeminism and works against it as the implicit background for her more technology-friendly arguments. Departing from most cosmic feminists in including the human-machine boundary as one that needs disruption, Haraway nonetheless shares their determination to locate the human within the natural world rather than on top of it. In discussing vision, for example, Haraway refers to "the eye of any ordinary primate like us."[27] In this and other passages she reminds her readers that we too are animals. Cosmic feminism shares with both praxis and linguistic feminisms an opposition to the conventional male-ordered hierarchies of living beings, but the cosmic position is unique in its employment of the language of the sacred to articulate its opposition.[28] Haraway, on the other hand, insists on prying open "the fiction of 'nature' with meanings unmediated by people's relations with each other"; this does not mean that one should not refer to the non-human plant and animal world, only that such references be reflective about the discursive and institutional filters through which they pass.[29] Haraway's ambiguous relation to cosmic feminism seems to combine an attraction to its politics with a suspicion of its metaphysics, a stance I discuss more fully below.

Cosmic feminist themes also provide the spiritual backdrop for critiques of racism in Audre Lorde's essays. In "An Open Letter to Mary Daly," Lorde receives with approval Daly's words on the Goddess, but points out the eurocentrism of taking images of women's spiritual power only from white history/mythology, while reserving for black women the role of victim: "Why doesn't Mary deal with Afrekete as an example? Why are her goddess images only white, western european, judeo-christian? Where was Afrekete, Yemanje, Oyo, and Mawulisa? Where were the warrior goddesses of the Vodun, the Dahomeian Amazons and the warrior-women of Dan?"[30] Lorde writes comfortably within the metaphors

of depth and divinity, and shares cosmic feminism's evocation of
darkness to reference timeless sources of inner power.

For each of us as women, there is a dark place within, where hidden and
growing our true spirit rises. . . . These places of possibility within ourselves are dark because they are ancient and hidden; they have survived
and grown strong through that darkness. Within these deep places, each
one of us holds an incredible reserve of creativity and power, of unexamined and unrecorded emotion and feeling. The woman's place of power
within each of us is neither white nor surface; it is dark, it is ancient, and
it is deep.[31]

Cosmic feminism's visions of a self-in-place with respect to a
larger scheme of things issue a radical challenge to the hubris of
humanism, which puts the human above all else. Refusing entry
into debates about how humans can best master the world, cosmic
feminists ask instead whether we should do so—and answer in the
negative. Invoking rather than sidestepping the realm of the prediscursive or nondiscursive, these views seek to loosen the hold of
language in order to bring into it the animal, the natural, and the
spiritual. Joining politically with a radical version of ecology, such
views generate compelling critiques of technology and of the reduction of the natural world to standing reserve. Cosmic feminism's bridging of the spiritual and the political has produced some
impressive radical feminist politics. The women who tried to levi-
tate the Pentagon in the Pentagon Action days may not have gotten
the building off the ground, but they helped to launch one of contemporary feminism's most radical confrontations with patriarchy.

Among the more political of the cosmic feminists is Starhawk, a
witch who brings her magic rituals to direct actions at the Lawrence Livermore weapons labs, Vandenberg Air Force Base, the
Diablo Canyon nuclear plant, and other sites of patriarchal mega-
power.[32] A further radical public dimension of cosmic feminism
involves the forms of alternative organization it creates; for example, Judi Chamberlin, Hayat Imam, and Spring Redd connect
their convictions about spiritual wholeness to radical, member-
operated mental health organizations such as the Elizabeth Stone
House.[33] Starhawk's insights into the daily structures and processes of radical politics—the problems of structurelessness, the
dilemmas of leadership without hierarchy, useful rules of thumb

for dealing with conflict—are often both helpful and amusing for those struggling with such immediate political challenges.[34]

Vandana Shiva's provocative analysis of "development" provides another example of the political power of a feminist analysis tilted toward the cosmic. I say *tilted* because her argument has significant praxis and linguistic dimensions as well; but these sit within a vocabulary of cosmic forces and sacred principles/personages. Attacking the "sacredness" of modern scientific knowledge and economic development, Shiva shows these to be not "universal categories of progress, but the special projects of modern western patriarchy." The violence to nature that seems intrinsic to what Shiva calls maldevelopment is associated with violence to the women who depend on nature to sustain themselves, their families, and their communities. Shiva's book, she explains, "is an attempt to articulate how rural Indian women, who are still embedded in nature, experience and perceive ecological destruction and its causes, and how they have conceived and initiated processes to arrest the destruction of nature and begin its regeneration."[35]

The argument parallels praxis feminism's in its analysis of the daily experiences of women who interact closely with trees, land, and water to get food, clothing, and shelter for their families. Shiva's analysis is most compelling when she follows in concrete detail the patterns of knowing and working of village women in certain areas of India and relates these patterns to the local environment. Rural Indian women's practices of water use and conservation are now being displaced by scientific water management; commercial forestry is destroying the environments in which local women traditionally foraged for food and fuel; peasant women are being displaced from the food chain through the so-called green and white revolutions. Shiva examines the collection and processing of the *mohwa* tree's fruit and the ethnobotanical knowledge of India's tribal peoples. She discusses Chipko, the resistance movement in rural India, and the tensions between the women and the men in Chipko (the men are more likely to be involved in the market economy and thus more positively inclined toward commercial forestry). She offers a chilling analysis of the relation of the green revolution to female infanticide and feticide. As increased commercialization leads to higher wages for men than for women (often twice as high), women's labor is devalued both in the labor market and outside it.

This trend, coupled with high dowry demands, increases the cost of raising girls while reducing their worth to their families.

Shiva has a keen eye for the ways in which science, through its utterances, constitutes the world to be conveniently suitable to its interventions and exploitations. Water that runs into the sea is "wasted."[36] Trees not marketable from an "industrial materials standpoint" are "clearly weeds."[37] Labor traditionally done by women to sustain life is disqualified from consideration, while the work of "experts" counts as productive:

it is assumed that "production" takes place only when mediated by technologies for commodity production, even when such technologies destroy life. A stable and clean river is not a productive resource in this view: it needs to be "developed" with dams in order to become so. Women, sharing the river as a commons to satisfy the water needs of their families and society, are not involved in productive labour: when substituted by the engineering man, water management and water use become productive activities. Natural forests remain unproductive till they are developed into monoculture plantations of commercial species.[38]

Although the unities of development and progress come under strict scrutiny in Shiva's arguments, other unities pass by unscathed. She invokes "Third World women" (or alternatively, "Indian women" or "women, peasants and tribals") as a group outside of modernity and in tune with nature: "In contemporary times, Third World women, whose minds have not yet been dispossessed or colonised, are in a privileged position to make visible the invisible oppositional categories that they are the custodians of. . . . Women embedded in nature, producing life with nature, are therefore taking the initiative in the recovery of nature."[39] Third-world women from elite and bourgeois backgrounds, who certainly don't live "closer to nature" than, say, a farm woman from Indiana, disappear from the scene. "Nature" is also an unproblematic unity, home for a "feminine principle" that has both agency and purpose. This feminine principle is "Prakriti, the living force that supports life." When women resist commercialization and insist on following the traditional practices of subsistence agriculture, "the feminine principle is stirring."[40]

Recognizing the problems with universal claims, Shiva calls instead for diversity: "They [women] are creating a feminist ideology

that transcends gender, and a political practice that is humanly
inclusive; they are challenging patriarchy's ideological claim to universalism, not with another universalising tendency, but with diversity; and they are challenging the dominant concept of power as
violence with the alternative concept of nonviolence as power."
Yet her disclaimers coexist with a heavy-handed globalizing rhetoric, one that finds a telos in the world, associated at least metaphorically with an ancient Indian goddess with whom one ought to
become properly attuned. Shiva advocates "reclaiming" and "recovering" the feminine principle "from which all life arises." The
longing for a return to a spiritual origin frames her arguments about
rural women's practices and the limits of science.[41]

What does this cosmic overlay on her arguments allow her to
accomplish? It facilitates an appealing humility before the interac-
tive ecosystems of forests, mountains, and oceans. It posits an alternative foundation (in the "primordial power," the "source of
abundance," the "will-to-become-many" and in "play," the various
forms of Prakriti in Indian cosmology) to her adversaries' telos of
redemption through progress.[42] It provides a spiritual anchor for
her political project that may well be significant for those whose
organizations she supports and whose causes she endorses.

It also brings her onto that very shaky ground where metaphors
of wholeness and transcendence carry an argument while relieving
proponents of cosmic feminism from the burden of actually articulating and defending their claims. Shiva's argument parallels genealogy in "the recognition that masculine and feminine as gendered concepts based on exclusiveness are ideologically defined
categories," but does so in the service of "a new wholeness in both
that transcends gender."[43] Wholeness and transcendence are reassuring tropes that promise completion while stilling questions
about its availability. Consider Shiva's critique of reductionism:

I characterise modern western patriarchy's special epistemological tradition of the "scientific revolution" as "reductionist" because it reduced the
capacity of humans to know nature both by excluding other knowers and
other ways of knowing, and it reduced the capacity of nature to creatively
regenerate and renew itself by manipulating it as inert and fragmented
matter. Reductionism has a set of distinctive characteristics which demar-
cates it from all other nonreductionist knowledge systems which it has
subjugated and replaced. The basic ontological and epistemological as-

sumptions of reductionism are based on homogeneity. It sees all systems as made up of the same basic constituents, discrete, unrelated and atomistic, and it assumes that all basic processes are mechanical. The mechanistic metaphors of reductionism have socially reconstituted nature and society. In contrast to the organic interconnectedness and reciprocity, the metaphor of nature as a machine was based on the assumption of separability and manipulability.

Her critique of reductionism is effective; the problem, of course, is that organic imagery is also metaphorical; it is not a literal description in one-to-one correspondence with its subject matter. Shiva seems to recognize this when she says "there is nothing like a neutral fact about nature *independent of the value determined by human cognitive and economic activity.*"[44] But she quickly forgets this insight in her deployment of organic metaphors through which meaning is said to reside in nature and to be discovered by the light of theory.

My point is not that cosmic feminism rides on poetic metaphor while other kinds of feminism make logical arguments. Rather, I am pointing to the necessary relationship between metaphor and argument, and the implicit politics involved in negotiating this relationship. One cannot articulate and defend a position without employing figures of speech—language consists largely of such figures. But one can attend as carefully as possible to the consequences of particular tropes and be wary of those that call on widely available cultural reassurances to make their case. Metaphors that are so familiar or legitimate that they sound like simple descriptions are the most powerful and dangerous of all. Such metaphors may have some immediate political advantage. They can recruit people into system-opposing practices by offering familiar points of access; perhaps cosmic feminism's popularity is due in part to its similarities to mainstream theological assumptions about an order written into the world with a divine hand.[45] Yet at the metatheoretical level, such metaphors are system-sustaining; they affirm the familiar, perhaps invisible, linguistic practices upon which claims to order ride. As Paul de Man has noted, figures of speech "tend to be smugglers and probably smugglers of stolen goods at that."[46] Cosmic metaphors of wholeness, depth, and completion tend to induce closure rather than to encourage further questioning. The goods they smuggle in are not unlike those Hegel clandestinely imports into his views of nature: both employ tropes that construe nature as receptive to the telos each wishes to project onto it. The content of the purposes each attributes to human-nature relations is different. Cosmic feminism's anti-hierarchical, pro-feminine stance is entirely incompatible with Hegel's masculine hierarchies. But the vision of ultimate reconciliation, and the assumption of a world suited to such reconciliations, is shared.

From a genealogical perspective, cosmic feminism presents an interesting and disturbing challenge. Its politics are impressive, but they are hopelessly mired in a serious essentialism (essentialism per se) and a pervasive metaphysics of presence. Like praxis feminism's, cosmic feminism's weaknesses mirror its strengths: the prediscursive is brought in by invoking the heavy hand of telos, by assuming a fit (at least potentially) between the prediscursive and the discursive that blinds one to one's own participation in constituting that fit. Attributing disjunctions and ruptures to the (unnecessary) effects of male power, cosmic feminism is not readily open to an appreciation of necessary ambiguities and dissonances between our articulations of life and the life being articulated. Animated by a quest for attunement with higher unities, such perspectives tend to turn away from examination of their own role in constituting such unities by the act of reaching for them.

Cosmic feminism's rhetoric of depth and wholeness is seductive. Especially when wielded with the poetic skills of a writer like Lorde, such metaphors beckon us with their promise. But as with most seductions, this one eventually raises our suspicions about the nature of its promises. Lorde's language privileges without actually making a case for a vision of the subject in which the superficial or imposed "outside" is contrasted with the authentic and true "inside." She argues that

when we begin to live from within outward, in touch with the power of the erotic within ourselves, and allowing that power to inform and illuminate our actions upon the world around us, then we begin to be responsible to ourselves in the deepest sense. For as we begin to recognize our deepest feelings, we begin to give up, of necessity, being satisfied with suffering and self-negation, and with the numbness which so often seems like their only alternative in our society. Our acts against oppression become integral with self, motivated and empowered from within.[47]

It is difficult to quarrel with this powerful equation of depth with virtue, especially when it is attached to such an important expression of political struggle. But that very difficulty can serve as a clue. Lorde's arguments ride piggyback on the conventional contrast between inner truth and outer deception, between deep feeling and surface behavior. But what is left unsaid, and unsayable, in this familiar formulation? Is the "inside" really so innocent? Perhaps the notion that what is dearest to us is "deep" is the product of a discursive constitution of selfhood that obscures the workings of power on desire. Power doesn't just say no, as Foucault and others have argued; it also says yes; it produces as well as constrains. My point is not that there are no important distinctions to make between greater and lesser intensity of feeling, or between greater claims to intimacy and lesser approximations. But it is not obvious that the contrasts of depth to surface or inner to outer best capture these distinctions. These are metaphors, not simple descriptions, and where there are metaphors there is power at work. To refer to an intense feeling or desire as deep does not excuse it from the web of power relations, once one considers power to be productive and not simply restrictive of our subjectivity. Power and resistance playing across the terrain of the self become more intertwined, less clearly opposed, more bound up with and implicated in one another. This does not make resistance impossible, but it may make it more complex, and less readily equated with some untouched inner territory.

Cosmic feminists tend to invoke premodern forms of faith in an order already inherent in nature. They hark back to what in another context has been called "an ancient philosophy of accommodation" that evokes disorder in the name of a higher order.[48] Griffin, for example, associates women with motion, fluidity, and the capacity to make change: "We are disorderly. We have often disturbed the peace. Indeed, we study chaos, it points to the future. The oldest and wisest among us can read disorder." But that disorder disrupts modern, humanist, rationalist understandings while it finds a fit within a higher order of things. In an account of forests that is simultaneously an account of women, Griffin observes: "Yet what you fail to know we know, and the knowing is in us, how we have grown this way, why these years were not one of them heedless, why we are shaped the way we are, not all straight to your purpose, but to ours."[49] Although cosmic feminists are quick to detect patriarchal strategies for smuggling male authority into language, they often seem blind to any similar process in the "picture thoughts" of their poetic, imprecise nature/woman imagery.[50] In their greater closeness to nature, Griffin argues, women are less dependent on the immediate crutch and veil of language. They are thus more in touch with the telos behind it: "Behind naming, beneath words, is something else. An existence named unnamed and unnameable."[51] The appreciation of the nondiscursive is strong, but the realm of the nondiscursive is read as having a consistent and available meaning, one that can absorb all apparent disruptions and mysteries into an inherent order of things. Difference—the concrete differences among/within women and men, and the elusive differences residing in the margins of any unified field of meaning—are easily lost in affirmations that subdue discrepancies by enveloping them.[52]

Kitsch, Appropriation, and Irony

Cosmic feminism lends itself to kitsch. Its emphasis on wholeness and completion and its promise of plenitude slide easily into a categorical agreement with being. While cosmic feminists are most radical in their criticism of modern social institutions and practices, the appeal to a stable backdrop of cosmic connections frequently degenerates into reassuring platitudes. Some of the contributions to *Woman of Power* mark it as the *Reader's Digest* of cosmic feminism. Kathryn Theatana, self-styled Dianic Witch and priestess of the Great Goddess, claims to have written her tribute to the goddess Hecate "during a Pluto transit." Z Budapest claims that her brand of witchcraft is popular on the West Coast because Californians "live closer to nature."[53] Lynn Andrews's best-selling novels (*Star Woman, Jaguar Woman, Medicine Woman, Crystal Woman, Wildhorse Woman,* and *Flight of the Seventh Moon*) read like a cross between Carlos Castaneda and the spacy New Age character Boopsie in the Doonesbury cartoons.[54] These glib and superficial paeans to blissful merger with the cosmos are often sold in upscale specialty stores along with overpriced crystals and other occult accessories.

A prominent example of cosmic kitsch is Riane Eisler's popular and much-translated book *The Chalice and the Blade*. Spanning, as Lillian Robinson observed, the period that "begins with prehistory and ends the day before yesterday," Eisler tells a cosmic feminist story of resurrection and return.[55] The earliest societies of Europe, Eisler tells us, were "partnership" societies—egalitarian and goddess worshipping. Then "nomadic invaders" from the "peripheral areas of our globe" (anywhere that is not Europe) "swarmed down" and overthrew the partnership societies in favor of patriarchy. The racial implications of centering "our globe" in Europe, while designating non-white peoples as those who "swarm," go uninvestigated. Eisler promises a return to partnership, fulfillment of a telos that predicts renewal of the good and defeat of the bad. Membership in this group return to the garden, however, can be costly: $5000 makes one a "Golden Chalice partner," $1000 gets you "Silver Chalice" status, and so forth.[56]

Through its commercial face cosmic feminism's fierce otherworldliness translates into a mundane this-worldliness.[57] This happens partly because late capitalism consumerizes everything, puts experiences, events, and ideas into circulation as objects to be purchased and displayed. But further, the opposites of this-worldliness and other-worldliness tend to reproduce each other. The spiritual answers that cosmic feminism promises assume the availability of such answers, and thus slide readily into offering them in profane forms: crystals to buy, seminars to attend, magazines to subscribe to, bumper stickers to display, platitudes to imbibe and repeat.

While this New Age razzle-dazzle gilds cosmic feminism with a coating of kitsch, it does not exhaust the political resources of the genre. Cosmic feminism attracts but is not contained by kitsch. It contains resources with which to critique its slide into a categorical agreement with consumerism. Cosmic feminists are the most likely of all feminists to talk readily about something one might call *felt truth*, that intuitive, gut-level feeling for the rightness or wrongness of a thing. Lorde describes felt truth as erotic, an understanding "firmly rooted in the power of our unexpressed or unrecognized feeling." She speaks of it as a richness, a fullness, an "internal requirement toward excellence." Lorde invokes her understanding of the erotic to critique, rather than to cooperate with, dominant economic systems: "The principal horror of any system which defines the good in terms of profit rather than in terms of human need, or which defines human need to the exclusion of the psychic and emotional components of that need—the principal horror of such a system is that it robs our work of its erotic value, its erotic power and life appeal and fulfillment."[58]

The codes of attunement with higher unities and discernment of the truth that waits to be found disturb those who are more comfortable with the empirical codes (just as problematic, it turns out) of praxis feminism or the code-consciousness of the genealogically inclined. But frank attention to felt truth might not only be a source of what William James called viciously acquired naivete, but also a protection against it.

The political face of cosmic feminism is indispensable; in its spiritually-based attacks on militarism and defenses of the environment it enacts radical and widely visible feminist politics. Feminism cannot afford to dismiss these most public manifestations of protest and struggle. So what's a non-believer to do?

Perhaps we can approach cosmic feminism ironically. While those who write the cosmological guidelines seem in deadly earnest, they are not entirely without humor. Some observers of ecofeminist direct actions have suggested that many of their members participate in the bewitchment rituals with their tongues firmly in their cheeks.[59] Standing back from the ontological and epistemological claims, a secular feminist can forge an alliance with her cosmic comrades by way of an appreciative chuckle at the audacity of the witches. Planting flowers on nuclear arsenals and dancing on missile silos may be forms of protest resting on cosmic kitsch, a playacting of defiance, a dramatization of resistance, but sometimes kitsch and melodrama are useful against the closed fist of power.[60] The women at Greenham Common, Seneca Falls, and the Lawrence Livermore labs are situated similarly to the defiant editor in Kundera's novel, who petitions the totalitarian state to free political prisoners: "His choice was not between playacting and action. His choice was between playacting and no action at all. There are situations in which people are condemned to playact. Their struggle with mute power . . . is the struggle of a theatre company that has attacked an army."[61]

Audacious women who use street theatre against nuclear nightmares have only their words, their rituals, their laughter and tears, and finally their bodies, to hurl against the state. A theatre company that attacks an army may well need its own comforting kitsch, its reassuring certainties and simple truths, to augment its meager arsenal, "to make the multitudes understand, to provoke collective tears."[62] The parables and fables that inspire cosmic feminists may sound like word salad to non-believers, but if there is a shared political agenda there is no reason for everyone to take them literally.[63] Feminist fables can have their place, and different kinds of feminists can hear them with different ears.

Starhawk seems to explore the possibilities of irony in her version of cosmic feminism. Alongside the self-deprecating good humor that dots her political discussions, her texts suggest an occasional ironic turn:

> When we are afraid, when it hurts too much
> We like to tell ourselves
> > stories of power
> > how we lost it
> > how we can reclaim it
> We tell ourselves
> > the cries we hear may be those of labor
> > the pain we feel may yet be that of birth.[64]

"We like to tell ourselves stories." Perhaps this is an implicit recognition of a will to power over truth, of a reach, produced out of need and pain, for origin stories. There is recognition of the act of telling, and of the hope and despair that prompt such acts. "The cries we hear may be those of labor / the pain we feel may yet be that of birth"—*may* and *may yet* introduce some doubt into the certainty of these organic metaphors, while calling attention to them *as* metaphors. Starhawk reflects on the political status of metaphor: "An overt metaphor is a map, a description we may find useful or not, may accept or reject. A covert metaphor is an attempt to restructure our reality by leading us to accept the map as the territory without questioning where we are going or whose interests are being served."[65]

Her recognition of the *desire* for stories, combined with her facility in telling them, could open a space for considering the fables of cosmic feminism ironically, as inspirational fictions rather than as metatruths. The stretch toward completion could then be viewed less as a belief in the ontological availability of such plenitude than as a political affirmation of the need for a visionary resource to guide political struggle.[66] "Our personal stories," Starhawk affirms, "can become the ground of the new myths we need in order to make our world anew."[67] This is not an unproblematic position since criteria are needed to decide which stories and which myths qualify for selection. Nor does it necessarily evade the sentimentalizations of kitsch: the most appealing stories and myths are likely to be those resonating with some familiar categorical agreement with being. But the acknowledgment of desire in relation to storytelling, and its inclusion in the actual telling of the stories, marks the possibility of an ironic turn in cosmic feminism. "We like to tell ourselves stories . . ."

The serious question of appropriation is a more difficult problem than kitsch for cosmic feminism. For people who reside, however reluctantly, within the modern western world, the invocation of premodern modes of understanding is at best problematic. First, there is substantial variation in what qualifies as premodern and substantial diversity within such categories: premodern consciousness is not a single entity. Second, efforts to apprehend such a consciousness are necessarily filtered through modern expectations, just as efforts to grasp the pre- or nondiscursive are filtered through language. Any premodern we can grasp is always *our* premodern. Third, the categories of modern and premodern, like any such dichotomy, are bound to leak; people are likely to be implicated to some extent in both. Contemporary Native Americans or native Hawaiians, for example, are likely to live in modernity, but not fully; some people love and reproduce across these boundaries, while others cross and re-cross them through education, occupation, and politics. Fourth, the modes of consciousness of various premodern worlds cannot readily be detached from their home cultures and transposed into the modern world.

Premodern notions of identity reside within their times and places and draw substance from their multiple rootedness in a geography, a history, an emotional and practical landscape of daily life. They are not commodities to be purchased, nor adornments to be embraced or discarded by outsiders. Cultural categories may leak, but they do not fully blend, especially when they are antagonistic to one another. Norbert Elias makes this point in his discussion of the cultural rootedness of language. Central notions of identity in particular societies "take form on the basis of common experiences. They grow and change with the group whose expression they are.

The situation and history of the group are mirrored in them. And they remain colorless, they never become fully alive for those who do not share these experiences, who do not speak from the same tradition and the same situation."[68]

Cosmic feminists are often aware of the dangers of appropriation. Carol Christ warns against it: "We can't just take off what we want from Native American culture and assimilate it, which is a typical imperialist posture of Americans."[69] But this caution does not make its way very far into the arguments or the textual practices cosmic feminists employ. Take, for example, efforts to transpose the rituals surrounding menstruation from Native American cultures into contemporary U.S. society. For Native Americans, the celebration of a young woman's first menses takes place within the context of a larger set of accomplishments: learning to run and swim in particular skilled ways, to live off the land, and to understand the stories of one's ancestors. Menses is a symbolic coming of age for many Native Americans, the culmination of years of physical, mental and spiritual learning.[70] But attempts by contemporary western feminists to celebrate the menses seem artificial because they lack context: they are unconnected to a larger set of daily practices and rituals. John (Fire) Lame Deer, medicine man for the Sioux, warns his white readers against such appropriation: "You can't take our beliefs out of our Badlands and prairies and put them into one of your factories or office buildings. . . . Our beliefs are rooted deep in our earth."[71] Feminism needs the resources to distinguish "temporary tourism" from respectful engagement.[72] Premodern ways, especially those that maintain a tenuous existence in the face of continued assaults, do not belong to moderns, feminist or not. But perhaps residents of modernity can learn from the histories or the descendants of premodern cultures how to curb modern society's tendencies toward expropriation and let other ways survive.

What stance toward the premodern is available to feminists in the modern world? What approach is open to its wisdom and respectful of its difference? Perhaps we can begin to formulate answers by considering a text that forces the reader to ask these questions. Anne Cameron's *Daughters of Copper Woman* confronts its readers with an inescapable problematic: how to approach the premodern without appropriating it.

Daughters of Copper Woman is a book of stories told to Cameron (a white woman) by the people of her husband's tribe, the Nootka of the village of Ahousat in Vancouver. The book immediately immerses the reader in its enormous contradictions. Cameron writes and the reader reads from an oral tradition that reaches back toward a culture far away and now nearly destroyed. In the preface and afterword, in the tone and timbre of the text, Cameron conveys the sense that she approaches an ancient wisdom with profound gratitude for its survival. Yet on the back cover, above the official ISBN number, the book is labeled fiction. What could this mean? For whom are these stories make-believe? Even the commitment to an alternative reality by Press Gang Publishers could not protect these stories from the hegemonic judgments of the modern western world. A declaration is printed on the last page of the book: "Press Gang Publishers is a feminist collective. We publish non-fiction and fiction that challenges traditional assumptions about women in society." The pursuit of that challenge violates distinctions between fiction and nonfiction, oral and written narrative, and author and reader. In the language of linguistic feminism, the book forces an active deconstruction of the categories of phallogocentrism.

In several beautiful stories and poems Cameron writes of the inherited memories of the women's secret society. The sacred connection to all life is expressed: "There are people who think that only people have emotions like pride, fear, and joy, but those who know will tell you all things are alive, perhaps not in the same way we are alive, but each in its own way, as should be, for we are not all the same. And though different from us in shape and life span, different in Time and Knowing, yet are trees alive. And rocks. And water. And all know emotion."[73] Dualisms of man/woman, life/death, human/animal, and material/spiritual are all challenged. The pervading opposition is between imperialist destroyers and those who protect "the soft power."

The stories set in contemporary time stress the need for the Native American women to share their understanding with other women, to unite around a shared ability to recognize the face of the enemy and a shared determination to resist:

We must reach out to our sisters, all of our sisters, and ask them to share their truth with us, offer to share our truth with them. And we can only trust that this gift, from woman to woman, be treated with love and respect, in a way opposite from the way the evil treated the other things this island had. Rivers are filthy that used to be clean. Mountains are naked that used to be covered with trees. The ocean is fighting for her life and there are no fish where there used to be millions, and this is the work of the cold evil. The last treasure we have, the secrets of the matriarchy, can be shared and honoured by women, and be proof there is another way, a better way, and some of us remember it.[74]

Yet the call for all women to learn from these stories is immensely complicated by the admonition in the afterword:

It is the tradition of the native people of North America, particularly all people of the west coast of Canada, that a story belongs to the one telling it, not to the one hearing or receiving it. A story can be passed on, retold, or shared by a listener Only if the person who Owns the story gives specific and personal permission. . . . Anyone who appropriates these stories by re-telling or adapting them is betraying the trust in which they were offered.[75]

This claim problematizes everything about the text. It makes it impossible for the modern reader to avoid confrontation with imperialism, the colonizing move implicit in even the most well-intentioned contact with premodern otherness. The contradiction cannot be resolved by turning away from the stories any more than it can be resolved by re-telling them. The plea that we listen and try to learn requires us to carry the stories with us, but the injunction that using is stealing problematizes any form of carrying.

This ironic doubleness sizzles with political tensions. And in relation to this book, a tension-filled position is precisely appropriate for feminists whose home is the modern western world. *Daughters of Copper Woman* forces the reader into an active collaboration with the text while warning her of the dangers of collaboration. The stories invite us with their many references to speaking to all women, with their conviction that white women, black women, Asian women and brown women all hold pieces of the "dance cape" of wisdom. And the ironic figure of the clown is provided as a way of mediating among the various ways, of living with their conflicts and imbalances; the clown uses parody and reversal to call attention to excess and to make it bearable. Within the context of a society in which much that the modern world views as profane was taken as sacred, there "wasn't nothin' sacred to a clown."[76] The clown was a constant reminder of limits, of the seriousness of absurdity, and she needed other clowns around to keep her so. The clown is also a figure of resistance. She uses humor as a point of entry to name and stand against the workings of power.

A similar ironic doubleness inhabits many of the texts in Moraga and Anzaldúa's volume, *This Bridge Called My Back: Writings of Radical Women of Color*, a collection of essays in which the claims of identity politics are both defended and questioned. Identity politics is itself a slippery term; slippery, that is, in relation to the categories of subjectivity I am offering. It is close to praxis feminism when it claims that women of color, or third-world women, or working-class women, or lesbians, because of the structure of circumstances and activities they are likely to share, gravitate toward a shared consciousness about themselves and their society. It leans more toward cosmic feminism when it posits some kernel of selfhood that adheres in those marked by color, class, passion, or world and can be elicited when the veil of colonization is lifted. Movement back and forth between these positions is only one of the many tensions within which these voices struggle: resentment about educating their oppressors alternates with the need to write "to anyone who will listen with their ears open (even if only a crack)";[77] the dream of a unified third-world women's movement struggles with recognition of the painful divisions among women of color; musing over the limits of words accompanies continued faith in communication; critiques of any form of elitism coexist with the need for "those of us who have more of anything: brains, physical strength, political power, spiritual energies . . . to share with those that don't have";[78] longings to be white do battle with irreverent claims for self-acceptance.

In "The Pathology of Racism: A Conversation with Third World Wimmin," doris davenport wields a biting irony/sarcasm to highlight racism through reversals: white women are ugly, she says, with stringy, straight hair, white lumpy bodies, "a strange body odor." "They can't dance," they like "bland food," they show themselves to be "juvenile and tasteless," "naive and myopic."[79] She speculates on a "real inferiority complex" in white feminists that translates into their pretensions of superiority. She then suggests that black and white feminists have " 'c.r.' [consciousness-raising] conversations about and with each other. If done with a sense of honesty, and a sense of *humor*, we might accomplish something."[80] For a non-Afro/Asian/Latina feminist reading these texts, every opportunity is dangerous: if I analyze them, bring to bear the tools of my intellectual trade, am I intellectualizing (evading and trivializing, as davenport suggests) or am I taking the texts seriously and offering the resources I possess for common use? If I embrace these arguments, am I entering sympathetically into these contexts or denying my whiteness? Every trap is also a promise, a slippery possibility that opens as it closes. This position of ironic doubleness can be productive for a white feminist reader; it gives one pause while it demands action. The alertness required to negotiate this terrain is best sustained with an ironic stance toward the difficulty of moving coupled with the need to go on.

In arguments like davenport's, feminists with a cosmic orientation might find resources to connect a determination to rebel with an appreciation of the persistent manyness of things. In texts like *Daughters of Copper Woman*, cosmic feminism can perhaps find inspiration to resist the temptation to appropriation as well as the lure of kitsch. Politically, we might learn not that residents of modernity can or should assimilate traditional cultures, but that we can work toward changes in our own society that will curb its enormous expropriating power and allow these other societies and the otherness within our own society to survive and flourish. More than any other face of feminism, cosmic feminism calls into question the project of mastery over nature presumed by Hegel and central to modernity. The otherness of the premodern can help to stimulate this challenge, to demonstrate its urgency, but it cannot be transcribed wholesale into the modern world. We moderns can approach premodern otherness with a variety of postures, including respect, awe, humility, and gratitude, but not with the confident expectation that it is for us.

Chapter Five

Linguistic Feminism

Feminism's third alternative perspective on subjectivity challenges the dominance of the speaking subject by calling upon the energies of semiotics and deconstruction, a deliberately unfocused invocation of multiple sites of meaning in identities, bodies, and pleasures. Countering "the masculine obsession with classification, systematization, and hierarchization," this code tries to evade binary divisions by opening itself to difference, marginality, and contrast.[1] Like praxis and cosmic feminism, linguistic feminism is an umbrella category that contains many different kinds of arguments; despite the contention within it, the category brings together arguments that stress subjectivity as the production rather than the discovery or originator of discourse. Linguistic feminism calls vigorously upon genealogical strategies: deconstructing unities, problematizing comfortable relations, attending to that which does not or will not fit into established categories. It employs what Donna Haraway calls "the acid tools of post-modernist theory" to encourage "polyweality" and to stand against totalizations.[2]

The aim of this chapter is to sketch the contours of linguistic feminism as a kind of thinking about subjectivity and knowledge. Linguistic feminism emphasizes the power of discourse as an economy, that is, the power to produce and distribute opportunities and resources that make available or deny entry into various subject-positions. This view does not produce an alternative vision of subjectivity so much as it offers a subversion of the categories of identity, a counter-subjectivity. Such moves typically raise difficult questions of agency (who could be doing this subverting?) and of political commitment (toward what ends do these subversions pro-

ceed?). Linguistic feminism, like its cosmic and praxis counterparts, is not without resources to critique its own limits. Similarly,
this face of feminism can engage in some fruitful, contentious encounters with the arguments and insistencies of its neighbors. In
these arguments irony and kitsch can serve as political resources
and warnings: ironic practices are right at home in linguistic feminism, and kitsch, while viewed as distasteful, is not unknown. Linguistic feminism offers an irreverent politics of subversion in relation both to male-ordered subjectivities and to their feminist
opponents.

Creating Linguistic Feminism

One important trait shared by linguistic feminists is a genealogical
approach to asking questions about subjectivity and knowledge.
This approach proceeds by making the familiar strange. Foucault,
for example, takes up the widely accepted notion of the unified,
desiring subject and finds it odd, finds its very acceptance to be in
need of explanation. He then sets out "to analyze the practices by
which individuals were led to focus their attention on themselves,
to decipher, recognize, and acknowledge themselves as subjects of
desire, bringing into play between themselves and themselves a
certain relationship that allows them to discover, in desire, the
truth of their being, be it natural or fallen."[3]

Another way to make a puzzle out of what seems self-explanatory is to take a category of understanding that seems atemporal
and give it a history, as Nietzsche does with morality and truth.
This move disrupts the certitude of fixed definitions, since "only
that which has no history can be defined."[4] A third, and related
approach is to take a question that is widely asked—e.g., what is
the proper morality of sexuality?—and ask why people ask that
question. Thus Foucault asks how the Greeks asked questions about
sexuality, how this arena of life became "an object of concern, an
element for reflection, and a material for stylization" in their discourses.[5] A fourth approach entails re-historicizing an idea that may
reside too securely in an available narrative structure: one might
find continuities and persistent themes where the hegemonic account sees clear breaks, as Foucault does between antiquity and

Christian morality.[6] Or conversely, one might find disruptions and breaks where the accepted view finds a single unfolding story.[7]

A fifth strategy, one helped along by the others, entails breaking apart apparently unified categories or secure dyads to allow differences and tensions within them to emerge. For example, Foucault's encounters with the prevailing categories governing Greek thought on sexuality allow him to break up the category of homosexuality: love of boys by adult men signaled, he argues, not a different kind of person but a special stylization of practices.[8] It becomes more difficult, in light of this deconstruction, to think of homosexuality as a label for what a person *is*, and more possible to think of homosexuality as a particular cultural practice. Similarly, Foucault argues that the ancients organized their sexual discourse not according to the opposition between permitted and forbidden acts but around "a constant oscillation between more and less."[9] This move relocates moral discussion about sexual practices out of the familiar dyad of good and bad and onto a less securely dualistic terrain.

Linguistic feminism uses these and other strategies of defamiliarizing and deconstructing to call into question male-ordered accounts of gender. In order to agitate into existence a different approach to categorization, it also destabilizes the categories that fellow feminists hold dear, including many that praxis and cosmic feminisms take for granted. Teresa Ebert designates "postmodern cultural feminist theory" as that which "refuses to reify 'female experience,' 'woman,' or the 'feminine' (whether as the 'natural' body or as the 'body' of writing, as in *l'écriture feminine*) nor does it essentialize the binarism of male/female."[10] Linguistic feminism struggles against categorization-by-negation: that is, the familiar practice of establishing something by contrasting it to its absence, for example, X to not-X, light to non-light/dark, man to non-man/woman.

Such resistance has complicated political implications: the struggle against the oppressive unities imposed by the "bad isms"— sexism, capitalism, orientalism—also sabotages the "good isms"— feminism, socialism, anarchism—that were formulated as counterpoint. Easy distinctions between oppression and resistance become foggy; complicity reigns. Cynthia Enloe gives a powerful example of this complexity in her discussion of western white female

explorers in colonial realms. These women, often to free themselves from significant patriarchal restrictions in their home nations, left behind domestic arenas to enter the nearly all-male world
of geographic exploration; meanwhile, their unconventional acts
helped "tighten the colonial noose" by contributing to the definition of "natives" as exotic, appealing in their place, but in need of
a civilizing influence.[11] A struggle against sexism that contributes
to empire undoes any clean opposition between power and resistance and suggests that reinscription of conventional power strategies can occur even in places where one might most confidently
expect liberation.

Linguistic feminists are not the only ones who attend closely to
language, but they do so in a distinctive way. The importance of
language in praxis and cosmic feminisms tends to lie in the things
that are said about women, or in the things that women have to
say; in linguistic feminism, the focus is on how women *get said.*
Judith Butler remarks that "language is not an *exterior medium or
instrument* into which I pour a self and from which I glean a reflection of that self."[12] Gayatri Spivak also locates identity in discourse:
"We know no world that is not organized as a language, we operate
with no other consciousness but one structured as language—languages that we cannot possess, for we are operated by those languages as well. The category of language, then, embraces the categories of world and consciousness even as it is determined by
them."[13] One consequence of the insistence that language is always already there in relation to meaning is that feminism loses the
option of starting from scratch: Denise Riley points out that feminist understandings of women and/or gender "are illuminated in
certain lights in advance; are already in some alliance with other
political and philosophical languages which colour them."[14] The
power that linguistic feminism attributes to language resides not
only in what gets said or who gets to talk, but in what is sayable at
all.

Arguments usually labeled postmodern or poststructural figure
prominently in linguistic feminism's claims about the constitutive
power of language. Julia Kristeva, for example, distinguishes between two moments of language: the symbolic, which functions to
represent and define; and the semiotic, where ambiguities, nu-
ances, and multiple possible meanings emerge. Kristeva views the

semiotic as innocent of sexual difference; it can thus weaken the dualism of male and female while evoking that which is marginal to power. To speak of the semiotic is to engage in paradox, marshaling the ordering capacities of symbolic systems to talk about that which resists order. Efforts to approach this system-shaking moment require that we resist the quiet seduction of familiar categories, that we become exiles: "How can one avoid sinking into the mire of common sense, if not by becoming a stranger to one's own country, language, sex and identity? Writing is impossible without some kind of exile."[15]

Luce Irigaray attempts a deconstruction of the subject who loves authority into a fluid and musical semiotic play, calling upon a multiplication of sites of pleasure in female bodies to counter the singleness and propriety of the male. "Woman," she says, "is neither open nor closed. She is indefinite, in-finite, *form is never complete in her.* She is not infinite but neither is she a unit(y), such as letter, number, figure in a series, proper noun, unique object (in a) world of the senses, single ideality in an intelligible whole, entity of a foundation, etc. . . . No metaphor completes her."[16] The difference of women's interiority, the fluidity of their identities, and the multiplicity of their desires, are repressed and denied in patriarchy. Setting maleness as the standard of humanness, phallocratic approaches to subjectivity *"reduce all others to the economy of the Same."*[17] Both Kristeva and Irigaray view western culture as having repressed the playful and sonorous in language in favor of the rational and representative, in the same way that it represses the body in favor of the mind and women in the service of men. While Irigaray's project focuses more on the articulation of difference, and Kristeva's on the deconstruction of gender, both share this turn to the semiotic and to bodies-and-pleasures.

The textual codes employed by linguistic feminists are better thought of as counter-codes, as disrupters, as codes out to disrobe other codes. Irigaray, for example, disrupts the orderings of narratives upon which praxis and cosmic feminisms depend with her reliance on analogy. Analogy can disrupt narratives by bringing together pieces from one story with pieces from another. In "The 'Mechanics' of Fluids," Irigaray draws an analogy between the resistance of fluids to a mechanics based on solids alone and the resistance of women to the dominant symbolization of male discourse. In fluids she finds "a physical reality that continues to resist adequate symbolization and/or that signifies the powerlessness of logic to incorporate in its writings all the characteristic features of nature."[18] The complicity between accepted rationality and solid mechanics excludes fluids, just as the complicity between reason and male discourse excludes women; women/fluid is continuous, diffusible, traversable, evading boundaries and identities. By juxtaposing the contrasting configurations of mechanics and gender, Irigaray's "textual impertinences" create an analogical space in which a new set of connections might be made.[19]

While some of its critics accuse linguistic feminism of reinscribing essentialism into its texts, most expressions of the genre seek to do the opposite—to show that any claim to a stable resting place, a firm grounding of identity or truth, is a production rather than a discovery of language. The version of subjectivity linguistic feminism offers is one of counter-subjectivity, aware of itself as the outcome rather than the originator of discursive strategies and signifying practices. The dominant discourses and institutions seek to harness the multiple possibilities of identity and desire into the categories that enable its modes of domination: this sex or that one; this race or that one; this erotic identity or that one. These power-laden definitions of self as *this* sex, *this* color, *this* class are then naturalized by the prevailing discourses, made to appear as simple manifestations of the way things are rather than as disputed outcomes of power relations. So linguistic feminism seeks to denaturalize prevailing subjectivities in order to create a space for more fluid and active constitutions of identity and desire to emerge.

Linguistic feminism has no patience at all with identity politics in either its praxis or cosmic forms. Spivak points out that the pursuit of one's "real identity" leads back to the worst aspects of male-ordered modernity: she objects to "the sort of obsession with one's proper identity as property that is both the self-duping and the oppressive power of humanism."[20] Butler argues that feminists should stop trying to specify identity as a basis for politics because we need to ask political questions about identity itself, and because any closure on identity constrains our politics. For Butler, "it is no longer clear that feminist theory ought to try to settle the questions of primary identity in order to get on with the task of politics. Instead, we ought to ask, what political possibilities are the consequence of a radical critique of the categories of identity? What new shape of politics emerges when identity as a common ground no longer constrains the discourse on feminist politics?"[21]

Here identity is presumed to be only constraining, never enabling, for feminism (a point I return to below). Butler asks Nietzsche's question about the metaphysics of substance: she questions "the belief that the grammatical formulation of subject and predicate reflects the prior ontological reality of substance and attribute."[22] Spivak refers to this as the subject-effect:

A subject-effect can be briefly plotted as follows: that which seems to operate as a subject may be part of an immense discontinuous network ("text" in the general sense) of strands that may be termed politics, ideology, economics, history, sexuality, language, and so on. (Each of these strands, if they are isolated, can also be seen as woven of many strands.) Different knottings and configurations of these strands, determined by heterogeneous determinations which are themselves dependent upon myriad circumstances, produce the effect of an operating subject. Yet the continuist and homogenist deliberative consciousness symptomatically requires a continuous and homogeneous cause for this effect and thus posits a sovereign and determining subject. The latter is, then, the effect of an effect, and is positing a metalepsis, or the substitution of an effect for a cause.[23]

Any search for some defining feature that establishes a person and maintains her continuity through time and space short-circuits the investigation of identity claims as "regulatory practices" that produce and valorize that which they claim only to discover and report.[24]

Along with identity, experience is another category cherished in cosmic and praxis feminisms and questioned in the linguistic version. Experience is a problematic ground for knowledge not only because different members of a group have different versions of that group's experience, but more fundamentally because experience does not come in neat segments: one can't confidently distinguish those labeled *female* from those labeled *white*, or *heterosexual* or *working class*.[25] The arbitrariness that accompanies the delineation of particular events, encounters, or practices as units of experience confounds efforts to draw direct causal links between those units and the ideas or identities thought to issue from them (for example, arguments such as "X happened to me, therefore I think Y"). The seamlessness of claims about "women's experience" suggests to a linguistic feminist that a very selective reading of a life world is taking place, that highlighted pieces of complex, contiguous, fluid, messy agglomerations of temporalities are being snatched out of context and patched together to create the desired story.

Instead of looking to gender as an origin of identity or an expression of authentic experience, Butler figures gender as "a kind of persistent impersonation that passes as the real . . . a cultural performance." Gender, in short, becomes something we *do;* and if we do enough of it, long enough, with great enough selectivity and consistency, it takes on the guise of nature: "Gender is the repeated stylization of the body, a set of repeated acts within a highly rigid regulatory frame that congeal over time to produce the appearance of substance, of a natural sort of being." An illusion with no reality behind it, gender is a "perpetual displacement." This face of linguistic feminism resembles its praxis counterpart in its stress on doing as constitutive of being. The difference between them is in the level at which this doing takes place. Most praxis feminists start with women, and looking at what they do, their practices, draw conclusions about their identity. Most linguistic feminists take women themselves to be a doing: "to understand identity as a *practice,* and as a signifying practice, is to understand culturally intelligible subjects as a resulting effect of a rule-bound discourse that inserts itself in the pervasive and mundane signifying acts of linguistic life."[26]

An example of gender as productive displacement can be drawn from an arena of life commonly thought to reveal foundations: early childhood. When my son was born I began a determined campaign to speak to and about him in a non-stereotypical fashion. I told him often that he is a sweet boy, a gentle boy, a beautiful boy, as well as a smart and strong boy. The range of adjectives may have been impressive, but there was a predictability in the nouns: whatever variation existed, it rotated around that anchor word, boy. The substitution of gender-neutral nouns ("you're such a terrific infant, such an adorable child, such a wonderful kid"), was unsustainable—those were not the conversations that were having me. A friend commented on this story with an exasperated appeal to reality: "So, what's the problem? He *is* a boy!" Well, yes, he has a penis; he also has fingernails, but I don't remind him of it every day. It is only a short distance (although I insist that it is a critical one) to the formulation favored by his grandparents, aunts, and uncles: he's "all boy."

My point is that the stage was being set, via the verbal displays of nouns and descriptors, for a lifetime of gender performances. Add to these verbal productions of boyness layers and layers of gestures, postures, intonations, costumes, amusements, and habits of speech (not to mention a skewed reward system) and you have the ingredients of a sedimented corporeal style.[27] It is not simply that my son is being socialized; rather, a subject upon whom socialization can do its work is being produced. Nor is it the case that his gendered corporeal style will necessarily become a prison for him; the temporal repetition of gender performances is not seamless; its very repetitiousness suggests the likelihood of irregularities and cracks.[28] But neither the consistencies nor the irregularities can be traced back to an origin; instead, they flow out of a set of "productions that create the effect of the natural, the original and the inevitable."[29]

Continuing in this vein of orneriness, linguistic feminism problematizes an evaluative category that is dear to the hearts of many praxis and cosmic feminists: authenticity. There are frequent appeals to notions of authentic identity, a true or whole self, in *This Bridge Called My Back*. Benjamin engages in loose talk about an "authentic self"; Ruddick avoids making any direct claims for authentic mothering, but does criticize inauthenticity in mothers who become too docile before authority.[30] Authenticity has an honorable history in feminist theory; de Beauvoir, along with Sartre, appeals to authenticity as the antidote to bad faith under conditions of existential freedom, as a way to save the process of choice from total indirection. Those whose suspicions of positivism make them uneasy about words like *objective* or *true* can take comfort in *authentic*, which sidesteps questions of verification but still somehow sounds like the real thing. Claims to authenticity are often associated with that which is genuine and has integrity; who could quarrel with such appeals?

Not surprisingly, linguistic feminists do. Partly, they ask who decides what counts as fully authentic. Trinh Minh-ha observes caustically that western expectations for the third-world people recruited to speak for their kind require them to paint themselves "thick with authenticity." This demand generates a "planned authenticity" that is the perfect counterpart and guarantee of strategies of universal standardization: a place for everyone, and everyone in her place. More fundamentally, linguistic feminism's suspicions are raised by the implicit promise of completion, of a final resting place or original home. Trinh points out that the search for "that genuine layer of myself to which I can always cling" pretends to hold constant that which is always in motion.[31] Depending on circumstances and interactions, dimensions of oneself that seemed most secure can become unmoored; "the superfluous can become real; the authentic can prove fake."[32] Desire for authenticity may well be strong, but desire is not a guarantee; it is neither a map nor a receipt; it is not even a down payment.

Linguistic feminism offers a radical challenge to the fixity of juridico-legal discourse by attacking hierarchy and authority where they reside in language. The discourse of the modern subject seeks to pin things down, to specify, to hold them still for examination and judgment. Linguistic feminism loosens the hold of the symbolic and representational, taking language itself as a model of experience that is patterned and structured but without a center, without a beginning or an ending. Language that attends to the semiotic "moves and twists, starts over again from different perspectives, does not go straight to the point."[33] It accepts and plays with the paradox of using language to point to the limits and excessiveness of language, invoking indirect strategies of metonymy and metaphor to indicate its own gaps, doublings, and fissures. By featuring various semiotic moments in art, music, poetry, dance, and other symbol-defying expressions, linguistic feminism seeks to facilitate "the ensuing fracture of a symbolic code which can no longer 'hold' its speaking subjects."[34] Recognizing the incompleteness of our organizations of life in relation to the life being organized, this view takes to heart Foucault's admonition that one "does not inhabit the whole of his [sic] language."[35] The bounded self-as-subject is rejected in favor of a dislocating and co-mingling of identities, a play of possibilities across undisciplined bodies.

The counter-subjectivity articulated in linguistic feminism counsels a vacation from subjectivity, an effort to disengage from the available paths to identity in order to scrutinize them as the productions rather than the producers of our worlds. However, it is difficult to hear this advice without asking, Who is it, then, who is going on vacation? and to enter into an infinite regress of agency. The genealogical hope here, as expressed by Foucault and others, is that the loosening of the boundaries of selfness might enable one to recast questions of subjectivity in a fresh light: Foucault urges us "to promote new forms of subjectivity through the refusal of this kind of individuality which has been imposed on us for several centuries."[36] The call for more porous boundaries and permeable differentiations in our notions of subjectivity may suggest that such a self would be either leaking or taking on water; but part of linguistic feminism's project is to challenge the idea that the self is a container in the first place, to mix up the distinctions of inside and outside.

Many feminists have commented on the paradoxical combination of publicity and secrecy that gender identity entails. Marilyn Frye notes that "the matter of our sexes must be very profound indeed if it must, on pain of shame and ostracism, be covered up and must, on pain of shame and ostracism, be boldly advertised by every means and medium one can devise."[37] Linguistic feminists take this insistence on a single gender identity to be a sign not simply of the exaggeration of biological givens but of the production of two opposing categories, male and female, out of the multiplicity and diversity of bodies and desires. Reflecting on Freud's assertion that having two sexes is basic to organic life, Irigaray asks: "Could this not be a difference thus clearly cut out in the service of argument? Once the heterogenous is found to be reduced in sexual practice, would we not observe a proliferation of differences, a compulsion to differentiate, either to retain the pleasure or to calm the anguish of indifference, at least in the art or science of dialectic?"[38]

In her analysis of the production of female desire in popular romance novels, Ebert argues that the most radical challenge to the patriarchal deployment of sexual dualism is to defy its terms entirely, to be "ungendered."[39] But the patriarchal mandate that we all be clearly either male or female is so hegemonic that it is extremely difficult to talk about what might appear were the mandate sufficiently shaken. Nongendered subjectivity "is concealed and rendered unsaid, even unknowable: it is not possible to articulate this alternative (taboo) organization of signification, merely to mark it."[40] What is being marked is a possibility, a potential space for naming differences among people in ways that do not privilege either possession of the biological penis or participation in phallic authority.

As with the other thematizations of subjectivity in contemporary feminist theory, there are characteristic weaknesses in linguistic feminism that are counterpoint to its strengths. Its insistence on the total maleness of the symbolic order and on men's successful exclusion of women from thinking and speaking leaves us to wonder why such a miserable creature as woman, one so fully dominated, should command our attention at all. If the hegemonic discourses are so total in their insistence on the existing state of things, how can an alternative possibility even be marked? How can that which lies unthought within reigning categories ever be approached in thinking? Both Irigaray and Kristeva tend to conceptualize the dominant discourse in a way that seems to disqualify the resistances they seek. In "Commodities among Themselves," for example, Irigaray posits the dominant discourse as total: "The exchanges upon which patriarchal societies are based take place exclusively among men. Women, signs, commodities and currency always pass from one man to another."[41] Kristeva also argues that the realm of the symbolic is completely ruled by phallogocentrism: although semiotic resistances occasionally peep out, no submerged discourse can be articulated. They overstate the stability and closure of the reigning symbolic systems, denying women any salient territory or efficacious words of our own.

Unlike Irigaray and Kristeva, Butler does not figure the dominant order as totally closed; on the contrary, she finds within the domain of gender performances the possibility of variations and displacements. However, Butler does tend to bring premature closure to her discussion of the subject by equating subjectivity with juridico-legal subjects. "The question of 'the subject,' " she maintains, "is crucial for politics, and for feminist politics in particular, because *juridical subjects* are invariably produced through certain exclusionary practices that do not 'show' once the juridical structure of politics has been established."[42] And again: "To trace the political operations that produce and conceal what qualifies as the *juridical subject* of feminism is precisely the task of *a feminist ge-nealogy* of the category of women."[43] Butler's total rejection of any liberating dimension to identity, noted above, seems to stem from this equation of subjectivity with the juridical subject of moder-nity.

But that construal of subjectivity does not exhaust the field. Praxis feminism's self-in-relation and cosmic feminism's self-in-place are two other coherent possibilities; in the next chapter I will suggest mobile subjectivities as another lucid alternative. While all these visions of subjectivity share the fact of their production—they are all produced by sets of exclusionary practices that provide their boundaries—they are not the same in all significant ways. If we grant the argument that all claims to identity are dangerous impo-sitions, what approaches are available to minimize or negotiate these dangers? What reasons are there to try? Butler does not consider these questions. She features constraint because she is most inter-ested in freeing feminist theory "from the necessity of having to construct a single or abiding ground which is invariably contested" by what it excludes.[44] Fine; but have we established that every identity claim would take such a form? Butler's ruthless pursuit of the deconstructive move vis-à-vis identity forecloses the need to ask these questions, or even to name the possibility of doing so.

Linguistic feminism is often accused by its critics of providing no sense of agency for women.[45] Just when feminists begin claim-ing a subjectivity for women, the argument goes, poststructuralism arrives on the scene to inform us that claims to subjectivity are passé.[46] But this criticism misses the mark; the problem is not that counter-subjectivity abandons agency or lacks politics, but that its politics lack adequate direction. Butler argues persuasively that the subject-effect suggests a refreshing approach to agency, one that sees in the prolific repetition of gender performances the possibil-ity of skewing those performances, of entering into the daily prac-tices of doing one's gender in a slanted way and thereby making a difference:

Paradoxically, the reconceptualization of identity as an *effect,* that is, as *produced* or *generated,* opens up possibilities of "agency" that are insidi-ously foreclosed by positions that take identity categories as foundational and fixed. For an identity to be an effect means that it is neither fatally determined nor fully artificial and arbitrary. That the *constituted* status of identity is misconstrued along these two conflicting lines suggests the ways in which the feminist discourse on cultural construction remains trapped within the unnecessary binarism of free will and determinism. Construction is not opposed to agency; it is the necessary scene of agency, the very terms in which agency is articulated and becomes culturally intelligible.[47]

Those who see in genealogy the destruction of agency are perhaps doing what Butler also does: they are reducing all possibilities of agency and subjectivity to the parameters of the juridico-legal subject, so that genealogy's attack on that subject seems to them to be an attack on all subjects. When Rosi Braidotti, Nancy Hartsock, and Christine Di Stefano perform this reduction, they find genealogy at fault for undermining the ground upon which they wish to stand. When Butler does it, she finds identity at fault for fixing the ground too firmly. Between these two positions, the possibilities of a genealogically enabled identity lie unexplored. Juridico-legal subjects are not the only agents in town.

Linguistic feminism's intense focus on language sometimes takes feminism too far away from the material realm in which bodies inhabit locations, structures distribute power and resources, and political judgments about collective life are necessary. One manifestation of this problem is the tendency to overthematize bodies in the direction of sexuality. One of linguistic feminism's characteristic moves is to privilege women's erotic passions, which are viewed as multiple in site and direction, in contrast to the singlemindedness of the male. Irigaray is particularly well known for her vaginal metaphors.[48] But the focus on pleasures in bodies can narrow one's notion of embodiment to the specifically sexual, leaving out, for example, the arena in which most people experience their bodies every day—labor. There is more to embodiment than sexual desire, no matter how diffuse and multiple we acknowledge it to be: there is grace, strength, relaxation, exertion, pain. Although Irigaray's goal is to multiply our vision of the body, she speaks rather relentlessly about the genitals, ignoring arms, legs, backs, shoulders, the parts of our bodies called upon most by those who do physical labor for a living. Also omitted are bodily metonyms that might symbolize playing, eating, aging, sleeping, or other embodied practices. Irigaray's vaginal metaphors, meant to multiply meaning, end up constricting it. Patriarchy too has defined women primarily in terms of their sexuality. Where is the line between reclaiming (or claiming in the first place) our sexuality and cooperating with male power?

Another manifestation of this limitation appears in a tendency to celebrate difference without considering which differences are most worthy of our attention. Consider Irigaray's appeal for connections among women:

> We can do without models, standards, or examples. Let's never give ourselves orders, commands, or prohibitions. Let our imperatives be only appeals to move, to be moved, together. Let's never lay down the law to each other, or moralize, or make war. Let's not claim to be right, or claim the right to criticize one another. If one of us sits in judgement, our existence comes to an end.[49]

This appeal to evade judgment and division in the name of connection is both liberating in its openness and disabling in its lack of distinctions. The world does not oblige us by leaving us alone, and some of those who do the work of power (for whatever reason) are women. If we forfeit the option of opposing those women, we are likely to be their victims. This is not to say that there is no vision of revolt in linguistic feminism. Kristeva appeals to all those marginalized by power to subvert phallogocentrism's hierarchical closure on meaning. Irigaray appeals to women to *"Overthrow syntax by suspending its eternally teleological order, by snipping the wires, cutting the current, breaking the circuits, switching the connections, by modifying continuity, alternation, frequency, intensity."* Seeing the established order as capable of colonizing any clear and straightforward utterance, she urges women "to speak only in riddles, allusions, hints, parables."[50] Through this confounding and distorting of the representational and the symbolic, "something of the difference of the sexes would have taken place in language also."[51]

There is much that is compelling here. Given the power of discourse to constitute the realities it then claims merely to describe, an indirect approach is often better able to loosen the hold of discursive hegemonies. Inciting the discrepancies and silences within the domain of the already-said is a political act that helps us to see, within the language events that make us what we are, the possibilities for being otherwise.[52] My complaint is not that linguistic feminism lacks politics altogether, but that its politics lacks sufficient formulation, and that its critique of phallogocentrism gives far too much to men. Theory is not their domain alone, even if they control the main vehicles of legitimation; and our response can invoke play and the loosening of language without degenerating into self-indulgence. Irigaray often writes as if she believes clarity is a capitulation to patriarchy. There are ways to evade the language strategies of male power without being driven by it into hostility toward communication. The move toward deconstructing male power in language need not take place at the expense of the historical and the material.

Kitsch, Irony, and
the Traffic In Between

The characteristic form of kitsch that emerges within linguistic feminism is a particularly academic variety. Although linguistic feminism's anti-foundationalism sabotages most promises of global plenitude or categorical agreement with being, it has not protected very well against a categorical agreement with the academy. Praxis feminism and cosmic feminism have found substantial audiences outside the university; linguistic feminism's home is firmly within academic journals, professional monographs, and graduate seminars. It seems to spawn an endless supply of secondary and tertiary literature in which esoteric debates among specialists crowd out any effort to speak to a broader audience. Academic kitsch carries its own forms of comforting reassurance: one's ideas must be profound because few can understand them; one's writing must be political because it calls for sabotage of the symbolic. I don't argue that theory should be simple. But the effort one puts into understanding theoretical arguments should pay off. My point is not that academics should not debate with one another, only that we should not speak solely to one another; not that we do not need specialized languages to help refine arguments and differentiate concepts, but that those languages become prisons if they are completely inaccessible to the uninitiated. Linguistic feminism's kitsch displays a curious resemblance to cosmic feminism's, not in promising global plenitude but in offering a cosmopolitan redemption via entry into the esteemed elite of those who are in the know.

However, if linguistic feminism tends toward self-containment in the academy, its resources are nonetheless not exhausted in in-house debates. One of the potent dimensions of linguistic feminism is the ease with which its own tools can be turned upon itself. Sometimes this move is put to good feminist use, to locate and name moves within an ostensibly deconstructive analysis that act to shore up conventional phallocentric power. At other times this move can constitute evasion rather than subversion. Deconstruction ruthlessly pursued tends to deflect inquiry into its own limitations by its determined search-and-destroy missions against any claims to wholeness. The difference between these two uses of the "acid tools of postmodernism" can be illustrated in contrasting arguments Butler makes with regard to her genealogical fellow travelers Kristeva and Foucault.[53]

Butler makes sense of periodic anti-lesbian lines in Kristeva by tying them to a naturalization of the maternal body and of the heterosexual commerce that generally produces such a body. At the same time, she finds Kristeva's valorization of the semiotic moments in discourse to be self-defeating in that semiotic impulses are given nowhere, politically, to go. Butler's critique of Kristeva makes the same deconstructive move against Kristeva that Kristeva makes against Jacques Lacan:

> Julia Kristeva attempts to expose the limits of Lacan's theory of language by revealing the semiotic dimension of language that it excludes. She argues that the semiotic potential of language is subversive, and describes the semiotic as a poetic-maternal linguistic practice that disrupts the symbolic, understood as culturally intelligible rule-governed speech. In the course of arguing that the semiotic contests the universality of the Symbolic, Kristeva makes several theoretical moves which end up consolidating the power of the Symbolic and paternal authority generally. She defends a maternal instinct as a pre-discursive biological necessity, thereby naturalizing a specific cultural configuration of maternity. In her use of psychoanalytic theory, she ends up claiming the cultural unintelligibility of lesbianism. Her distinction between the semiotic and the Symbolic operates to foreclose a cultural investigation into the genesis of precisely those feminine principles for which she claims a pre-discursive, naturalistic ontology.

Butler's critique of Kristeva makes the classic deconstructive move: it shows Kristeva's dependency upon and reproduction of precisely that which she sought to oppose and displace. Butler calls upon genealogical argument to critique Kristeva for naturalizing motherhood and heterosexuality, for claiming to discover conclusions that her discourse helped to create. Finding in Kristeva an "ascription of a teleological aim to maternal drives prior to their constitution in language or culture," Butler asks "how do we know that the instinctual object of Kristeva's discourse is not a construction of the discourse itself?" She makes good use of genealogy's destabilizing practices to push linguistic feminism to critique itself from within. Denaturalizing the maternal, which Kristeva employed as a stable resting place, Butler wants us "to cure ourselves of the illusion of a true body beyond the law." What Kristeva takes to be the producer of discourses and practices of sexuality (the maternal body), Butler takes as the product, as an effect rather than a cause:

The female body that she [Kristeva] seeks to express is itself a construct produced by the very law it is supposed to undermine. In no way do these criticisms of Kristeva's conception of the paternal law necessarily invalidate her general position that culture or the symbolic is predicated upon a repudiation of women's bodies. I want to suggest, however, that any theory that asserts that signification is predicated upon the denial or repression of a female principle ought to consider whether that femaleness is really external to the cultural norms by which it is repressed. . . . repression may be understood to produce the object that it comes to deny.[54]

Butler's genealogical critique is directed toward making more space within the realm of the symbolic for subversion, for unexpected permutations and inconsistencies, for submerged discourses and competing thematizations that challenge phallocentrism's hegemony. Kristeva's claim to have found meaning in the female body prior to culture does the opposite: it works to privilege maternity and to exclude lesbianism as a possible identity or practice for women. Not only does Kristeva take one dimension of a phenomenon (maternity as a dimension of being a woman) to stand for all; she goes on to naturalize this limited account so that those who fall outside it are disqualified from full participation. Kristeva's account of lesbianism is fully contained by conventional Freudian categories: lesbianism becomes a kind of difference that simply does not fit, so she dispenses with it by equating it with psychosis.[55] Her account of desire could, from a point of view more attentive to and respectful of difference, shed doubt on itself by its exclusion of lesbianism; but instead Kristeva holds to her account and accepts the delegitimation of lesbians. She cooperates with phallocentrism by finding lesbianism odd, rather than problematizing phallocentrism's rejection of lesbians as the odd move that requires explanation. Butler rightly calls Kristeva to task for this naturalizing move by showing both its ontological difficulties and its unpalatable political implications.

On the surface, Butler's arguments against Foucault are similar; again she plays the genealogical trump card, showing his dependence on that which he claims to oppose. But in this case the critique operates somewhat differently, to close down rather than open up the interpretive terrain and to draw attention away from a characteristic deconstructive difficulty rather than to illuminate it.

Butler criticizes Foucault's introduction to *Herculine Barbin: Being the Recently Discovered Memoirs of a Nineteenth-Century French Hermaphrodite* for harboring an "unacknowledged emancipatory ideal" that contradicts his insistence on sexuality as a historical system of power/knowledge producing sexual understandings and practices.[56] The memoirs tell the story of an intersexed individual, one with ambiguous genitalia, who was raised as a female and committed suicide soon after being reassigned to manhood as a young adult. Butler finds Foucault guilty of a "sentimental indulgence" in a discourse of innocent pleasures, an indulgence that she sees as both disqualified and prefigured in Foucault's earlier work: "On the one hand, Foucault wants to argue that there is no 'sex' in itself which is not produced by complex interactions of discourse and power, and yet there does seem to be a 'multiplicity of pleasures' *in itself* which is not the effect of any specific discourse/power exchange. In other words, Foucault invokes a trope of prediscursive libidinal multiplicity that effectively presupposes a sexuality 'before the law,' indeed a sexuality waiting for emancipation from the shackles of 'sex.' "[57]

Foucault, in other words, has been caught in the act of kitsch; Butler finds him guilty of romanticizing and appropriating Herculine's indefinite sexuality and in the process refusing to take seriously Herculine's own account of the miseries imposed by this life of indefiniteness.[58]

Butler bases her argument against Foucault on some questionable rhetorical strategies. First, she introduces her critique by charging that Foucault "appears to romanticize" Herculine's world, that he "appears to think that the journals provide insight into precisely that unregulated field of pleasures prior to the imposition of the law," that he "seems to laugh" in a manner that suggests difficulties.[59] *Appears* and *seems* make their suggestions tentatively; they allow for the possibility that things may look one way but be another. These qualifiers disappear, once the suggestions have been planted, so that the subsequent argument asserts without reservation that Foucault *does* romanticize, think, and laugh in the suggested ways. With this linguistic sleight of hand Butler slides from tentative observations to firm conclusions, offering little bridge between them. Second, Butler hangs her reading of Foucault's introduction largely on one phrase, "the happy limbo of a non-identity," which Foucault invokes to describe Herculine's early life.[60] She takes this phrase to mean, among other things, that Foucault sentimentalizes Herculine's story by finding her/him far too happy. Meanwhile, Foucault's other characterizations of Herculine as "unfortunate" and "unhappy" go unremarked.[61]

Third, Butler sustains several silences in her discussion that, if articulated, would problematize her account. She neglects to point out the brevity of Foucault's introduction, which might be taken as an effort on his part to refrain from interpreting too much, to let the text speak for itself. She takes no note of the problematic retrospectiveness of Herculine's text: Herculine was writing/creating her/his story when she/he had endured gender reassignment by the authorities and was near suicide. Herculine is not simply narrating her/his life as she/he experienced it; she/he is constructing that life, and is likely to read into past encounters the meanings inscribed on her/his body by more recent interactions. Butler takes certain of Herculine's claims—that she/he was always different from other girls;[62] that she/he knew her/his position was a transgression;[63] that her/his body never fit in [64]—as evidence that Herculine knew all along that she/he had no place in the sexual order. But these reflections could as easily be read as the laments of a self-conscious adolescent, reinscribed after-the-fact into a narrative of ambivalent sexuality.

What might be an alternative reading of *Herculine Barbin*? Foucault offers a starting point when he refers to Herculine as "one of those unfortunate heroes of the quest for identity."[65] *Unfortunate* helps the reader to avoid the too-easy idealization that Butler finds. *Quest for identity* reminds the reader that identity is not a self-evident state in which one finds oneself, but a problematic production requiring extensive maintenance. *Hero* is very suggestive. Foucault also refers to Herculine, in the context of her/his education and employment in Catholic schools for girls, as "this puny Achilles hidden in their boarding school."[66] One might take this to refer to the girl/boy as the Achilles heel of the female boarding school, the fatal flaw triggering subsequent disgrace. Or one might, as Moti Shojania has suggested, be reminded of the story of Achilles hiding among the women to avoid going to war. Ferreted out by Odysseus, Achilles is brought out of the company of women and into the manly and deadly arena of war.[67] Herculine could be read as this Achilles, propelled by male authorities out of the women's realm and into that of men, not quite belonging to the former, yet condemned to death in the latter. One might call on Sherri Tepper's feminist retelling of the *Iliad* and see a hero as a male who becomes a man by acts of conquest, defeating other men and putting women and children to the sword. Herculine could be the unfortunate hero who slays the woman and the child within the self in order to become the man, to enter into manly arenas and there to die.[68]

My point is not that *unfortunate hero* is the proper starting point for interpretation, while *happy limbo* is not; only that the two are quite different, and that both are findable within the pages of the text. The possibilities suggested by the heroic metaphors do not lead in the direction of sentimentalization; they employ more irony than kitsch, suggesting that to be a hero, usually thought of as lauded and admired, is to be unfortunate indeed. There is more than one story here, and Butler's reading of Foucault forecloses alternative interpretations rather than inviting them.

One can see why the tendency toward academic kitsch inhabits linguistic feminism: deconstructive readings are capable of endless self-perpetuation. Butler deconstructs Foucault's reading of *Herculine Barbin*; I deconstruct Butler's reading of Foucault's reading of *Herculine Barbin*; someone can now deconstruct my reading; and so on. But multiple readings also allow one to see the contending possibilities that reside within a text, to follow the political implications and ontological predispositions of different interpretations, to inquire into the relations between speech and silence that constitute the available maps of the text, to imagine others not yet articulated and pursue their possibilities.

A final question about Butler's critiques of Kristeva and Foucault: ought feminism to be equally suspicious of all efforts to reference some phenomenon standing outside our accounts of it? Kristeva finds a specific prediscursive meaning in the maternal body that operates to reinforce phallocentric categories by naturalizing mothering and delegitimating lesbianism. Foucault suggests a vague arena of multiple pleasures that exceeds the confines of any particular regulatory sexuality. But are these the same? A genealogical perspective does not necessarily hold that nothing exists outside language; but it does insist that such phenomena can only make an appearance to human participants by being brought into language, by being recruited out of the recalcitrant flux of being and into the realm of the nameable.

Any reference to a prediscursive or nondiscursive realm is problematic, not because such realms can be shown not to exist, but because one cannot get to them through the available language practices by which referencing proceeds. Perhaps Nietzsche uses that troubling word *instinct* (troubling especially to feminists for its accustomed patriarchal baggage) as an incoherent way to gesture toward some realm of bodily energies that precedes any particular ordering of those energies.[69] Perhaps Foucault evokes the enigmatic phrase *bodies and pleasures* in the same way, as a vague gesture toward that inchoate material upon which the ordering powers of discourse do their work.[70] Caught in the bind of using language to refer outside itself, perhaps this is the best one can do. Butler's single-minded attack on any suggestions about what stands before or outside language fails to distinguish between arguments that enshrine a particular naturalization, such as Kristeva's, and arguments such as Foucault's that merely gesture toward a pre- or nondiscursive terrain that necessarily remains unarticulated. Linguistic feminists are persuasive in demonstrating the difficulties one gets into by trying to encounter via language a place outside language, as their cosmic counterparts are wont to do; but such cautions do not and cannot eliminate the possibility of such a place, nor still curiosities about it.

If linguistic and cosmic feminists seem completely at odds with regard to questions of the pre- or nondiscursive, they evince some interesting common ground in other respects. Despite the widespread genealogical suspicion of totalization, there is a certain nostalgia for wholeness operating in Kristeva and Irigaray. They seem to have absorbed from Lacan and other psychoanalytic thinkers the idea that desire is always for something lost, for the impossible reunion with the mother that offered such blissful plenitude to the infant.[71] Ebert also adopts this view: "Desire is the repressed and unattainable wish for that which the subject loses upon entry into signification: the separation of the self from its unconsciousness, its own body, the other—a disjunction it views as a loss of unity, loss of fullness of being, loss of oneness with another. It is the unrealizeable longing for wholeness of self and unity of oneness with another."[72]

Here desire is never future-oriented, never inclined toward new possibilities, but always toward the past that is forever lost. Agnes Heller argues that "nostalgia for lost simplicity and sublimity" is "a typically bourgeois feeling: the problematic individual looks back with painful yearning and respect to the non-problematic individual."[73] Perhaps a society as bound up in separation, inequality, and self-scrutiny as the modern western world cannot help but produce visions of desire as longings for earlier and total self-acceptance via merger with another. But what is missing here is any idea that desire could look forward or sideways as well as backward. Perhaps the infant's experiences of connection with another continue to have a presence in adult consciousness; perhaps the experiences of infancy are not the only source of imagination and longing. Other genealogically-oriented thinkers, including Deleuze and Nietzsche, have articulated more life-affirming, forward-looking, open-ended notions of desire; but many linguistic feminists seem to affiliate themselves with Lacan's insistence on a desire that is always already unavailable.[74] The reconstitution of desire as nostalgia is reminiscent of cosmic feminism's nostalgia for an alleged matriarchal past or a return to the old ways. The psychoanalytic imaginary functions rather like the mythic garden as the lost source of plenitude; perhaps the original wholeness cannot be recovered in either case, but the search for it motivates much of the understanding of identity and desire operating in both thematizations of subjectivity.

There are other interesting similarities between cosmic and linguistic feminism. Both appeal to the power of art, music and poetry for their political promise. Speaking of the heterogeneity of the semiotic, Kristeva argues that "poetic language making free with the language code; music, dancing, painting, reordering the psychic drives which have not been harnessed by the dominant symbolization systems and thus renewing their own traditions; and (in a different mode) experiences with drugs—all seek out and make use of this heterogeneity and the ensuing fracture of a symbolic code which can no longer 'hold' its speaking subjects."[75] While Butler's criticism here—that the subversiveness of the poetic is too thin because Kristeva gives too much to the wholeness and imperviousness of the symbolic order—is still a good one, nonetheless the poetic is the home of important subversions and displacements of phallogocentric law. Audre Lorde makes a similar appeal to poetry, but connects it to a much more robust vision of resistance: "For women, then, poetry is not a luxury. It is a vital necessity of our existence. It forms the quality of the light within which we predicate our hopes and dreams toward survival and change, first made into language, then into idea, then into more tangible action. Poetry is the way we help give name to the nameless so it can be thought. The farthest horizons of our hopes and fears are cobbled by our poems, carved from the rock experiences of our daily lives."[76] Lorde argues that poetry can be the avenue for bringing inchoate desire into the ordered symbol systems of ordinary language "so it can be thought," while Kristeva argues that the poetic would be immediately colonized were it to make such an appearance. But both writers look to the poetic for some liberating potential.

Both cosmic and linguistic feminisms play in the realm of the semiotic; cosmic picture thoughts and linguistic analogies are not that far apart. Mary Daly's delightful word-tumblings about laughing crones are a match for any of linguistic feminism's semiotic enjoyments:

As Self-conscious Seers, Be-Laughing women are engaged in the Meta-mysterious work of Metafooling. Disdaining the fooling of snools, we learn to See and Act in ways that transcend the rules of fools. Refusing Foolfill-ment, we escape the state of totaled women. Refuting the foolproofs of foolosophical re-search, we avoid absorption by academentia. In short, Metafooling is Outrageous Contagious Departure from phallic fixations. It consists of riotous transformations.[77]

Meanwhile, praxis feminism plods along in the symbolic. Perhaps what the appeal to the premodern and the stretch toward the post-modern have in common is simply that neither of them embraces the modern.

Both linguistic and cosmic feminisms sometimes valorize mysti-cism, although to somewhat different ends. Irigaray's essay "La Mystérique" (a neologism formed from a fusion of mysticism, hys-teria, mystery and femaleness) finds potency in women mystics who speak "about the dazzling glare which comes from the source of light that has been logically repressed, about 'subject' and 'Other' flowing into an embrace of fire that mingles one term with another, about contempt for form as such, about mistrust for understanding as an obstacle along the path of jouissance and mistrust for the dry desolation of reason."[78] Irigaray seems to suggest that mysticism may be a disruptive discourse. While many cosmic feminists ap-pear simply to embrace (some version of) mysticism as an unprob-lematic answer to patriarchal logos, the shared willingness at least to consider the mystical is there.

What is one to make of the common terrain between linguistic and cosmic feminisms? An approach to subjectivity animated by a strong quest for attunement and another motivated by an equally strong suspicion of such quests might well be expected to share little. Yet the face of feminism that calls for the return to the god-dess seems not unlike another face that asserts that, not just god, but the goddess as well, is dead.[79]

Perhaps one can make sense of this perplexity by reconsidering the various kinds of essentialism discussed earlier. Both cosmic feminists and linguistic feminists have been found guilty of essen-tialism by their critics. Both contribute to this perception by their tendency to employ picture thoughts, imprecise images that in-voke an affective response while defying particular differentiations.

Part of the appeal of Irigaray and Griffin is their use of picture thoughts to talk about women in a way that bonds us together in a struggle against male power. Irigaray's use of *we* in her lovely essay "When Our Lips Speak Together" is very like Griffin's use of *we say* to articulate women's resistance. Irigaray asks:

How can I say it? That we are women from the start. That we don't have to be turned into women by them, made holy and profaned by them. That that has always already happened, without their efforts. And that their history, their stories, constitute the locus of our displacement. It's not that we have a territory of our own; but their fatherland, family, home, discourse, imprison us in enclosed spaces where we cannot keep on moving, living, as ourselves. Their properties are our exile. Their enclosures, the death of our love. Their words, the gag upon our lips.[80]

Compare Griffin:

Suddenly we find we are no longer straining against all the old conclusions. We are no longer pleading for the right to speak: we have spoken; space has changed; we are living in a matrix of our own sounds; our words resonate, by our echoes we chart a new geography; we recognize this new landscape as our birthplace, where we invented names for ourselves; here language does not contradict what we know; by what we hear, we are moved again and again to speech.[81]

Important differences remain between these positions: Irigaray argues against the very possibility of the home beyond appearances that Griffin seeks. Griffin finds a voice for women that Irigaray can only indirectly indicate. But does this matter in the face of the overwhelming discursive power of that shared *we*, that overweight pronoun suggesting that all women are the same?

This is a very complex question. Irigaray's *we* inhabits a different discursive terrain from Griffin's. In keeping with the common textual strategies of cosmic feminism, Griffin's *we* unproblematically refers to women, a collective noun recruiting its members from those alleged to sustain a particular relation to the non-human world. Irigaray, in contrast, nearly always accompanies her invocations of all women with reminders that women are not all the same: "We are always open . . . we have so many voices to invent in order to express all of us everywhere . . . we have so many dimensions."[82] Her project always entails attention to difference in the face of the tyranny of sameness in phallogocentrism. But the attention to difference becomes abstract and unconnected to the particular kinds of differences—racial, sexual, economic, geographic, historical—that inhabit people's concrete lives.

Linguistic feminism tends, paradoxically, to cloud our vision of material differences in its effort to bring linguistic difference into focus. Perhaps one can understand Irigaray's *we* as an instance of the third aspect of essentialism posited earlier—not really essentialism at all, but a textual gesture that constitutes a unity of *women* or *men* in order to enable discussion. Unlike many cosmic feminists, Irigaray does not seem to posit a natural or spiritual essence prior to culture that characterizes all women.[83] Although there may be some inconsistency on this point in her writings, for the most part Irigaray's conceptual unities are self-consciously constituted, not simply discovered: she wants to be able to speak of women as a coherent category in contrast to men. Her mistake, then, is not one of essentialism per se. Instead she loses sight of the provisionality of her categories and lets the unifying power of her figures of speech take over the text.

This is not to say that no traces of essentialism per se inhabit linguistic feminism. Butler's case against Kristeva, for example, is persuasive on this point. But Irigaray's global language does not, for the most part, act to naturalize convention in the same way Kristeva's writing does. If Irigaray can be found innocent of that charge, she nevertheless manifests a troubling tendency to applaud difference in the abstract but attend little to it in the concrete. What could prevent or at least modify this situation? Perhaps if Irigaray and theorists like her were to participate more vigorously in praxis feminism's strategy of close attention to particular practices and events, they would stray less easily into that global and timeless *we*. Rosemary Hennessy and Rajeswari Mohan are quick to point out that linguistic feminism tends to be ahistorical.[84] Praxis and linguistic feminisms frequently work together, as in Ong's use of Foucault and Pierre Bourdieu to investigate the productive power of discourse, or Hennessy and Mohan's acknowledgment of Foucault's contributions to figuring the power/knowledge/subject matrix. But in both these cases, Foucault makes an early appearance whereas Marx gets the last word.[85] Spivak is more successful at holding praxis and linguistic claims in a productive tension; she calls for them to "become persistent interruptions of each other."[86]

Irigaray urges psychoanalysts to look more to historical, cultural, and political/economic explanations, and criticizes Lacan for not doing so; but such explanations are not evident in much of her own work.[87] Chandra Mohanty has noted a tendency in western feminist theory to marginalize difference by first positing women as a category and then qualifying that category with other adjectives: working-class, black, third-world. Mohanty's point is that gender is not always the starting point for constituting whatever unities a particular group of women or men work with to understand themselves.[88] Lorde takes the same position: "I find I am constantly being encouraged to pluck out some one aspect of myself and present this as the meaningful whole, eclipsing or denying the other parts of myself. But this is a destructive and fragmenting way to live. My fullest concentration of energy is available to me only when I integrate all the parts of who I am, openly, allowing power from particular sources of my living to flow back and forth freely through all my different selves, without the restrictions of externally imposed definition."[89] While the word *integrate* is problematic here, suggesting a harmonious and conciliatory resolution, nonetheless Lorde's primary point still stands: any reference to *all women* is a contestable figure of speech, not a discovered unity. Sometimes it is a serviceable trope, inciting a unification among women-as-a-group in contrast with the power of men-as-a-group. But it is also a dangerous trope, and should be deployed with caution.

The caution that linguistic feminism most often evinces is ironic in form. Linguistic feminists find themselves in the paradoxical position of needing what they oppose, or depending upon what they have exposed as undependable: using language to explore the limits of language, calling experience into question while still wanting to hear what people have to say, deconstructing identity while continuing to use pronouns. In fact, irony has become so closely associated with linguistic feminism that other feminisms may have trouble entertaining it (or being entertained by it) at all.[90] Irony provides an alternative to the search for (and presumption of) solid foundations for ethics and politics; it provides a way to throw out one's hermeneutic anchor in the absence of a safe harbor. Irony allows linguistic feminists to acknowledge the limits of their practices but to proceed with them nonetheless.

Linguistic feminism's ironies appear in many ways. Butler is emphatic in her call not simply for irony, but for laughter: "laughter in the face of serious categories is indispensable for feminism. Without a doubt, feminism continues to require its own forms of serious play."[91] Irigaray urges women to engage in mimicry, whereby repetition can disrupt hegemonic formulations through ridicule.[92] Butler suggests the possibilities of parody in which "truly troubling" repetitions interrupt business as usual.[93] William Callahan opts for irony as juggling: "Relentless irony is like juggling. It is a skill; something capable of being learned, one which some do well, and which some will never be able to do. But also something that is temporal. Timing is crucial for skillful juggling. And more importantly, one cannot do it all the time. Everyone needs a rest, a break, from the trying struggle of ironic identity. To settle into one of its facets as a (mobile) home."[94]

I want to close this chapter with two vignettes about the workings of irony in linguistically oriented feminisms. The first is to be found (more accurately, is findable) in Trinh's considerations of the act of writing; the second in Haraway's intimations of an animalcentric (that is, non-human animal-centered) perspective on taxidermy and hunting. I use words like *findable* and *intimation* here because irony is a tricky thing to locate; in John Seery's words, "reading irony is an ongoing process of interpretation: posing questions, making guesses, reflecting further, inclining perhaps toward an answer."[95] Even when a writer states that her mode is ironic, as Haraway does, the particular workings of the ironic doublings and triplings, turnings and twistings, evasions and confrontations, remain unstable. Recognizing the irony of trying to reach some conclusions about irony, I nonetheless have a few to offer.

Like many women of color, Trinh is self-reflective about the politics of writing.[96] She anticipates and responds to the problem of access in academic kitsch:

Clarity as a purely rhetorical attribute serves the purpose of a classical feature in language, namely, its instrumentality. To write is to communicate, express, witness, impose, instruct, redeem, or save—at any rate to *mean* and to send out *an unambiguous message*. Writing thus reduced to a mere vehicle of thought may be used to orient toward a goal or to sustain an act, but it does not constitute an act in itself. This is how the division between the writer/the intellectual and the activists/the masses becomes possible. To use the language well, says the voice of literacy, cherish its classic form. Do not choose the offbeat at the cost of clarity. Obscurity is an imposition on the reader. True, but beware when you cross railroad tracks for one train may hide another train. Clarity is a means of subjection, a quality both of official, taught language and of correct writing, two old mates of power: together they flow, together they flower, vertically, to impose an order.[97]

What relation can be sustained between writerly acts disruptive of the conventions of order and the desire to communicate effectively with others? Trinh raises suspicions about those who "continue to preach conformity to the norms of well-behaved writing" yet she seems to want to get through to her readers somehow.[98]

Perhaps the relationship can be constituted ironically. Disruptions of narrative order are necessary for *linguistic* feminism to make space for its genealogical practices to do their work. It is precisely the power of familiar narratives—their power to carry us toward certain conclusions without ever having to argue for those conclusions—that is being challenged. At the same time, it is necessary for linguistic *feminism* to reach its audience, not only those who already participate fully, but also those who approach it tentatively, skeptically, or fearfully. The political task of confounding order and the pedagogical task of communicating effectively and in a trustworthy manner (which is also political, and central to the creation of solidarities) might meet on the playing field of irony.

Trinh's book is multi-coded in many respects. For starters, the words are accompanied by pictures, stills from Trinh's films, which are themselves multi-coded; scenes that seem to be interviews are actually staged and scripted, characters who seem to be real turn out to be actresses, and so forth.[99] The angle and positioning of the camera periodically call attention to its own productions, further undermining the viewer's ability to sit passively as a voyeur of truthtelling; instead, the audience is recruited actively into the productions of imagery and meaning, enjoined to help sort them out. Further, the various chapters are coded differently: the first is a genealogically inspired analysis of writing as a third-world woman; the second is a caustic rendition/echo of the colonialism of anthropology, which always posits "natives" as endless material for study, "a pace behind their white saviors"; the third, a pained and powerful meditation on identity and difference, "A Special Third World Women Issue"; the fourth, an appreciative, participatory account of storytelling.[100] Trinh characterizes her work: "From jagged transitions between the analytical and the poetical to the disruptive, always shifting fluidity of a headless and bottomless storytelling, what is exposed in this text is the inscription and de-scription of a non-unitary female subject of color through her engagement, therefore also disengagement, with master discourses."[101] There are many points of entry into Trinh's tales of engagement and disengagement, many powerful (if slippery) places of access. If you can't get in at one point, there are others to try. Here the text disrupts and confounds; there it takes pains to explain its disruptions and confoundments. There's work required to enter this text, but it's work with a payoff, and remarkably little kitsch.

My second example of the workings of irony in linguistically-oriented feminism comes from Haraway's "Metaphors Into Hardware: Harry Harlow and the Technology of Love." Here Haraway juxtaposes two apparently distinct narrative schemes of humanism and of sadism to open up a space for their mutual enablement to appear. Harlow investigated mother-infant bonding in rhesus monkeys by separating newborn monkey infants from their birth mothers and putting them in a variety of laboratory situations: with surrogate "cloth mothers," with rejecting and harsh "mothers," in nuclear families, in total isolation. Haraway introduces sadism into her account not directly to accuse Harlow and his researchers of enjoying the monkeys' pain, but to talk about the kind of vision of otherness that enables such research to take place, to win prestigious awards, to be counted as progress. Sadism works "by reducing the other to a flawless, perfectly controlled mirror of the self"; it is a way of marking the other as that which rightfully receives its meaning from elsewhere.[102] Sadism organizes a narrative of investigation in which the choice between kindness and cruelty is secondary to the prior claim to an unqualified right to define. Humanism, that seemingly innocent quest for self-knowledge, intersects obligingly with sadism via science: *Know thyself* turns readily into *Everything is for me!* Haraway comments:

The mother surrogate and infant isolation experiments in the Harlow labs were part of this stunning project of humanistic self-knowledge. It was in this context that one must see the TV scientists talking calmly to the camera about love, while the visual field behind and around them is full of self-clutching, autistic infant monkeys, experimentally produced to show the "touching" adequacy of a mother surrogate in a liberal, rational society. Sadism demands a story.[103]

Haraway's dismal ironies irrevocably blur the distinction between humanistic good guys and sadistic bad guys. Her discussion is punctuated by photos of the monkeys that accomplish indirectly what a more direct appeal would endanger: an empathetic connection with the monkeys that dislocates smug presumptions about necessary sacrifices in the cause of science. In one photo a baby monkey clings to its cloth and wire "surrogate mother": the grip is stressed, clutching; the animal's face, desperate.[104] In a later photo illustrating a very different kind of research project, a baby ringtail lemur holds onto its mother; the embrace is casual, comfortable; the faces of mother and young are relaxed.[105] Haraway offers no comment on these photos. Any effort to do so, as I have just done, risks interpretive disaster, not to mention immediate descent into kitsch. How could the human viewer confidently attribute desperation to one monkey, comfort to another? What familiar human narrative about mothers and babies is being recruited and imposed onto these scenes? Haraway's wordless juxtapositions accomplish, by way of indirection, a questioning of the other-engulfing vision that enables humanism's intersections with sadism to produce the practices of science.

Haraway's approach to narrative and perspective, and Trinh's stance toward accessibility, have something in common: they make it possible to inhabit, however tenuously, the unfamiliar; they enable an indirect coming-to-terms with something (disorderly counter-narrative strategies or imagined othernesses) that would dissipate under more direct assault. Genealogy's ironic multiplications prove fertile for enabling linguistically-oriented feminist inquiries.

Chapter Six

Mobile Subjectivities

This discussion of subjectivity began with a consideration of Hegel's views on the subject and of feminists' relations to Hegel's account. An exemplary figure in the articulation of modern western male-ordered notions of subjectivity, Hegel can serve as a point of entry into the discourse feminists wish to contest (although they work from it and sometimes duplicate it as well). The kinds of desires Hegel attributes to his subject are instructive: desire for the consumption and control of nature; desire for recognition via domination; desire for the other's desire. The kind of person who could have these desires turns out to be characteristically modern, western, and male: an intersubjectively impoverished individual locked into a variety of combative stances, seeking dominance in relationships, mastery over nature, and absorption of difference.

Hegel's account of subjectivity served as the vehicle for raising the man question and problematizing the assumptions and conclusions of a male-ordered view of identity. The process of making Hegel strange, of troubling the theoretical terrain upon which his account operates, opens up spaces for the articulation of alternative thematizations of subjectivity. Praxis feminism challenges Hegel's account of self-other relations by stressing affirmation in connection (although not without encountering its own difficulties with universalizations). Cosmic feminism counters Hegel's subordination and objectification of nature by locating the human self/soul in more egalitarian relation to a larger natural/spiritual order (even while raising serious questions about appropriation). Linguistic feminism contests Hegel's faith in the capacities of language to apprehend being and his absorption of difference by elucidating the productive power of discourse (although not without sometimes overstating the hegemony of dominant discourses and neglecting the particularity of lived differences).

Different thematizations of subjectivity within feminism suggest alternatives that respond to the Hegelian model of subjectivity in different ways. Taking the relations among praxis, cosmic, and linguistic feminist understandings of identity and desire to reside in a productive field of frictions and invitations, this chapter offers one more thematization of subjectivity for feminism. Mobile subjectivities ride on the ready-made conversations/contestations among linguistic, praxis, and cosmic feminisms, on the struggles of interpretive and genealogical metatheories, but with an ironic twist—they trouble fixed boundaries, antagonize true believers, create new possibilities for themselves.[1] Mobile subjectivities are temporal, moving across and along axes of power (which are themselves in motion) without fully residing in them. They are relational, produced through shifting yet enduring encounters and connections, never fully captured by them. They are ambiguous: messy and multiple, unstable but perservering. They are ironic, attentive to the manyness of things. They respect the local, tend toward the specific, but without eliminating the cosmopolitan. They are politically difficult in their refusal to stick consistently to one stable identity claim; yet they are politically advantageous because they are less pressed to police their own boundaries, more able to negotiate respectfully with contentious others.

My notion of mobile subjectivities is inspired by other contenders for redefining subjectivity—Haraway's cyborgs/situated knowledges, Trinh's splitting and re-connecting pronouns, de Lauretis's eccentric subjects, Spivak's intersections of Marxism, feminism, and deconstruction, Riley's contentious identities, and Butler's local possibilities.[2] The attraction of mobile subjectivities is at heart political and ethical, not simply epistemological. Thematizing ourselves as mobile subjectivities eschews the search for an essential reality to which our representations correspond, while claiming an historical residence in the contentious fields of late modernity and seeking strategies by which to stay honest about our affirmations while we keep moving toward them.

Tragic Choices, Happy Endings, or
Ironic Encounters

Sketching the parameters of mobile subjectivities requires attention to the difficult problem of relating the different faces of feminism to one another. What relationship can praxis, cosmic, and linguistic feminism sustain?

I see three approaches to this question. One possibility is simply to select the least problematic perspective and defend its virtues against the criticisms of the others. Stressing the ways in which each perspective disqualifies the others, this strategy abandons the possibility of creating a coherent relationship among praxis, cosmic, and linguistic feminisms. Why not just pick one perspective on subjectivity and be done with it?

If this were the most tenable option I would be likely to find myself defending linguistic feminism as the best of the three.[3] Although it may neglect the historical and the particular and devalue the ecological impulse, at least it is on the right track with its suspicion of foundations and origins. But my arguments to this point have made this strategy unappealing. I have insisted that each of these thematizations of subjectivity has qualities in its favor, strengths that turn out to be valuable in the struggle against the hegemony of male-ordered discourses on subjectivity and desire. The strategy of cutting one's losses by embracing the least problematic perspective is a tragic approach; each of them has something precious to offer, something to make one protest against their mere dismissal.

On to possibility number two: Why not attempt a synthesis of the three feminist perspectives? This strategy calls for a wedding of the strengths of each of the positions, a merger that would call out the "good" aspects of each set of arguments while divorcing the "bad." Certainly praxis, cosmic, and linguistic feminisms share a great deal: they all evince a concern with language, with the ways women and men take up and are taken up by language. They all evoke disorder in their struggles against the confinement of patriarchy, urging us to heed the multiple voices within us. They all affirm an anti-dualistic posture, and they all focus on women's bodies—our reproductive experiences, our sexuality, or our labor—as central both to knowledge and to politics. They all participate to some extent in the deconstruction of rationality, re-reading the claims of reason in light of desire, including the desire for reason itself. They all invoke the capacity to imagine beyond the familiar, and name (some of) the obstacles to the cultivation of that capacity. They all look to women to resist male power.

These and other similarities allow those who participate in one or more of the three thematizations to recognize one another as feminists. Might we concentrate on this shared ground, constituting feminism as a unity and celebrating its harmonies? My project instead has been to incite the discrepancies (as well as the unexpected agreements) among the various views, to force open a space within feminist discourses for greater acknowledgment of discontinuity, incompleteness, and tension. The move toward synthesis and transcendence, however comforting, is not fully available because, as I have argued, the weaknesses of the positions shadow their strengths. Following Heidegger, each of these theoretical formations enables a revealing by simultaneously imposing a concealing; that is, in each case the sharpness of vision offered comes at the expense of that which is unnamed or engulfed. Further, the call to transcend limitations and go beyond contraints toward a larger and happier merger is a call deeply bound to interpretive strategies of argument, which assume that a more profound whole stands behind disparate visible parts. The genealogical impulse so strong in linguistic feminism and sometimes present in praxis and cosmic feminism as well cannot readily be absorbed into a call for unity.

My articulation of the strengths and weaknesses of each thematization of subjectivity has made me a partisan: I long to hold onto some aspects of praxis, cosmic, and linguistic feminisms and to be rid of others. But I recognize the problems of such selectiveness. It invents a recipe for mobile subjectivities: take two parts linguistic feminism, fold in one part praxis, and add a dash of cosmic. Start with linguistic feminism's anti-foundationalism (minus its political vagueness), add praxis feminism's focus on relationships and on specific, perspective-shaping practices (eschewing its tendencies toward universalism), and mix in cosmic feminism's acknowledgment of the earth itself as a mysterious agent (with strict avoidance of its faith in attunement). Separate the yolks from the whites, and whip until smooth. Evidently, one does not escape easily from the longing for synthesis. But perhaps the longing is not itself the problem. Perhaps the problem comes from the assumption that a desire for synthesis of virtues or transcendence of limitations guarantees or even indicates the availability of synthesis or transcendence. There are good reasons to suspect that the strengths of each perspective will come attached to its weaknesses, for shadows are hard to detach from their places of residence. The expectation of synthesis and transcendence, William Connolly has argued, can only be sustained by assuming a creator to guarantee it, one who designed the world so that fulfillment accompanies longing. Otherwise it would be a farfetched coincidence to inhabit a world where desire is so conveniently matched with its completion.[4] Acknowledging, even honoring, a desire one cannot believe will be fully met could produce/reflect despair; or it could hitch itself to a wry shrug and a concomitant willingness to struggle nonetheless.

Eschewing both the tragic resolution entailed by the first possibility and the happy ending promised by the second, what's left? Not surprisingly, it's irony. Irony makes it possible for me to reside within the unstable theoretical space I have created. It enables a contentious conversation among praxis, cosmic, and linguistic feminisms, one in which they continuously argue and interrupt each other yet find enough worth listening to so that they continue to talk. Irony allows contending thematizations of subjectivity to negotiate a political relationship that does not depend upon unanimity, consensus, or even majority agreement to any particular configuration of identity, gender, or nature, or to any one metatheoretical stance. Ironic conversations enable the competing claims for identity and desire to undercut as well as enable one another and produce an enhanced appreciation of each. Ironic encounters illuminate differences while they enable connections to be made.[5] Armed with irony, mobile subjectivities have a resource for handling the tensions entailed in appreciation of the virtues of each thematization of subjectivity, awareness of its limitations, and determination to explore/explode the contentious field its interactions create.

The effort to incite multiplicity against the somnolent hand of totalization and to mobilize the arts of irony to do so, need not weaken feminisms' strategies of political struggle; rather, it may multiply the levels of knowing and doing upon which resistance can act. The conversations possible among feminisms can engage as well as irritate. For example, the explicit political commitments of the first two thematizations can strengthen the third by naming the differences most worthy of articulation and struggle: differences that name historically and materially specific dimensions of gender; differences that locate the self within relationships and the human within the natural; differences that let other differences be. Linguistic feminism's enhanced attention to the practices of theorizing could prod the others into greater alertness concerning their own patterns of insistence, their own will to truth.[6] Further, attention to the contestable connections within and among thematizations of subjectivity can alert us to the ruptures and discontinuities within seemingly harmonious points of view. Looking at Hegel's phenomenology of identity, Jane Bennett argues that "every figure of consciousness is always in struggle with competing modes."[7] The same can be said for visions of subjectivity within feminisms. Cosmic feminism, for example, makes no sense at all outside the steady incursion of modernity into non-human nature; praxis feminism's stress on intersubjectivity is counterpoint to male-ordered notions of the self as walled city; linguistic feminism is dependent on the various hermeneutics it deconstructs. The struggles are internal to feminist conversations as well: praxis and linguistic feminisms often scorn their cosmic counterparts for a certain embarrassing tendency toward flakiness; linguistic feminists frequently find the others to be naive and unsophisticated about the metatheories they employ; cosmic feminists often allege that their neighbors are insensitive to the spiritual dimensions of life.

An argument for multiplicity and undecidability in feminist discourses on subjectivity creates a space for partial identities and mobile subjectivities. Sandra Harding notes that an anti-totalizing posture "encourages us to cherish and defend our 'hyphens'—those theoretical expressions of our multiple struggles."[8] Theresa de Lauretis notes a move within some feminist theories toward "reconceptualization of the subject as shifting and multiply organized across variable axes of difference."[9] I have chosen the term *mobile* rather than *multiple* to avoid the implication of movement from one to another stable resting place, and instead to problematize the contours of the resting one does.

Linda Alcoff uses the term *positionality* to look at the "moving historical context" within which different people take up their relationship to constituted entities such as women or men.[10] I find *positionalization* to be a better term, despite its awkwardness. It names an outcome of a positionalizing practice; the evocation of the verb form stresses the activity that is involved, both in the ways that power acts upon us and in the ways we resist it. Identity is something one *does*, an active corralling of practices, events, desires, contingencies, a regulatory semiotic and material operation. Commenting on the shift from nouns to verbs, Butler remarks that "gender ought not to be conceived as a noun or a substantial thing or a static cultural marker, but rather as an incessant and repeated action of some sort." [11] Attention to mobile subjectivities requires one to heed both the repeated doings that underwrite claims to "be," and the structures that produce those doings, including the possibilities of doing otherwise. Particular positionalizations are both the products and the producers of discursive and institutional practices, both the outcomes of the operations of power and the starting points for the practices of resistance. Thematizing the subject as mobile suggests a way to harness respect for difference with attention to the concrete, without eliminating either the desire for or the recognition of commonalities.

Respect for difference is a call that can work in more than one way. It can affirm differences between women whose specific racial, class, erotic, or geographical circumstances (and the identities those circumstances produce) vary. Audre Lorde calls for the affirmation of this kind of difference: "Difference must be not merely tolerated, but seen as a fund of necessary polarities between which our creativity can spark like a dialectic. Only then does the necessity for interdependency become unthreatening. Only within that interdependency of different strengths, acknowledged and equal, can the power to seek new ways of being in the world generate, as well as the courage and sustenance to act where there are no charters." [12] This dimension of difference is crucial for any coalition politics. To attend to it involves "a shared responsibility, which requires a minimum of willingness to reach out to the unknown." [13] There is another face of difference, however, which stands in tension with this one: a difference that does not separate or relate one identity to another but instead explodes the very idea of identity. Trinh focuses on the second aspect of difference:

Difference in such an insituable context is *that which undermines the very idea of identity*, deferring to infinity the layers whose totality forms "I." It subverts the foundations of any affirmation or vindication of value and cannot, thereby, ever bear in itself an absolute value. The difference (within) between difference itself and identity has so often been ignored and the use of the two terms so readily confused, that claiming a female/ ethnic identity/difference is commonly tantamount to reviving a kind of naive "male-tinted" romanticism. If feminism is set forth as a demystifying force, then it will have to question thoroughly the belief in its own identity. [14]

These two dimensions of difference seem contradictory. To attend to differences between women in the name of feminism seems to tighten the boundaries around specific identities by taking them for granted: for example, if you're a woman of color and I'm a white woman, what creative politics can make our differences productive rather than merely threatening? Attention to differences *within* identity-claims destabilizes the take-off points of the prior argument: woman of color and white woman become unstable categories, shaky representations, regulatory impositions concealing enormous turbulence. The trick for mobile subjectivities is to bring those two together in ironic juxtaposition. The first throws out a hermeneutic anchor in the name of classed, colored, gendered, or some other identity; the second questions the stability of that resting place from within. Trinh gestures toward this pairing when she speaks of "identity as points of re-departure of the critical processes by which I have come to understand how the personal—the ethnic me, the female me [the classed me]—is political. Difference does not annul identity. It is beyond and alongside identity." [15]

In the writings of some working-class women, lesbians, and women of color one often finds expression of what might be called mobile subjectivities. Class, race, gender, and erotic choice are some of the central trajectories along which mobile subjects move and are moved. They are axes of power/domination/resistance that run across and are traversed by mobile subjects. Although the categories working-class women, lesbians, and women of color are themselves constitutions rather than discoveries, it is precisely the processes of that constitution that make them potent. When we attend to the production of these categories in different circumstances for different purposes, we recognize that the list of such categories is inexhaustible. As Butler so wonderfully points out, the "embarrassed etc." at the end of every list of oppressions should alert us to the inevitable failure of closure. [16]

Women who are aware that factors like race, class, gender, and erotic identity may be held against them are less likely to invest themselves completely in any single dimension and more likely to be attentive to the multiplicities within them. They are more likely to realize that their likenesses to others—male workers, men of color, white people who are female, gay men—are never complete, that they are similarly situated in some ways but not in others. Their resistances can be grounded, as Haraway remarks, "not on the basis of original innocence, but on the basis of seizing the tools to mark the world that marked them as other."[17] Hyphenated identities that combine class and gender, class and color, and erotic identity and ethnicity can remind other women and men that even the more privileged (and therefore less problematic) positionalizations—as white, as middle or upper class, as first-world, as heterosexual, as male—are likely to be deceptive homogenizations concealing some turbulence. Hyphenated identities that range along particular axes of definition, such as used-to-be-working-class-now-professional, or divorced-mother-now-lesbian, mark the ordering trajectories across which mobile subjects roam as also in motion. Mobile subjectivities locate themselves in relation to the moving trajectories of power and resistance via circumstances of proximity and distance, restlessness and rootedness, separation and connection.

Mobile subjectivities are too concrete and dirty to claim innocence, too much in-process to claim closure, too interdependent to claim fixed boundaries. Unstable but potent, diverse but not incomprehensible to one another, mobile subjectivities could play across the terrains mapped out by praxis, cosmic, and linguistic feminisms, refusing stable memberships while insisting on affiliations. They stand in a relation of "antagonistic indebtedness" both to interpretively and genealogically informed feminisms and are enabled by the arguments among them.[18] Amply indebted to linguistic feminism for its counter-ontology, to praxis feminism for its enhanced appreciation of sociality and of the specifics of time and place, and to cosmic feminism for recognition of the earth as another subjectivity, "a coding trickster with whom we must learn to converse," mobile subjectivities pay their debts irreverently, with little regard for interest accumulated but much gratitude for contentious beginnings made available.[19] Interpretation and geneal-

ogy engage in "persistent interruptions" of one another and in that
space of aggravated encounters mobile subjectivities emerge.[20]

Mobile subjectivities appear not just in discourse but in institutions as well; they are material as well as semiotic actors.[21] In their
relations to the social spaces that help to constitute them, mobile
subjectivities incline toward the local. Greselda Pollock's description of the "spaces of femininity" can also serve mobile subjects:
"They are the product of a lived sense of social locatedness, mobility and visibility, in the social relations of seeing and being seen."[22]
Articulation of mobile subjectivities requires careful attention to
the specifics of social and geographical location, to the spaces inhabited by individuals, groups, and relationships. Suspicious of global
theory for its totalizing tendencies, mobile subjectivities prefer a
"specifying" gesture. In her analysis of specifying in the context of
the lives of black women in the U.S., Susan Willis conveys a sense
of emphaticness, of being *specific* about things.[23] I want to retain
her sense of the term, and also to include the notion of appealing
to particular, local settings for meaning. The globalizing move seeks
a unity based on sameness, while the specifying move seeks a more
contentious solidarity based on a political and moral commitment
to defend the margins against the center while simultaneously
struggling against centeredness. Spivak finds a specifying move in
a deconstructive attention to "the repeated agenda of the situa-
tional production of those concepts [gender, race and class] and
our complicity in such a production. This aspect of deconstruction
will not allow the establishment of a hegemonic 'global theory.' "[24]

The globalizing tendency moves in the direction of some set of
umbrella claims and seeks to encompass particulars under a larger
and more complete category, such as humanity, nature, or rights.
This move suggests both "the will to annihilate the Other through
a false incorporation" (Hegel, for example),[25] and Butler's description of the closing down of agitations and incommensurabilities within
subjects: "the epistemological paradigm that presumes the priority
of the doer to the deed establishes a global and globalizing subject
who disavows its own locality as well as the conditions for local
intervention."[26] The practices by which mobile subjectivities produce their provisional identities open up the possibility of producing against the grain, of participating in the daily practices that
mark gender, race, and class in an unpredictable way, on a slant,

and thus making a difference. Even the most hegemonic insistences that we *be* a certain way must be negotiated, not simply absorbed and regurgitated. Local possibilities for undoing and redoing naturalized identity claims are a starting point (not a final resting place) enabling mobile subjectivities to do their work.

Attention to "practices which are directly stitched into the place and time which give rise to them" do not disallow efforts at generalization.[27] Similarities among places and times can suggest themselves through careful attention to their requirements and possibilities. For example, Aihwa Ong's account of the colonization of Malaysia rings bells of recognition for feminists living in Hawai'i: the metamorphosis of land from spiritual home to saleable commodity; the colonial production of the "lazy native"; the politics of "squatting"; the use of immigrant labor to create complex race/class structures (the Tamils in Malaysia being similarly situated to the Filipinos in Hawai'i); the bureaucratic struggle over who actually "counts" as Malay or Hawaiian; the explicit connections of the schools to the factories in the free-trade zones (in Hawai'i, to the giant tourist hotels).[28] This process could result in the creation of a global account of colonialism that would be helpful in the simplifying sense that models can be helpful; but there is no pristine locale for such models to represent: "it would be tempting to offer a map of the local, something that would point out 'you are here,' with arrows to indicate the path to be followed. But . . . the local exists nowhere in a pure state. The local is only a fragmented set of possibilities that can be articulated into a momentary politics of time and place."[29] In the shifting temporal and spatial possibilities offered by specific locales, mobile subjectivities find the resources for de-articulating and re-articulating themselves.

Irony is an important resource for feminists (and others) struggling toward mobile subjectivities. In a world made by and for solid subjects (more accurately, by and for those who believe themselves to be solid subjects), the pull of competing fragments and partial affiliations can be uncomfortable. Mobile subjectivities offer no guarantees. They are likely to be testy and argumentative (but need not be imperialistic). Mobile subjectivities are not necessarily always on the go; their mobility comes in part from their relation to the places where they rest, and from the kind of resting they do.

Without an ironic stance toward the contrary pull of needed incompatibilities, despair or rigidity are likely. Mobile subjectivities require a certain modesty to acknowledge their limits and a strong dose of chutzpah to pursue their possibilities.

I want to pursue the possibilities made available through mobile subjectivities by considering three arguments that could be made against them. The first and second come from the interpretive orientation of praxis and cosmic feminism, and maintain that mobile subjectivities undervalue a stable identity; the third expresses linguistic feminism's genealogical suspicions that mobile subjectivities overvalue identity.

The first criticism suggests the viewpoint of one who has already tired of all the multiplicity and motion; she wants to be stable and whole. This point of view suggests that the mobility I am praising has been forced upon us by a society bent upon division and conquest, classification and control. For example, Rosario Morales recognizes the multiplicities of identity, but does so with regret and rejection:

I am a whole circus by myself　　　　a whole dance company with stance
and posture for being in middle class homes　　　　in upper class
buildings　　　　for talking to men　　　　for speaking with blacks
for carefully angling and directing　　　　for choreographing my way
thru the maze of classes of people and places thru the little boxes of
sex　　　　race　　　　class　　　　nationality　　　　sexual
orientation　　　　intellectual standing　　　　political
preference　　　　the automatic contortions　　　　the exhausting
camouflage with which I go thru this social space called

CAPITALIST PATRIARCHY

Multiplicity is forced upon her: "this is no way to live."[30] Morales does not argue for a compression of identity into single categories. She asserts, angrily, against those who would do so: *"Color and class don't define people or politics."* Her appeal is not for a diminution of identity but for its expansion into a coherent whole that can comfortably contain all its parts:

I want to be whole. I want to claim my self to be puertorican, and U.S. american, working class & middle class, housewife and intellectual, feminist, marxist, and anti-imperialist.[31]

Despite its eloquence, this appeal for wholeness is looking for respite in all the wrong places. The pain and humiliation, the suffering and loss, that come with being thought of/treated as/made to be lesser may suggest that some secure residence in a stable subjectivity, a home, is the answer. But such homes always end up requiring much policing to monitor the fringes and basements, to stabilize the points of rupture and erosion. The border patrol is kept busy erasing and denying whatever does not or will not fit. Mobile subjects celebrate multivocality not to embrace what has been thrust upon them but to lighten the grasp of order, to alleviate the requirements of closure, and to evade the administrative requirements of stabilized, once-and-for-all identities. Self-regulation tightened to the point of suffocation is the price of the search for wholeness.

The second objection to mobile subjectivities is also concerned with wholeness, but from a more therapeutic point of view. This criticism finds talk about de-centered subjects to be ignorant and disrespectful of the suffering of the mentally ill, whose lack of a core identity brings no emancipation. Flax, for example, scolds postmodernists for abandoning a necessary core self:

I work with people suffering from "borderline syndrome." In this illness the self is in painful and disabling fragments. Borderline patients lack a core self without which the registering of and pleasure in a variety of experiencing of ourselves, others, and the outer world are simply not possible. Those who celebrate or call for a "decentered" self seem self-deceptively naive and unaware of the basic cohesion within themselves that makes the fragmentation of experiences something other than a terrifying slide into psychosis. These writers seem to confirm the very claims of those they have contempt for, that a sense of continuity or "going on being" is so much a part of the core self that it becomes a taken-for-granted background. Persons who have a core self find the experiences of those who lack or have lacked it almost unimaginable.[32]

Flax's concern for the well-being of her patients leads her to set up a dichotomy between therapeutic practices that can help to treat the "false self" and find the "true self" (as in D. W. Winnicott's analytic approach) versus those that merely reconcile patients to their self-estrangement (as in Lacan's strategy).[33]

But are these the only two options? Mobile subjectivities must negotiate their incompatibilities, but they are not confined solely to them. They have continuities and stabilities as well; but they attempt to refrain from shoring these up with the reigning status of truth. Mobile subjectivities are not anchorless; their mobility lies in the status they give to anchors, not in a lack of them. Mobile subjectivities need not be cavalier about responsibilities to themselves, other persons, or the earth. Such responsibilities provide anchors around which one stabilizes oneself and is stabilized by others. The self does not have to revolve around an immutable core to have coherence, continuities, or patterns; the question is, What is the status of those continuities, and against what discontinuities do they jostle and persist? To thematize subjectivity as mobile is to seek a way of talking about identity as a stabilization of energies and events constantly in motion, as a location, and also as a stance toward the act of locating. Concern for the mental health of the seriously disturbed need not lead back to the abandonment of mobile subjectivities in favor of an alleged true self.

The third criticism issues from the linguistically oriented and proceeds in the opposite direction. From this perspective mobile subjectivities may be too enthusiastic about their (partial) identities, too intent on staking out their (intersecting and colliding) turfs. Identities of any kind are here viewed, at best, as strategies for political change, without any intrinsic value. Spivak, for example, argues that "claiming a *positive* subject-position for the subaltern might be reinscribed as a strategy for our time."[34] Riley agrees; arguing "from the territory of pragmatism," she holds that "it is compatible to suggest that 'women' don't exist—while maintaining a politics of 'as if they existed'—since the world behaves as if they unambiguously did."[35]

Riley's position might qualify as a feminist version of the old saw: "Women—can't live with 'em, can't live without 'em." Butler critiques the unintended consequences of such strategies. She argues that feminism cannot invoke a "seamless category of women," not even for strategic purposes, because "strategies always have meanings that exceed the purposes for which they are intended."[36] However, I want to part company with Butler here and take up the opposite direction of inquiry. The deep ambivalence toward identity that mobile subjectivities carry and that irony is recruited to sustain is not an ambivalence between values on the one hand and tactics on the other, but between competing sets of values. It is the painful and rewarding tension between longing for and wariness of a home. Minnie Bruce Pratt exemplifies this tension in her reflections on the ambivalences of her racially defined locations: describing life in a largely black neighborhood of Washington, D.C. (Pratt is white), she is refreshed by the way her neighbors speak to her: "I am comforted by any of these speakings for, to tell you the truth, they make me feel at home." But home is here the south of her childhood, with its inescapable racial viciousness: "The pain, of course, is the other side of this speaking, and the sorrow." She questions whether she just wants to "stay a child: to be known by others, but to know nothing, to feel no responsibility" and she relentlessly scrutinizes the legacy of her childish understandings for the unacknowledged privilege whiteness bestows upon them. Yet a memory of childhood can still sustain her: "The place that I missed sometimes seemed like a memory of childhood, though it was not a childish place. It was a place of mutuality, companionship, creativity, sensuousness, easiness in the body, curiosity in what new thing might be making in the world, hope from that curiosity, safety, and love."[37] Pratt's ruminations on identity are thoroughly informed and sustained by her simultaneous interrogation of and appreciation for her homesickness. Return is impossible; and so is severance of the tie. To further investigate this ambivalence in the constitution of identity I want to move onto the terrain staked out by one of mobile subjectivity's trajectories: class.[38]

Class Encounters of a Third Kind

Class is curiously under-thematized in contemporary feminist theory; curiously because it is mentioned all the time in the litany of *isms* we are against or oppressions we wish to recognize. Class disappears from our analyses far too often, much like race—and often, paradoxically, in discussions *of* race. In Trinh's otherwise excellent analysis of identity and colonialism, for example, gender and ethnicity are thoroughly intertwined but class seldom makes an appearance.[39] Similarly, in Pratt's intense discussions of race and gender, class recedes to indistinctness: specifically, white working-class women drop out of the picture; all the white women become middle-class.[40] One might protest that, after all, no one can attend to every important topic at once, that one has to be selective (as I am here by bringing the class/gender nexus to the fore while back-grounding erotic choice, race, and others. My point is that, some-how, feminist selections seem underinclined in the direction of class. The outcome is predictable. Only poor and working-class people are seen to have a class; like whites who don't know they have a color, bourgeois and elite women take their circumstances as nor-mal. It takes the perspectives of working-class people to thematize class—for the dominants it is the invisible ground of their privi-lege. According certain privilege to the situated knowledge of the oppressed is a valid political and epistemological move because coming out on the short end of the stick, so to speak, gives one a broader view of things (at least with regard to that particular stick). This does not mean that oppression makes a person virtuous; but it may mean that the creative strategies required to cope with cir-cumstances of oppression offer promising possibilities for knowl-edge and politics.

Two difficult examples of the underthematization of class come to mind. The first deals with class as a casualty of a race/gender nexus too narrowly drawn; the second with the class fallout of a too-tight intersection of gender and erotic choice.

Many white women who inhabit working-class regions, or who struggled out of them, seethe with rage when they confront women of color from third-world elites or from the rare bourgeois family of color in the U.S. who stress race alone as the salient divider of privileged from unprivileged women. But the fear of being called racist and the accompanying taboo against criticizing women of color is sufficiently strong in contemporary feminism that white working-class women often express their anger only privately, to each other. And there are few ways to talk about these glitches in the hierarchy of oppressions (white women not privileged by class; women of color who are) that don't quickly degenerate into a contest for "more oppressed than thou."

Heterosexual working-class women encounter similar obstacles in interactions with lesbians inclined toward separatism. The latter group often cannot understand the former's loyalties to the men of their class, much like white women who evince incomprehension at minority women's loyalties to the men of their color. Homopho-bia, like racism, is thoroughly articulated in contemporary femi-nism as something to avoid; working-class women find themselves engaged in considerable contortions to articulate their class experiences in an environment in which men are never considered to be sufficiently oppressed to merit attention.

One of the problems with this discussion is that the categories marking subject positions seem anything but mobile. The challenge for mobile subjectivities is to name these positionalizations in ways that mark their fluidity, their interactiveness, their ambivalences. Nouns can readily change places with adjectives: sometimes I am a woman from the working class, at other times a female white person, at still other times a female heterosexual or a straight woman. Gender, class, and race are things that happen to us, positions through which we move and which move through us and through each other. Riley makes this point with regard to gender: "Can anyone fully inhabit a gender without a degree of horror? How could someone 'be a woman' through and through, make a final home in that classification without suffering claustrophobia? To lead a life soaked in the passionate consciousness of one's gender at every single moment, to will [to] be a sex with a vengeance—these are impossibilities, and far from the aims of feminism."[41]

The placements of identity's descriptors shift, sometimes unpredictably. Through interactions, practices, confrontations, and accidents of history or circumstance, different positionalizations are mobilized, put on temporary alert. They come to the fore and do their work, but always with the persistent jostling of their own histories and of the contending positionalizations against which they are deployed. Some examples might help make this point. The first two illustrate Riley's point about "becoming a woman"; the third illustrates the complex, sometimes indecipherable, collisions of race and class.

First scenario: I am standing with a male friend who is in a heated argument with a much smaller but energetically aggressive man. The second man's "girlfriend" stands nearby. As the two men come close to blows, I intervene to try to prevent a fight—and for a second she and I glance at each other, a mutual flicker of recognition is exchanged, acknowledgment of our similarity in relation to their strangeness. The circumstances of our interaction produced us as women in that event, that moment.

Second scenario: At a predominantly male faculty union board meeting, an official announces that the university is proposing a new plan called TOPS. One woman on the board asks the meaning of the acronym. No one knows, and the inquirer allows as how in her world TOPS stands for "take off pounds sensibly" but she doubts that was what the administration had in mind. The room roars with laughter, but within that laughter the few female persons in the room exchange glances of recognition, combining acknowledgment of a shared experience with some embarrassment that such a potentially humiliating subject, one so thoroughly female, was broached in mixed company. For that instant, in relation to that set of events and practices, we became women—only to slip out of that identity when a particularly outrageous administrative maneuver propelled us into the identity of faculty members vis-à-vis university bureaucrats. My point is not that we had been temporarily something else (in these cases, neighbors or union members) and had returned to our foundational female state. Rather, we moved among positionalizations that were in place in advance, some politically loaded, others rather trivial, but none able to claim to be the founding condition. In both these stories of becoming a woman, woman is constituted in opposition to, sometimes in conflict with, another unity called men. Identities are not always adversarial, although they often are required to be; but they are always relational, temporal, contiguous, temporary yet durable, simultaneously fragile and flexible.

My third example is textual rather than experiential. It comes from Shula Marks's reflections on South African women in "Not Either an Experimental Doll." Evidently intended as a critique of racism, this piece unwittingly reproduces it. The topic seems to be Eurocentrism and one young black woman's struggle against it. Highlighting the relationship between a white woman and two black women in the South Africa of the early 1950s, Marks reports tracking down one of the black women long afterwards to find that she had spent the last 25 years of her life in mental institutions: "by the time I met her she was a shadow of her former self, her English all but forgotten." How can these two things—forgetting a foreign tongue and declining in health—be equated, unless the language somehow stands in for normality? "Most of my subsequent interviews were, perforce, with her remarkably articulate and vivacious younger sister, a fully trained nurse."[42] To whom would a young

African woman's ability to express herself seem remarkable, except to a western white person who implicitly equates whiteness/English with ability to speak? Marks's statements recall Barbara Cameron's biting comments on language: "Articulate. Articulate. I've heard that word used many times to describe third world people. White people seem so surprised to find brown people who can speak fluent english and are even perhaps educated. We then become 'articulate.' I think I spend a lot of time being articulate with white people. Or as one person said to me a few years ago, 'Gee, you don't seem like an Indian from the reservation.' "[43]

The racism performed or remarked upon in these two accounts stands out as the primary axis upon which the ability to express oneself is calculated. My point is not to contest the significance of a racial positionalization, but to ask it to make room for, and consider its relations to, one anchored in class. Class and race interdigitate in such a complex manner that sometimes race comes to stand for a class/race nexus. This problem is not resolved, of course, by trying to separate class and race: every person comes marked with both. Yet access to the privileged language is also a classed access. This dimension can easily slip away, especially in texts in which the markings of color are more readily identifiable while class location steps back into invisibility. In the case of the two sisters, and of Barbara Cameron, class is not incidental to their placement outside authorized speech.

My desire to incline feminist theory more vigorously in the direction of class does not reflect a claim to have discovered a solid new identity for myself. Class, like race and gender, is something I move through, that moves through me. Geographic location, figures of speech, habits of interacting, culinary practices, courtship patterns, sexual desires, leisure activities, distributions of housework and childcare, expectations of parents and children, attitudes toward the workplace, relations with kin, conversational styles—class is a lot more than location in the labor force. These elusive yet persistent traits are anchors, however mutable through "interclass travel," locating a class-defined way of life.[44]

The class positionalization of women from the working class is called to center stage when one encounters the sense of entitlement that often goes with class advantage. A remark by Spivak about her own class background is illustrative. Speaking of her education as "an upper-class young woman in the Calcutta of the fifties," she refers to her schooling as "highly over-determined."[45] The structural production of that classed sense of entitlement surfaces here: if she had missed or rejected one set of opportunities, there would have been plenty more. For working-class sons and daughters, there may well be only one (or none)—lack of resources, absence of role models, or failure of imagination or nerve can seal it off forever. Working-class parents do not "deny" their children intellectual encouragement; they generally don't know what it is. They may encourage reading as an alternative to television, and they may even contrive to send their children to college, but the opportunities of higher education are often seen, with ambivalence, as primarily marital for the daughters, financial for the sons. Positionalization in the middle and upper classes brings enhanced access to the symbolic capital of a society, to "the cumulative structure of dispositions (*habitus*) cultivated through education, acquired values, and practices"; class privilege allows one to invest in and accumulate the cultural currency that enhances one's own status and degrades others.[46] The circulation of symbolic capital creates or forecloses opportunities; it distinguishes between the merely eccentric and the deviant; it marks off those who belong from those who trespass. People from privileged class backgrounds tend to make easy assumptions about opportunity, assumptions that appear as arrogant claims about what the world owes them to working-class eyes.[47]

A powerful thematization of gender/class/race intersections appears in Michael Moore's film about General Motors in Flint, Michigan, "Roger and Me."[48] Moore situates himself as a white working-class kid who set out to escape and succeeded. Everyone else in the family worked for GM; he "got out." Much as prisoners speak of escaping, or former citizens of repressive regimes talk of secretive emigration, successful children of the working class mark their geographical, social, and economic escape. You don't just leave; you get out.

The film situates GM in the context of international capital: runaway shops, union cooptation, management profiteering (half of Flint is on some form of welfare, and Roger Smith, president of GM, gives himself a $2 million raise), exploited labor in the third world, and unemployment at home. It shows, both through interview material and through filmic techniques, the insulation, arrogance, and viciously acquired naivete of the local well-to-do, the casual mixture of pity and contempt for the economically marginal: unemployed workers should "go out and do something with your hands" (Anita Bryant); "The key becomes attitude" (Pat Boone); "They just don't want to work," "Everybody should try to find another job," "They take the easy way out" (rich ladies on the golf course). Moore employs irony to establish class contrasts. Camera angles show the rich standing at a slant and background music highlights the melodramatic pomp and circumstance surrounding corporate authority. The filmmaker's earnest pursuit of Roger Smith, the chummy juxtaposition of first name/first-person pronoun in the title, ironically mark the vast gulf that separates workers from top management. Sometimes the irony slides into sarcasm: "The name Smith was a common one among these people."

Visual media allow the contrasts of gendered class differences to appear in ways that are hard to capture in words. The film portrays the geography of working-class life in hard times—closed-down factories, boarded-up shops, empty houses, evicted families. Against this backdrop comes the parade scene: the bystanders, including many overweight women with stringy hair and postures of resignation, surrounded by children; and the passing Miss Michigan, with her vacuous good looks and trained smile. The beauty queen's self-absorption is astounding; her message for the people of Flint: "Keep your fingers crossed for me" in the upcoming Miss America pageant.

The two heroes of the film are people caught in the contradictions of their class and struggling to survive them with a measure of dignity. Deputy Fred is a middle-aged black man, a former auto worker, now a sheriff's deputy assigned to evict those who fall behind with their rent payments. Most of the people he evicts are black; many are his friends. "The system's gotta change," he insists, as he puts families out on the street. With resignation: "I put out some of my best friends. If they're lucky enough to draw me, at least they got somebody to talk to." Deputy Fred's combination of insight into and continued participation in the political economy of eviction reveals a complex mixture of class loyalty and class treason.

The other hero is the nameless white woman who supplements

her meager social security income by raising and selling rabbits. The sign outside her house reads "Rabbits and Bunnies—Pets or Meat." From many perspectives—vegetarian, or middle-class, or merely urban—she may seem heartless, perhaps even a bit crazy. From the point of view of the rural working class (I'm sure she was a former country gal) she makes a coherent, comprehensible, even admirable peace with the structural circumstances of her marginality. She combines a casual affection for the rabbits with an equally casual ability to kill them; *casual* here means ordinary, not superficial. Her attitude makes perfect sense within the political economy of farm life, where one often has affection for the animals one must kill, or sell for killing. She treats them as well as she can, tries to sell them as babies for pets, but readily takes those not sold out of the category of pet and into that of meat. She uses every part of the animals—the meat for eating, the hides for a coat—and she does the dirty work herself. "I was brought up to learn to survive," she remarks. Michael Moore asks: "Do you think it's hard to survive in Flint these days?" Her answer, emphatically: "Yes."

From a perspective sympathetic to the exigencies of working-class life, the woman's laughter as she strokes the rabbit she intends to kill for dinner is understandable: a combination of nervousness in front of the camera and recognition of the uncomfortable ambivalence of her situation. The theatre audiences I observed did not find it understandable; they manifested an audible disgust at her attitudes as well as her activities. When asked about the future, the woman talks/dreams of going to school to be a veterinary assistant and dog groomer: "There's a lot of animals that need takin' care of." [The audience roars with scorn and disbelief.] She recognizes the contradiction she inhabits—pets or meat—and would prefer to resolve it in the kinder direction. (She did not, for example, want to become a butcher.) But that does not stop her from having dinner. Like Deputy Fred, she tries to be compassionate, and to think of ways to change her circumstances, but she continues to do her job. The unfortunate heroes of the struggle for survival have few other options.

Deputy Fred and the woman with the rabbits provide clues to some of the ambivalences of working-class life. It is a prison, a place of oppression and victimization; it denies opportunity, takes too great a toll from its members. It is produced by the operations of power, it is recruited to maintain power, it cooperates in its own confinements. The working class confines us. We have to forget. Yet it is a home, a community, roots; a place of selves-in-relation that is empowering, strengthening; it provides an anchor; it deserves valorization. We have to remember.[49]

Remember. Forget. Pets or meat. A self hoping for stable boundaries, secure identities, and readily-available criteria for membership doesn't stand a chance. Why not simply embrace working-class identity, claim residence there, and be done with it? Partly because it takes too great a toll, in parents dead before their time from the work they do or in children confined to that same work. But also because *working class* is not a category that stands still, not a container that can hold identity without excising that which does not or will not fit. Then, why not simply regret identity and reduce it to a mere strategy of politics? Because of the gratitude I feel to those with whom I share or have shared working-class positionalizations, those with whom I have come to be who I am. The relations among family, kin, friends, community; the ties to land, crops, animals, machines; the pleasant familiarity of certain practices, smells, the roughness and smoothness of things. The landscape of my home pleases my eye. I have strategies for approaching identity; but identity itself is not a strategy. It is an ambiguous achievement and its ambiguities need to be theorized in ironic relation to one another.[50] Pets or meat.

What keeps this reading of class from degenerating into a proletarian categorical agreement with being, a kind of working-class kitsch? After all, the sentiments affirmed here can easily become sentimentalized—loyalty can slide into nostalgia, or anger into self-righteousness. Maintaining allegiances without enshrining the circumstances of their production is a tricky business. The doubleness/manyness of irony is a partial corrective to the temptations of kitsch, since irony disrupts the singleness and purity of kitsch's sentimentalizations. But there are no guarantees against kitsch. Awareness of the pitfalls of self-indulgence, even when such awareness itself threatens to become another form of self-indulgence, is simply the best one can do.

The identity practices of mobile subjectivities are produced by institutional realignments and material circumstances as well as by discursive deployments and shifts. When the structural arrangements of collective life change, the people inhabiting them are often forced to resituate themselves and to renegotiate some elements of their identities. Imagine, for example, the changes in the roles and events producing subjectivities that might occur were affirmative-action policy in the United States to include class as a preferred category for social intervention. Social spaces require mapping; affirmative-action policy is one discursive mapping of the spaces of inequality and opportunity in U.S. institutional life. This policy charts the conventional distribution of various resources (which is also the outcome of the material and semiotic practices mapped by, at least, the dynamics of capitalism, patriarchy, colonialism, slavery and war) and calls into question selected elements of the older map in the name of principles hidden within it: equality, liberty, citizenship. Affirmative action names race and gender as unfairly disadvantaged identities; it stops short of naming class, although of course class differences are implicated in racial and gender categories.

Identities constituted primarily around race and gender can find grounds for objecting to their circumstances in the very system that produces those circumstances: unfettered opportunity is supposed to be a reward for individual merit and perseverance, regardless of color or sex. But identities constituted primarily around class have no such grounds, since class is understood within the dominant discourse and institutions as the outcome, rather than the starting point, of individual effort. Class disadvantage, then, is one that people can still be officially held to "deserve." Absent this ideology of just desserts, the legitimacy of the entire socio-economic system would be called into question. Affirmative action does not accomplish this (nor should it be expected to—it is not likely that any government policy will call government itself into question). My point is that the social space for embracing or eschewing particular identity positionalizations would shift in interesting ways if class were to be included in affirmative-action policy.

Some of the consequences of such a move would be unsavory, perhaps even ridiculous: people might begin to jockey for inherited or acquired working-class status; accoutrements of disadvantaged class status would be produced and displayed to compensate for the relative invisibility of class markings (compared to those of race or gender) on bodies. Some of the consequences would be entertaining: for example, the implicit contradiction between equal-opportunity policy (which promises not to discriminate against any-one, and therefore forbids one to inquire into the race, ethnicity, or national origin of a person) and affirmative action (which prom-ises to favor those from the underrepresented groups, thus requir-ing one to know the racial, ethnic or national identity of a person) would be highlighted. Claims to class discrimination would en-hance this contradiction because there would be fewer non-intru-sive strategies for organizations to use in getting the required in-formation without appearing to ask for it.

Whatever else it might do, naming class in this manner would dislocate the grounds of legitimacy upon which contemporary eco-nomic inequalities reside, and it would remap the social spaces within which identities are claimed, negotiated, and disallowed. Standards of merit in professions would be seriously challenged if claims to class discrimination were given legitimacy. Relations be-tween white working-class men, people of color, and women might well shift, perhaps lessening the resentments of the first group toward the others and making political alliances built on a common per-ception of dispossession more likely. Further, the inclusion of class in affirmative action would probably have a greater effect on racial and gender inequalities than existing policies can claim, since race and gender are so intimately tied up with class. Other shifts and repositionings would surely occur as well; I don't want to exhaust the predictable consequences of such a move, but only to illustrate a potential identity-shaking institutional change. When social spaces are remapped, so are resident identities; prevailing subjectivities are likely to become loosened (and perhaps, eventually, tightened again) as individuals can no longer "attach themselves like limpets to the old arrangements."[51]

Mobile subjectivities can recognize more intimate or profound or consequential moments in their processes, can attend to them, without claiming to have found a true home or bedrock anchor of authentic identity. Class, like race, gender, erotic identity, "etc.," can be a crucial but still temporary and shifting resting place for subjects always in motion and in relation. To make this claim for class is not to say that class is more important, for example, than race or gender (such claims are always contextual, never final); nor is it to discern in class an unmoving foundation around which all else rotates (class too mutates, lightens, intensifies, hides, shifts, splits, overlaps, and undermines other trajectories of power). It is to claim a place in feminism for attending to the rages and griefs that are produced by class, and for honoring the ambivalent understandings that negotiation of the class structure can offer. For mobile subjectivities class is a troubled resting place. Articulation of its complexities offers no final resolution, but rewards persistence; there are many pauses, but no end.

Ironic Convergences, Coalition Politics, and Kitsch

Mobile subjectivities need irony to survive the manyness of things. The political communities into which mobile subjectivities can enter require ironic recognition of the partiality and mutability of both the groups and their members. They are not utterly groundless, but their grounds are shifting, provisional, passionately felt yet unreliable. Coalition politics makes sense for mobile subjectivities, which can feel empathy with many different perspectives but find themselves fully at home in none. The ironist can prod both the skeptic and the true believer into political conversation by appealing to their irreverent tendencies, marking points of potential overlap, and eschewing demands for unity. The arts of irony are subversive of unity, but crucial for solidarity across differences.

An ironic ethic allows mobile subjectivities to affirm without secure foundations for those affirmations. Thoroughly attuned both to the differences between people and to the differences within, mobile subjectivities tend toward an ethic of letting difference be. Letting difference be is not the outcome of "the fuzzy ambiguity of pluralism" but an active attention to multiplicity;[52] not the claim that all claims are equally valid, but the call to attend to all calls to order with a sympathetic ear for what does not or will not fit. This ethic does not dispense with the need for governing norms or intelligible rules for ordering collective life, but it does call attention to the status of those norms and rules as contestable outcomes of negotiations, as artifice rather than discovery.

Enhanced appreciation of difference can come from many sources, sources honored by praxis and cosmic feminism as well as by linguistic feminism. It can issue from learning the light touch needed to guide another life without crushing it, as Sara Ruddick argues: "Attention lets difference emerge without searching for comforting commonalities, dwells upon the other, and lets otherness be. Acts of attention strengthen a love that does not clutch at or cling to the beloved but lets her grow." And further: mothers train themselves "to look, imagine, and then to accept what is different."[53] Alternatively, appreciation of difference can grow from stretching oneself toward the nearly extinct life worlds of premodern peoples, from imagining residence in a cosmology in which the world comes alive through the stories of one's ancestors.[54] Or from a genealogical understanding of the arbitrariness of all categories and the costs of all demands for stability and order. My point is not, finally, that a happy convergence of praxis, cosmic, and linguistic feminisms produces a common ethic (synthesis, at last!). Rather, I am arguing that the desire to let difference be, to lighten the hand of order so that difference can reside in greater safety and with greater honor, can come from more than one direction and rest upon more than one dimension of subjectivity.

The call to let difference be may seem to lead to political quietism and protection for all positionalizations, including those that oppress. But mobile subjectivities seek to combine appreciation of difference with involvement for change; more specifically, it is their appreciation of difference that insists on involvement for change. The prevailing order of modernity calls vigorously for innovation, but resists difference; that is, modernity is always in need of new, improved stuff (including, perhaps, postmodernity) but it immediately brings it to order around the prevailing norms and rules. Letting difference be does not entail indifference to oppression and suffering, nor tolerance for oppressors as just another difference. Loosening the hand of order and abating the drive to mastery require mobile subjectivities to let be the differences that let difference be, while opposing those that call for greater uniformity, consistency, and regulation.

When we push past tolerance to appreciation of difference between us and within us, we take mobile subjectivities in the direction of coalition politics. Mobile subjectivities are skilled at detecting affinities with others, but inept at achieving total correspondence with them. Men who moved their self-constructions onto the terrain of mobile subjectivity would not necessarily be feminist; nor would whites necessarily be anti-racist; but it's likely that they would be more open to the shifts involved in attending to feminist or anti-racist claims. In this process, the solidity of the categories *men* and *white* could deteriorate, as the available material and semiotic conditions work to loosen the hold of conventional categories (although not to eradicate them entirely). Affinities detected and honored can provide the tentative grounds for coalitions; coalitions struck out of possibility or necessity can provoke affinities.[55] Coalition politics does not replace identity politics so much as it displaces it, moving it in the direction of multivocal subjects engaging specific issues, particular actions, concrete grievances.

Coalition politics have been advocated for other reasons. Women of color have often turned to coalitions out of recognition of the powerlessness of small, isolated groups. Barbara Smith recognizes the strength of this move: "I do feel that the strongest politics are coalition politics that cover a broad base of issues. There is no way that one oppressed group is going to topple a system by itself. Forming principled coalitions around specific issues is very important. You don't necessarily have to like or love the people you're in coalition with."[56] Bernice Johnson Reagon contrasts work in coalitions with work at home: "Coalition work is not work done in your home. Coalition work has to be done in the streets. And it is some of the most dangerous work you can do. And you shouldn't look for comfort. Some people will come to a coalition and they rate the success of the coalition on whether or not they feel good when they get there. They're not looking for a coalition; they're looking for a home!"[57]

Mobile subjectivities turn to coalitions for a somewhat different reason: not as a necessary venture outside a stable home base, but in lieu of such a stable base. These two endorsements of coalitions have in common their recognition that political power is collective, and that ways must be found to bring dissimilar people together. But they differ significantly in their understanding of the relation of coalitions to identity. Butler argues for coalition politics as follows:

Without the presupposition or goal of "unity," which is, in either case, always instituted at a conceptual level, provisional unities might emerge in the context of concrete actions that have purposes other than the articulation of identity. . . . when agreed-upon identities or agreed-upon dialogic structures, through which already established identities are communicated, no longer constitute the theme or subject of politics, then identities can come into being and dissolve depending on the concrete practices that constitute them. Certain political practices institute identities on a contingent basis in order to accomplish whatever aims are in view. . . . An open coalition, then, will affirm identities that are alternately instituted and relinquished according to the purposes at hand; it will be an open assemblage that permits of multiple convergences and divergences without obedience to a normative telos of definitional closure.[58]

What's missing from this argument about coalition politics as productive of subjectivity is sufficient recognition of the continuing importance of *some* notion of identity. Coalition politics lightens the claims of identity by shifting away from "Who am I?" and toward "What can we do about X?" But *What can we do?* is always preinformed by some sense of *we*. Butler sidesteps this dilemma with phrases like *whatever aims are in view* and *according to the purposes at hand*; she uses indirect grammar and passive constructions to avoid saying *what we have in view* or *our purposes*. But some group of people who believe they have enough in common to use first-person plural pronouns is presumed to exist. Coalition politics cannot turn completely away from identity, but must keep identity in motion.

Yet the typical problems of identity politics have already warned us about the difficulties of keeping identity in motion, including the problem of settling into a comfortable claim and using it to take on the world. Irony can be a useful tool in the struggle against this sort of kitsch, since the maintenance of any categorical agreement with being requires great seriousness. In the incomplete and unsettled worlds of mobile subjectivities, sometimes one simply has to laugh. Kitsch does not fare well in the messy realm of mobile subjectivities, where ragged pluralities and multivocalities both contest one another and seek out affinities. Kundera points out that kitsch grows better in a thinner and more compliant soil:

The feeling induced by kitsch must be a kind the multitude can share. Kitsch may not, therefore, depend on an unusual situation; it must derive from the basic images people have engraved in their memories: the ungrateful daughter, the neglected father, children running on the grass, the motherland betrayed, first love.

Kitsch causes two tears to flow in quick succession. The first tear says:

How nice to see children running on the grass! The second tear says: How nice to be moved, together with all mankind, by children running on the grass!

It is the second tear that makes kitsch kitsch.

The brotherhood of man on earth will be possible only on a base of kitsch. [59]

Mobile subjectivities do not seek a brotherhood or sisterhood of all. They do seek coalitions with other similarly situated localities: "affinity, not identity." [60] Mobile subjectivities can learn from the thematizations of subjectivity in feminist theory to attend to daily practices, to privilege interconnection, to resist the project of mastery over nature, to be conscious of themselves as in part the productions of that which they resist. Mobile subjectivities can also be edified by the various ways that feminisms slide into kitsch: the glorification of motherhood, the quest for attunement with a higher order, the ready adjustment to the institutional constraints and inducements of the academy. This stance is not the same as throwing out the bad dimensions of praxis, cosmic, and linguistic feminisms, while retaining the good. It is, rather, a recognition of the complex mix of possibility and constraint in each portrait, and a strategic effort to pursue the promise of each with full consciousness of the shadow each one casts. Living with the tensions and incompatibilities that result from such a strategy requires an ironic stance, a wry shrug at the impossibility of complete resolution and a concomitant willingness to keep struggling for partial victories.

The kitsch formula can, to some extent, be refused through acknowledgment that it promises too much and delivers too little. Kitsch can be understood as the betrayal of feeling; it is feeling good about feeling, then cooperating in producing the feeling one can feel good about. The original feeling itself, its spontaneity, immediacy, its pulse, is lost. To protect itself from kitsch, feeling needs its particularities and its contradictions. Thought itself does not protect against kitsch, since thought can be recruited into kitsch: one can think a certain thing, then feel good about thinking that thing. Knowing that kitsch is a "beautiful lie" is helpful only if we want to protect the initial, particular feeling. Otherwise, why not believe the beautiful lie? Because when it is an attack on, or subversion of, the feelings it enshrines, it is not so beautiful anymore.

But even with such a brave effort to accept partiality and work within particularities, a certain amount of kitsch is likely to follow. Sometimes the best one can do is to be conscious of kitsch's distasteful seductions and aware of its echo in oneself. The act of identifying and naming kitsch, Kundera argues, does not eliminate it from one's political vocabulary but does disarm it to some extent: "As soon as kitsch is recognized for the lie it is, it moves into the context of non-kitsch, thus losing its authoritarian power and becoming as touching as any other human weakness. For none of us is superman enough to escape kitsch completely. No matter how we scorn it, kitsch is an integral part of the human condition."[61]

To return to Nietzsche's formulations, mobile subjectivities, like every other kind, are likely to make up their claims to knowledge and then forget they made them up; but they don't forget that they forgot (or at least they strive not to). By short-circuiting the second move, mobile subjectivities call attention to the patterns of insistence that compel them. Mobile subjectivities can both valorize their particular affirmations and stay open to that which is potentially disruptive of them. Already aware of themselves as incorporating contestation, mobile subjectivities could be prepared to accept the partiality of any set of solutions to public problems and the necessity of continued political struggle. Accepting the tug of contending identities within themselves, mobile subjectivities are able to approach otherness from some stance other than mastery or absorption. Ironic recognition of their own patterns of insistence can help to balance their desires for a stable and simple home in the world with recognition that neither stability nor simplicity is available. Interpretation and genealogy can serve feminism well as ironic allies in the constitution and continuous reconstitution of shifting but powerful mobile subjectivities.

Notes

Chapter One

1. Karl Marx et al., *The Woman Question*, 89–90.

2. Luce Irigaray, "This Sex Which Is Not One," in Irigaray, *This Sex Which Is Not One*, 26.

3. Julia Kristeva, "Stabat Mater," in *The Kristeva Reader*, ed. Toril Moi, 179.

4. G. W. F. Hegel, quoted in Edith Wyschogrod, *Spirit in Ashes: Hegel, Heidegger, and Man-Made Mass Death*, 113. See Hegel, *The Phenomenology of Mind*, 496.

5. Irigaray, "Women on the Market," in Irigaray, *This Sex Which Is Not One*, 171. See also Nancy C. M. Hartsock, *Money, Sex and Power*, appendix 1.

6. Irigaray, "The Power of Discourse and the Subordination of the Feminine," in *This Sex Which Is Not One*, 69–71.

7. Following Toril Moi, I use *phallocentrism* to denote a symbolic system that "privileges the phallus as the symbolic source of power." (*Sexual/Textual Politics: Feminist Literary Theory*, 179). By *patriarchy* I mean a set of institutions and practices that asserts and enforces the power of men as a group over women as a group. Patriarchy has been a much-disputed concept in feminist theory because some use it to claim a universality that others rightly suspect. I use patriarchy in a fairly limited way to mean institutionalized male power, and my specific topic is modern patriarchy in the west.

8. Sandra Harding makes this argument in *The Science Question in Feminism*, 138.

9. In discussing gender in terms of an opposition of male and female, I am transgressing the common (though contested) practice of using *masculine/feminine* to refer to social and cultural differences (gender), and

male/female to refer to biological differences (sex). I want to connect the many different dimensions of sexual opposition and difference, and to suggest that all, including the biological, are at least to some extent negotiated meanings rather than fixed truths.

10. Michel Foucault, *An Introduction*, vol. 1 of *The History of Sexuality*; and the introduction by Foucault to *Herculine Barbin: Being the Recently Discovered Memoirs of a Nineteenth Century French Hermaphrodite*. For Foucault's explanation of the strategy of reversal, see "The Order of Discourse," in *Untying the Text*, ed. Robert Young, 67–73 passim.

11. Gayatri Chakravorty Spivak, "Subaltern Studies: Deconstructing Historiography," in Spivak, *In Other Worlds*, 204.

12. Spivak, "Displacement and the Discourse of Woman," in *Displacement: Derrida and After*, ed. Mark Krupnick, 184.

13. Jacques Derrida and Christie McDonald, "Choreographies," 66–76. For another effort to break up familiar dyads, this time with regard to the injunctures of proper female appearance, see Carole Spitzack, *Confessing Excess: Women and the Politics of Body Reduction*. For a fascinating discussion of erotic multiplicity and its tendency to disappear into familiar sexual dyads, see Valerie Traub, "Desire and the Differences It Makes," in *The Matter of Difference: Materialist Feminist Criticism of Shakespeare*, ed. Valerie Wayne, 81–114.

14. Michel Foucault and Gilles Deleuze, "Intellectuals and Power," in Foucault, *Language, Counter-memory, Practice: Selected Essays and Interviews*, 208.

15. See Wendy Brown, *Manhood and Politics: A Feminist Reading in Political Theory* and Christine Di Stefano, *Configurations of Masculinity: A Feminist Perspective on Modern Political Theory* for discussions of contemporary and historical masculinity. While I have been greatly edified by these analyses of the construction of masculinity in history and theory, such questions are not, primarily, the ones I am pursuing here.

16. Martin Heidegger, "The Question Concerning Technology," in *Basic Writings*, ed. David F. Krell, 308–309.

17. William E. Connolly, *Political Theory and Modernity*, 2.

18. Spivak, "Explanation and Culture: Marginalia," in Spivak, *In Other Worlds*, 107.

19. Foucault, *Language, Counter-memory, Practice*, preface by Donald F. Bouchard, 9.

20. Connolly, *Political Theory and Modernity*, 138.

21. Donna Haraway, "Situated Knowledges: The Science Question in Feminism and the Privilege of Partial Perspective," 577.

22. Roland Barthes, "On Reading," in Barthes, *The Rustle of Language*, 54.

23. Connolly, *Political Theory and Modernity*, 10, 136.

24. Hartsock, *Money, Sex and Power*, 9, 10.

25. Irigaray, "The Power of Discourse and the Subordination of the Feminine," 78.

26. Harding, *The Science Question in Feminism*, 195, 246, 244, 141.

27. Fatima Mernissi, *Beyond the Veil: Male-Female Dynamics in Modern Muslim Society*, 137, 140.

28. Ibid., viii.

29. For a somewhat different but compatible critique of orientialism, especially in feminist guises, see Marnia Lazreg, "Feminism and Difference: The Perils of Writing as a Woman on Women in Algeria," in *Conflicts in Feminism*, ed. Marianne Hirsch and Evelyn Fox Keller, 326–48.

30. Ibid., 149, 94, 154.

31. From Jürgen Habermas, *The Theory of Communicative Action*, quoted in Stephen K. White, "Foucault's Challenge to Critical Theory," 423.

32. Friedrich Nietzsche, *The Geneaology of Morals*, 149.

33. Ibid., 178–179.

34. Foucault, "What Is An Author?" in Foucault, *Language, Counter-memory, Practice*, 137–38.

35. Irigaray, "The Power of Discourse and the Subordination of the Feminine," 78 (italics in original).

36. Irigaray, "Questions," in Irigaray, *This Sex Which Is Not One*, 162.

37. Moi, *Sexual/Textual Politics*, 142; Julie Wuthnow, "Feminism and Post-Structuralism: A Marriage of Convenience."

38. Moi, *Sexual/Textual Politics*, 114.

39. Kristeva, "The System and the Speaking Subject," 25–34.

40. Teresa Ebert, "The Romance of Patriarchy: Ideology, Subjectivity, and Postmodern Feminist Cultural Theory," 23.

41. Alice Walker, "My Father's Country Is the Poor," in Walker, *In Search of Our Mothers' Gardens*, 212 (italics in original).

42. Derrida, "Plato's Pharmacy," in *Dissemination*, 65.

43. Moi, *Sexual/Textual Politics*, 106.

44. Connolly, *Politics and Ambiguity*, 153.

45. Nietzsche, "On Truth and Falsity in their Ultramoral Sense," in *The Complete Works of Friedrich Nietzsche*, vol. 2, *Early Greek Philosophy*, ed. Oscar Levy, 180.

46. Spivak, "Explanation and Culture: Marginalia," 105.

47. Ibid., 114.

48. Foucault, "A Preface to Transgression," in Foucault, *Language, Counter-memory, Practice*, 50.

49. Irigaray, "This Sex Which Is Not One," 29 (italics in original).

50. Carol Gilligan, *In a Different Voice*, 25–39.

51. Kristeva, "The System and the Speaking Subject," 25.

52. Hartsock, *Money, Sex and Power*, 255.

53. Marilyn Frye, *The Politics of Reality: Essays in Feminist Theory*, xi–xii.

54. Foucault, "Nietzsche, Genealogy, History," in Foucault, *Language, Counter-memory, Practice*, 145.

55. Ibid., 155, 146.

56. Ibid., 142.

57. Donna Haraway, "A Manifesto for Cyborgs: Science, Technology, and Socialist Feminism in the 1980s," 75.

58. Judith Butler, *Gender Trouble: Feminism and the Subversion of Identity*, 36.

59. Hartsock, *Money, Sex and Power*, 233, 234.

60. Irigaray, "This Sex Which Is Not One," 30.

61. Butler, *Gender Trouble*, xi, x. Butler is one of the few feminist writers who shares my inclination toward the term *genealogy* rather than the more standard *poststructuralist* or *postmodern*.

62. Wuthnow pointed this out during a spirited discussion of Irigaray in the graduate seminar in feminist theory, Department of Political Science, University of Hawai'i, Fall 1988.

63. Spivak, "Displacement and the Discourse of Woman," in Krupnick, *Displacement: Derrida and After*, 184.

64. Elizabeth V. Spelman, *Inessential Woman: Problems of Exclusion in Feminist Thought*, 149, 142, 136.

65. Harding, *The Science Question in Feminism*, 28.

66. Butler, *Gender Trouble*, 16.

67. Foucault, "Revolutionary Action: Until Now," in Foucault, *Language, Counter-memory, Practice*, 230.

68. Irigaray, "Commodities Among Themselves," in *This Sex Which Is Not One*, 197.

69. Connolly, *Political Theory and Modernity*, 87, 130.

70. Hartsock, *Money, Sex and Power*, 261–62.

71. Haraway, "Situated Knowledges," 590.

72. Connolly, *Politics and Ambiguity*, 155.

73. Connolly, *Political Theory and Modernity*, 161. For an interesting discussion of the possibilities of a postmodern ethic of responsibility to otherness, see the following exchange: Stephen K. White, "Heidegger and the Difficulties of a Postmodern Ethics and Politics," 80–104; Michael T. Gibbons, "The Ethic of Postmodernism," 96–102; Stephen White,

"Paths to a Postmodern Ethics and Politics: A Reply to Gibbons," 103–104.

74. Ebert confuses these two dilemmas when she makes a case for the deconstruction of gender against a merely "egalitarian feminism," which "strives to achieve economic, political, educational, and occupational equality for women within the existing social structure" (p. 45). While most feminists, regardless of their politics, would find their lives severely hampered absent liberal feminist efforts at "mere reform," the tension between liberal and radical feminist politics is not as difficult as the tension between two different strains of radical feminist politics.

75. Connolly, *Politics and Ambiguity*, 158; Michael Shapiro, *The Politics of Representation*, 54.

76. Haraway, "Reprise: Science Fiction, Fictions of Science, and Primatology," in Haraway, *Primate Visions: Gender, Race, and Nature in the World of Modern Science*, 377.

77. Haraway, "Introduction: The Persistence of Vision," in Haraway, *Primate Visions*, 8.

78. Derrida, *Plato's Pharmacy*, 65–73, 96, 98–99, passim.

79. Derrida, *Spurs: Nietzsche's Styles*, 39–41, 37 passim.

80. Alice A. Jardine, *Gynesis*, 180.

81. Shapiro, *Politics of Representation*, 19.

82. White, "Foucault's Challenge to Critical Theory," 423.

83. The terms *interanimated* and *interruption* are Spivak's. For the first, see "Explanation and Culture: Marginalia," 109; for the second, see "A Literary Representation of the Subaltern: A Woman's Text from the Third World," in Spivak, *In Other Worlds*, 241.

84. Connolly, *Politics and Ambiguity*, 159–60.

85. Shapiro, *The Politics of Representation*, ch. 1.

86. See Linda Alcoff, "Cultural Feminism Versus Post-Structuralism: The Identity Crisis in Feminist Theory," 428, for an argument in favor of transcendence.

87. Haraway, "A Manifesto for Cyborgs," 65.

88. John Evan Seery, *Political Returns: Irony in Politics and Theory from Plato to the Antinuclear Movement*, 137, 343.

89. bell hooks, "Stylish Nihilism at the Movies," 29.

90. Seery, *Political Returns*, 137–38.

91. Irigaray, "The 'Mechanics' of Fluids," in Irigaray, *This Sex Which Is Not One*, 106.

92. Seery, *Political Returns*, 170, 139.

93. Ibid., 62; Seery finds this approach to irony in Hayden White and Thomas Spragens, for example.

94. Seery finds this position in Richard Rorty's work. I depend heavily on Seery's characterizations, since I am not interested in cataloging what others have said about irony but in charting terrain that irony might enable feminisms to cover. Here too I have found Seery's work invaluable, both for suggesting the possibilities of an ironic politics and for indicating the limits of a male-ordered notion of irony. See Chapter 3 for further discussion.

95. Ibid., 89.

96. Ibid., 62.

97. Haraway, "Teddy Bear Patriarchy: Taxidermy in the Garden of Eden, New York City, 1908–36," in Haraway, *Primate Visions*, 26–58.

98. Haraway, "Women's Place Is in the Jungle," in Haraway, *Primate Visions*, 293.

99. Haraway, "Teddy Bear Patriarchy," 27.

100. Ibid., 30.

101. Ibid., 31.

102. Ibid., 33.

103. Ibid., 30.

104. From Carl Akeley, *In Brightest Africa*, 222, quoted in Haraway, "Teddy Bear Patriarchy," 33.

105. Akeley, 235, quoted in Haraway, "Teddy Bear Patriarchy," 34.

106. Akeley, 230, quoted in Haraway, "Teddy Bear Patriarchy," 34.

107. Haraway, "Teddy Bear Patriarchy," 48.

108. The phrase *felt truth* is Laura Rice Sayers's.

Chapter Two

1. Framed as an investigation into the question of whether women had souls, thus qualifying for humanness, the debate began at the Council of Macon in 585. By the end of the sixteenth century the verdict came down in our favor. Chilton Latham Powell, *English Domestic Relations 1487–1653*, 150; and Cheris Kramarae and Paula A. Treichler, *A Feminist Dictionary*, 199. See also Ian Maclean, *The Renaissance Notion of Woman*, 12. The debate seems to reflect a continuation of Aristotle's conviction that women are incomplete beings; see Maryanne Cline Horowitz, "Aristotle and Woman," 183–213. My thanks to Valerie Wayne for her help with these citations.

2. Susan Bordo, "The Cartesian Masculinization of Thought," 439–56, esp 441; Hannah Pitkin, *Fortune Is a Woman*; Christine Di Stefano, "Masculinity As Ideology in Political Theory: Hobbesian Man Considered," 633–44. See also Carolyn Merchant, *The Death of Nature*. One might include Plato and Aristotle here as well, and others not yet named,

but I am limiting my considerations to modern and contemporary western political theory in order to avoid the unfortunate implication that patriarchal notions of subjectivity are everywhere the same. For the ancients, despite a shared tendency to separate women from the realm of the human, subjectivity meant something quite different than it did for those modern thinkers for whom common public space and vigorous civic life were distant recollections, dangerous fantasies, or desperate dreams.

   3. Irigaray, "Any Theory of the 'Subject' Has Always Been Appropriated by the 'Masculine,' " in Irigaray, *Speculum of the Other Woman*, 133–46.

   4. Edward Said, *Orientalism*, 7, 204.

   5. Said's gloss on Balfour's argument goes like this:

England knows Egypt; Egypt is what England knows; England knows that Egypt cannot have self-government; England confirms that by occupying Egypt; for the Egyptians, Egypt is what England has occupied and now governs; foreign occupation therefore becomes 'the very basis' of contemporary Egyptian civilization; Egypt requires, indeed insists upon, British occupation.

(Said, *Orientalism*, 34)

   The argument in *Orientalism* has a richly gendered dimension, one that Said marks but does not explore. Said notes that it is "by no means accidental" that female types figure strongly in orientalism (180); he then sets this insight aside: "it is not the province of my analysis here" (188). Perhaps he feared that to bring in gender would be to crowd out race; but it is precisely the race/gender intersections that are provocative for a feminist reading of orientalism. Eschewing hierarchical ranking, one could call in the gendered dimensions of orientalism to accompany, not to replace, its racial operations, allowing for inquiry into the complex intertwinings of strategic formations of power and resistance. One might even investigate the race/sex nexus for a key to a governing logic of discourses of domination in the west.

   Some key points where parallels to gender beg to be made: orientals, like women, are held to be "irrational, depraved (fallen) [like Eve], childlike, 'different'; thus the European [/male] is rational, virtuous, mature, 'normal' " (40). The west knows what is best for orientals, echoing male rights of "protection" over women (father knows best) (37). The belief that "orientals were almost everywhere nearly the same" mirrors the logic of the eternal feminine (38). Both the masculine and the western are given rights of penetration and definition: "because his was the stronger culture, he could penetrate, he could wrestle with, he could give shape and meaning to the great Asiatic [or female] mystery" (44). Both women and the orient are poor imitations: Islam is "a misguided version of Christianity"; women are defective men (61). The west/men have the gaze; the orient/women are watched (103). Anticolonialism/feminism is a nuisance and an insult to western democracy/humanism (108). And so on.

6. Foucault, "The Order of Discourse," in Young, *Untying the Text*, 74.

7. Seyla Benhabib, "On Hegel, Women and Irony," in *Feminist Interpretations and Political Theory*, ed. Mary Lyndon Shanley and Carole Pateman, 135.

8. For an interesting discussion of Hegel's encounters with the feminism of his time, and of contemporary debates on Hegel's relation to the prejudices of his age, see Benhabib, 129–45.

9. Some have gone so far as to see Hegel, with Marx, behind all critical thought! See Joan Cocks, *The Oppositional Imagination*, 15, 36.

10. My account of Hegel's subject owes a great deal to Judith Butler, *Subjects of Desire: Hegelian Reflections in Twentieth-Century France*; William E. Connolly, *Political Theory and Modernity*; Edith Wyschogrod, *Spirit in Ashes: Hegel, Heidegger, and Man-Made Mass Death*; and to Mulford Q. Sibley's graduate seminar on Marx and Hegel, Department of Political Science, University of Minnesota.

There are some interesting differences among these texts. Butler's Hegel is less totalizing than Connolly's, Wyschogrod's or Sibley's. Butler claims of Hegel that "his vision is less 'totalizing' than presumed" (x). She deemphasizes this aspect of Hegel by comparing him to other, even more totalizing, monistic thinkers, such as Spinoza. Connolly, comparing Hegel not with Spinoza but with Nietzsche, emphasizes the move toward including the many into the one, as Wyschogrod does when she compares Hegel to Heidegger and as Sibley does when he compares Hegel to Marx. Further, Butler emphasizes the differences between Hegel and Hobbes, stressing that the two philosophers' shared emphasis on conflict takes place within very different contexts (242–43). Wyschogrod, on the other hand, points to the shared fear of violent death as a common feature of Hegel's and Hobbes's understandings of the foundation of self-consciousness (120).

Finally, Connolly reads Hegel's account of gender as fundamental to Hegel's entire theory, while Butler's reading cooperates, until the last few pages, with the fiction that Hegel's subject is genderless. Connolly argues that

[Hegel's] account of gender difference, which completes itself by reserving the home to women and civil society to men, is not an incidental feature of Hegel's ontology of Spirit. It is fundamentally expressive of it . . . As long as the ontology of Spirit infuses the account, gender role differentiation cannot be defined as subordination; bodily differences which cut across and through gender lines are not given ontological weight; and the claim of the state upon the life of the family is not treated as intrusive.

(122–23)

Connolly's inclusion of feminist concerns at the outset makes an interesting contrast with Butler's late-breaking feminist turn; she waits until p. 231 to ask about the genderedness of Hegel's subject.

Butler's Hegel is also unusual in that he is portrayed as "an ironic artist" (x), whereas John Seery finds in Hegel, especially in his *Aesthetics*, a critique of irony as a self-destructive impulse that undermines the faith in truth needed for action. While judgments about ironic moves within texts are necessarily ambiguous, I tend to agree with Seery that "Hegel quite simply was not a friend of irony" (*Political Returns*, 230 n. 138).

11. Richard Bernstein, *Praxis and Action*, 28.

12. Charles Taylor, *Hegel*, 130.

13. Connolly, *Political Theory and Modernity*, 94.

14. G. W. F. Hegel, *The Phenomenology of Mind*, 229.

15. Ibid., 237.

16. Connolly, *Political Theory and Modernity*, 95.

17. Hegel, *The Phenomenology of Mind*, 237.

18. Butler, *Subjects of Desire*, 21.

19. Ibid., 55.

20. I am indebted to Marta Savigliano for pointing out the freight carried by the metaphor of the traveler.

21. Hegel, *The Phenomenology of Mind*, 233.

22. Butler, *Subjects of Desire*, 49–51.

23. Hegel, *The Phenomenology of Mind*, 230.

24. Hegel, *Lectures on the Philosophy of History*, 230.

25. Ibid., 230.

26. Connolly, *Political Theory and Modernity*, 94. I am indebted to Bill Connolly for calling my attention to the significance of this reading of Hegel for my arguments about subjectivity and feminism.

27. The phrase *abstract masculinity* is Nancy Hartsock's. See *Money, Sex and Power*, 240–47.

28. Caroline Whitback, "A Different Reality: Feminist Ontology," in *Beyond Domination*, ed. Carol Gould, 69; from Julia Kristeva, *Revolution in Poetic Language*, quoted in Butler, *Subjects of Desire*, 232; Jessica Benjamin, *The Bonds of Love: Psychoanalysis, Feminism, and the Problem of Domination*, 31–38; Hélène Cixous and Catherine Clément, *The Newly Born Woman*, 78, 79.

29. Butler, *Subjects of Desire*, 46.

30. Ibid., 47.

31. Ibid., 47.

32. Ibid., 48.

33. Ibid., 48.

34. The language of gift and appropriation comes from Cixous. See

"Sorties: Out and Out: Attacks/Ways Out/Forays," in Cixous and Clément, *The Newly Born Woman*, 63–132.

35. Wyschogrod, 106.

36. Hegel, *The Phenomenology of Mind*, 470.

37. Ibid., 496; see Wyschogrod, 113, for an interesting discussion of this passage in Hegel.

38. Nineteenth-century Anglo-American feminism, as Denise Riley points out, worked within this arrangement but effected a reversal of its priorities, anticipating a move in contemporary feminism. About this time Riley remarks, "If woman's sphere was to be the domestic, then let the social world become a great arena for domesticated intervention, on a broad and visible scale." (*Am I That Name?: Feminism and the Category of 'Women' in History*, 46). The attempt to fashion women's elevation out of their subordination is even more troubling in its class configurations: some women were empowered to keep others under surveillance in the name of reforming the social: " 'Women' both come under and direct the public gaze." (50)

39. Butler, *Subjects of Desire*, 42, 38.

40. Hegel, *The Phenomenology of Mind*, 478; for further discussion of this point, see Connolly, *Political Theory and Modernity*, 122–23.

41. Shulamith Firestone, *The Dialectic of Sex*; Simone de Beauvoir, *The Second Sex*; Nancy C. M. Hartsock, *Money, Sex and Power*; Sara Ruddick, "Maternal Thinking," 342–67; Arlie Russell Hochschild, *The Managed Heart*. For a feminist eco-theology, see Lois K. Daly, "Ecofeminism, Reverence for Life, and Feminist Theological Ethics." For evocations of female bodily pleasure, see Luce Irigaray, *This Sex Which Is Not One*. For ironic boundary-violation, see Donna Haraway, "A Manifesto for Cyborgs," 65–107; and Haraway, "Teddy Bear Patriarchy," 26–58.

42. Michael A. Gillespie, *Hegel, Heidegger, and the Ground of History*, 106.

43. Butler, *Subjects of Desire*, 10. See also Connolly, *Political Theory and Modernity*, 10.

44. Wyschogrod, 93.

45. I am again indebted to Bill Connolly for pointing out the hints of this restlessness in Hegel.

46. Gillespie, *Hegel, Heidegger and the Ground of History*, 116.

47. This philosophical *we* appears, for example, in the first few pages of the lordship and bondage section of the *Phenomenology*. For Richard Bernstein's comments on this rhetorical strategy, see *Praxis and Action*, 23.

48. See Teresa Ebert, "The Romance of Patriarchy," 19–57; Judith Butler, "The Body Politics of Julia Kristeva," 104–18. I also made this

argument in *The Feminist Case Against Bureaucracy*, 54–55. For those of us who found Foucault's first volume of *The History of Sexuality* to be intriguing but insufficiently attentive to gender differences, the second volume is more satisfactory; here Foucault's analysis is more explicit about the dynamics of male privilege and female subordination. See *The Use of Pleasure*, vol. 2 of *The History of Sexuality*, 6, 19, 22, 47, 82, 84, 128, 143, 147, 149, 151, 198, 216, and 253.

49. See, for example, Kim Chernin, *The Obsession*; and M. F. Belenky et al., *Women's Ways of Knowing*.

50. Harding, *The Science Question in Feminism*, 10.

51. From Michel de Montaigne, *Essays*, quoted in Bordo, 443.

52. For fuller discussion of the interiorization and rationalization of the self in modernity, see Norbert Elias, *The History of Manners* and Hans Peter Duerr, *Dreamtime: Concerning the Boundary Between Wilderness and Civilization*. Duerr disputes Elias's argument that the erosion of pre-Enlightenment sensibilities and the triumph of modernity in Europe was gradual and continuous. The transition to modernity that Elias describes consisted of the steady incremental accretion of stronger and stronger norms concerning self-control, increasing levels of differentiation and self-restraint, increasing prohibitions on sensuality and bodies, and an "expanding threshold of aversion" in behavior and emotion (83). Elias's delightful history of books on manners from Erasmus to Cabanes charts more or less steady movement "of the kind that we call 'progress' " (156). The middle ages, he argues, lacked

the invisible wall of affects which seems now to rise between one human body and another, repelling and separating, the [wall] which is often perceptible today at the mere approach of something that has been in contact with the mouth or hands of someone else and which manifests itself as embarrassment at the mere sight of many bodily functions of others, and often at their mere mention, or as a feeling of shame when one's own functions are exposed to the gaze of others, and by no means only then.

(69–70)

Duerr, in contrast, argues that this "progress" toward "civilization" was neither gradual nor steady. It was interrupted in the late middle ages by "rebellion in an epoch that is often considered to be merely the end of the preceding one" (56). Through this rebellion "a freeing of the senses occurred on all levels of life" (56). The main agents of this rebellion, it seems, were women:

This woman of the late middle ages had broached the domain of men. She was a woman, as one historian put it, whom one might encounter everywhere where there was activity, in the drinking halls of the guilds, at any kind of folk festival, at markets and fairs. . . . She was a woman who had found her way to a new consciousness. She was admitted to professions that formerly were reserved for men. She was allowed to learn a trade and attain the rank of a master. There were a number of trades organized into guilds that could be carried out only by women, such as extensive branches of the textile industry, beer brewing, bleaching, and baking. Women were also represented among furriers, harness makers, teachers and physicians. It was not until the dawn of the modern age that the trade and journeyman's organizations effectively stopped the work of women in the public domain in the course of domesticating them.

(56)

The "thumbscrews of this modern age," Duerr continues, were tightened simultaneously around women, wilderness, earth-mother imagery, and the remnants of goddess religions (56).

These arguments are interesting for feminists in part because in the late middle ages, the time during which Duerr sees a rebellion that Elias misses, there were many more women than men in Europe. (See Marcia Guttentag and Paul F. Secord, *Too Many Women?*, 62 passim.) The "women's movement" of the late middle ages could, according to some, be seen as predecessor of and inspiration for current feminist struggles. (See *Signs* 14 [Winter 1989]). Perhaps one lesson is that when there are "low" sex ratios (i.e., more women than men) the times are promising for feminism, and when there are equal numbers of women and men, there are too many men.

53. Connolly, *Political Theory and Modernity*, 2. See also Arturo Escobar, "Discourse and Power in Development: Michel Foucault and the Relevance of His Work to the Third World," 377–400.

54. Connolly, *Political Theory and Modernity*, 123.

55. Hegel, *The Phenomenology of Mind*, 463.

56. Connolly, *Political Theory and Modernity*, 94.

57. Hegel, *The Phenomenology of Mind*, 496.

58. Hegel, *The Philosophy of History*, 252–53 (italics in original).

59. See Audre Lorde, "The Master's Tools Will Never Dismantle the Master's House," in Lorde, *Sister/Outsider*, 110–113.

60. Elizabeth V. Spelman, *Inessential Woman*, 159.

61. Butler, *Subjects of Desire*, ix–x.

62. The phrase is Trinh Minh-Ha's. See *Woman, Native, Other*, 95.

63. Butler, *Subjects of Desire*, 13.

64. Ibid., 9.

65. This observation was made during an independent study session on subjectivity and desire, Department of Political Science, University of Hawai'i, Spring 1989.

66. Hegel, *The Phenomenology of Mind*, 233.

67. Butler, *Subjects of Desire*, 9.

68. Taylor, *Hegel*, 148.

69. Butler, *Subjects of Desire,* 184.

70. Iris M. Young, "Humanism, Gynocentrism, and Feminist Politics," 174.

71. De Beauvoir, *The Second Sex,* 52. De Beauvoir said more. Her insistence that women are made, not born, opened doors into the investigation of that making and thus enabled many kinds of radical feminisms to go about their business. Her genealogy of the "eternal feminine" showed it to be a construction of male power rather than a discovery within female nature. I am not claiming here to summarize all of de Beauvoir's founding contributions to feminist theory, only to indicate the similarity of her thematization of subjectivity in *The Second Sex* to Hegel's. It's important to acknowledge, not simply to attack, our foremothers.

72. Butler, *Gender Trouble,* 10, 19–20.

73. Gilligan, *In a Different Voice;* Chernin, *The Obsession.*

74. Belenky et al., 133.

75. This question is parallel to Arturo Escobar's. He argues that the ideas of "development" and "underdevelopment" constituted by post–World War II western discourse must be dismantled in order for Third-World peoples to pursue a "different type of development" (378). Similarly, the hegemonic ideas about subjectivity must be, if not dismantled, at least loosened and problematized in order for feminism to pursue a different kind of subjectivity.

76. Young, "Humanism, Gynocentrism, and Feminist Politics," 173.

77. Foucault, "Nietzsche, Genealogy, History," 145.

78. Nietzsche, *The Genealogy of Morals,* 160. Although Nietzsche is not the first or only theorist to discuss the power of naming, he is one of the most powerful and influential to do so. For a discussion of the power of definition as recognized by Hobbes, see Connolly, *Political Theory and Modernity,* 34–35.

79. Joan Cocks, for example, collapses praxis and cosmic feminisms by insisting that all arguments connecting women to a particular moral sensibility or political practice are the same (*The Oppositional Imagination*). Feminists who "flirt with notions of a sexualized moral dualism" are "joining the radical feminists" (123). By seeing in any such perspective the claim that "when women are what they truly are, they are nurturant, caring, co-operative and egalitarian," Cocks avoids recognition of complex arguments over the status of "women," "truly," and "are," and she reduces the richness of feminist interpretations to the level of caricature (178). This reduction allows her to include Mary Daly and Carol Gilligan, among others, in the same footnote as "feminist dualists" (233 n. 4).

80. Foucault, *The Use of Pleasure,* 6.

81. Idem, *The Archaeology of Knowledge,* 120.

82. Haraway, "A Manifesto for Cyborgs," 74.
83. Frye, *The Politics of Reality*, xii.
84. Foucault, "History of Systems of Thought," in Foucault, *Language, Counter-memory, Practice*, 199.
85. Diana Fuss, "Reading Like a Feminist," 88.
86. Milan Kundera, *The Unbearable Lightness of Being*, 261, 249.
87. Duerr, *Dreamtime*, 91. Moi, *Sexual/Textual Politics*, 7 passim.

Chapter Three

1. Connolly, *Politics and Ambiguity*, 154.
2. Benjamin, *The Bonds of Love*, 19, 19–20, 48. Benjamin is quoting *The Unbearable Lightness of Being*. Since I am cataloging arguments within feminist theory in these chapters, it might be worthwhile to note that my book *Self, Society and Womankind: The Dialectic of Liberation* developed a relational view of subjectivity akin to those of Gilligan, Chodorow, and Benjamin. I took my theoretical inspiration largely from George Herbert Mead, especially his neglected *Philosophy of the Present*. Benjamin also recognizes Mead's contribution to a relational subjectivity; however, since she cites only his better-known *Mind, Self, and Society*, she seems to miss the strongly temporal dimension to Mead's self.
3. Benjamin, *The Bonds of Love*, 185.
4. Ibid., 193; see also 9, 10, 130.
5. Aihwa Ong, *Spirits of Resistance and Capitalist Discipline: Factory Women in Malaysia*, xiii, 15, 123.
6. Ibid., 107; see also 25, 26, 99.
7. Ibid., 112, 137.
8. For a patient explanation of the usefulness of textual metaphors, see Gayatri Chakravorty Spivak, *The Post-Colonial Critic*, 1–2, 25.
9. Hannah F. Pitkin, *Fortune is a Woman*, 6, 7, 10.
10. Ibid., 22, 105, 109, 136, 165.
11. Ibid., 240, 292.
12. Ibid., 294.
13. DiPalma and Wuthnow presented these observations during our seminar on feminism and the history of political theory (cotaught with Manfred Henningsen), Department of Political Science, University of Hawai'i, Spring 1990.
14. Ruddick, *Maternal Thinking*, 11.
15. Ibid., 108, 121, 70; see also 72, 73, 79.
16. Ruddick's definition of a practice is tightly drawn, very goal-oriented, even somewhat technical: "To engage in a practice is, by definition, to accept connections that constitute the practice" (41). Why couldn't

practice be constituted more contingently, with more acknowledgment of layers and fissures? She claims that "thinking itself is often a solitary activity; its cooperative forms are the dialogue or conversation, not the chorus" (15). Why not the cacaphony?

17. Ibid., 83. See also 34; and Benjamin, *The Bonds of Love*, 16–18.

18. Ruddick, *Maternal Thinking*, 136; see also 57.

19. Ibid., 52.

20. Ibid., 53, 260 n. 24; Ruddick is quoting Noddings, "Shaping an Acceptable Child," in *Learning for Life: Moral Education Theory and Practice*, ed. Andrew Garrod.

21. Michael Shapiro, *Reading the Postmodern Polity*, ch. 1: 7, 9 passim.

22. Ibid., 57. Ruddick couples her position with Hartsock's standpoints via a shared focus on "the work itself and the political conditions in which it is undertaken" (133). Ruddick gets off the train, however, at the claim to have found "real" grounds for politics and ethics:

Epistemologically, I continue to believe that all reasons are tested by the practices from which they arise; hence justifications end in the commitments with which they begin. Although I envision a world organised by the values of caring labor, I cannot identify the grounds, reason, or god that would legitimate that vision. There is, for example, nothing above or below preservative love, only the ongoing intellectual-practical acts of seeing children as vulnerable and responding to that vulnerability with a determination to protect rather than to abandon or assault.

(p. 135)

This refreshing modesty in the face of the big questions does not deter her commitments; she cannot find secure grounds for her values, but she can give reasons for them: "I am confident that persistent efforts to see and act from the standpoint of care will reveal the greater safety, pleasure, and justice of a world where the values of care are dominant" (135–36).

23. Harding, *The Science Question in Feminism*, 142–58. Harding calls upon the work of Hilary Rose, Nancy Hartsock, Jane Flax, and Dorothy Smith in her discussion of feminist standpoints.

24. Hartsock, *Money, Sex and Power*, 242, 261.

25. Haunani-Kay Trask, *Eros and Power: The Promise of Feminist Theory*, xi.

26. Gilligan, *In a Different Voice*, 2. Many people have criticized Gilligan for failing to mention that the notions of rationality and identity in her "men's voice" sound a lot like classical liberalism, and that "women's voice" could be attributed to all groups excluded from that dominant paradigm. I agree with this criticism, but it does not negate Gilligan's importance in developing praxis feminism's arguments. In fact, it may enhance it: because perspective is seen as developing out of immersion in prac-

tices, similarities between "women's voice" and, for example, that of native Hawaiian men, working-class men, or others, could suggest their participation in comparable practices, including the practices necessary to survive subordination.

27. Nancy Chodorow, *The Reproduction of Mothering*, 3, 28, 3, 7, 166, 167.

28. Nancy Fraser and Linda Nicholson, "Social Criticism without Philosophy: An Encounter between Feminism and Postmodernism," 345; Young, "Humanism, Gynocentrism and Feminist Politics," 181; Alcoff, "Cultural Feminism versus Post-Structuralism," 408; Haraway, "A Manifesto for Cyborgs," 76, 77; Bordo, "The Cartesian Masculinization of Thought," 455; Harding, *The Science Question in Feminism*, 27; Jeffrey Weeks, *Sexuality and Its Discontents*, 204; Spelman, *Inessential Woman*, 159; Moi, *Sexual/Textual Politics*, 110, 112.

29. Some feminist peace activists, for example, make a rather simplistic connection between women's reproductive activities ("givers of life") and women's politics ("makers of peace"). See, for example, Alice Cook and Gwyn Kirk, *Greenham Women Everywhere*. But this link does not go uncontested in activist circles. For an interesting discussing of the theoretical dilemmas entailed in connecting women to peace, see Jean Bethke Elshtain, *Women and War*.

30. Jane Flax, "Postmodernism and Gender Relations in Feminist Theory," 638.

31. Benjamin, *The Bonds of Love*, 123; see also Chernin, *The Hungry Self*.

32. Haraway, "Manifesto for Cyborgs," 100.

33. One method by which this slide from recognized partiality to global wholes takes place is through the politics of footnotes and asides. For example, Benjamin offers a footnote in which she acknowledges that

Despite women's universal role as primary caretakers of small children, there is great variation in the organization of childrearing. Only in Western middle-class families do we see the typical pattern of babies attended by one lone mother. Thus our theory, unless amended, might strictly apply to such families. On the other hand, patterns of childrearing have been changing—in favor of paternal participation—in these families.

(75)

In a later footnote she notes that her analysis "assumes a heterosexual, two-parent family," and she comments on the difficulties of this assumption (104–5). Yet these reflections on the limitations of her analysis do not affect the analysis itself; instead they function as token acknowledgments that recognize an objection without actually taking it into account.

A second example of the slippery politics of footnotes and asides can be found in Sara Ruddick's discussion of the relation of mothering to nature. She puts quotation marks around "nature" for the first few usages, to remind the reader that "the idea of 'nature' I discuss is constructed within maternal practice" (*Maternal Thinking*, 76). Then she stops: "Having made this general epistemological point, I will now drop the quote marks for ease of reading" (76). But *nature* is a term already deeply and problematically embedded in the discursive arrangements of modern society, and is not so easily dislodged from them. Ruddick rescues women from being "closer to nature" in some essential way, only to put children there: "As a child is naturally meant to survive, so too her spirit is natural and naturally developing" (84). "Nature is a mother's ally, so long as she actively cooperates in its purposes." "If, even in the midst of social and personal disaster, children develop their wondrous resistance [it] suggests that spirited development is in a child's nature" (84). Like writers who claim in one footnote that the term *man* means everybody and then continue to use it, Ruddick has entered a discursive deployment of a loaded term, and she has ceased marking any effort or even any need to qualify her use of that term. This usage allows her to slide into a discussion of children's relation to nature that moves strongly in the direction of the cosmic, finding a telos in nature to which mothers can become attuned. One suspects that it is the convenience of the writer, not the reader, that is at stake.

(And another thing. Yet another kind of footnote politics can be found in Spivak's work. In "Feminism and Critical Theory," in *In Other Worlds*, 77–92, one-third of the footnotes [11 out of 33] cite Spivak herself. Why would a writer do this? For the convenience of the reader, one might reference herself to indicate places where particular arguments are developed more fully. But in that case a few broadly sketched references to other texts would suffice. Or a writer might wish to provide the interested reader with a list of related works elsewhere in the book. Spivak's excessive self-referencing suggests something else: a claim to authority. Footnotes are authorizing gestures, vehicles for claiming or bestowing validity in claims to knowledge. To place oneself prominently within them is implicitly to back up the merits of one's arguments with pleas to be considered the legitimate producer of the arguments. While simpler considerations of vanity or convenience might also be at work, the politics of the gesture should not be overlooked.)

34. Fraser and Nicholson, "Social Criticism Without Philosophy," 354, 355, 357, 358–59, 359.

35. Ibid., 360.

36. Gilligan, *In a Different Voice*, 2–3.

37. Ibid., 42, 65, 69, 100.

38. Fraser and Nicholson, "Social Criticism Without Philosophy," 359.

39. Chandra Mohanty, "Under Western Eyes: Feminist Scholarship and Colonial Discourses," 64, 62, 65, 72.

40. Fraser and Nicholson, "Social Criticism Without Philosophy," 362.

41. Mohanty, "Under Western Eyes," 67.

42. Ibid., 65, 62.

43. I develop this argument more fully in relation to Gilligan and Hartsock in "Knowledge, Politics and Persons in Feminist Theory," 302–14; with the help of Michael Shapiro, "Metaphor in the Philosophy of the Social Sciences," 197 passim.

44. Cocks, *The Oppositional Imagination*, 12.

45. I am indebted to Kathy Jones for this insight and for many others as well.

46. Jane Flax, *Thinking Fragments: Psychoanalysis, Feminism and Postmodernism in the Contemporary West*, 110, 249 n. 40.

47. Ibid., 120.

48. Ibid., 16, 182.

49. Connolly, *Political Theory and Modernity*, 136.

50. Flax, *Thinking Fragments*, 183.

51. Rosemary Hennessy and Rajeswari Mohan, "The Construction of Woman in Three Popular Texts of Empire: Toward a Critique of Materialist Feminism," 325, 337, 347, 352.

52. See, for example, Jackie St. Joan, "Female Leaders: Who Was Rembrandt's Mother?" in Charlotte Bunche et al., *Building Feminist Theory: Essays from Quest*, 230.

53. Ruddick, *Maternal Thinking*, 30.

54. For an argument for an alternative ethical theory see Joan C. Tronto, "Beyond Gender Difference to a Theory of Care," 644–63.

55. Audre Lorde, "Sexism: An American Disease in Blackface," in *Sister/Outsider*, 62.

56. Ruddick, *Maternal Thinking*, 78.

57. Ibid., pp. 72, 74, 71.

58. John Evan Seery, "Irony and Death (Or, Rorty contra Orpheus)," 8, 18.

59. Seery, *Political Returns*, 342, 11.

60. Ibid., 342.

61. Ong, *Spirits of Resistance*, xiii.

62. I am indebted to Marta Savigliano, "Political Economy of Passion: Tango, Exoticism and Decolonization," for her discussion of the intersections of exotic and erotic in western productions of the third world.

63. Ong, *Spirits of Resistance*, 207.

Chapter Four

1. Charlene E. Wheeler and Peggy L. Chinn, *Peace and Power: A Handbook of Feminist Process*.

2. Carol Ochs, *Women and Spirituality*; Starhawk, *The Spiral Dance*.

3. Susan Griffin, *Women and Nature*.

4. Jane Bennett, *Unthinking Faith and Enlightenment: Nature and the State in a Post-Hegelian Era*, 9.

5. Hans Blumenberg, *The Legitimacy of the Modern Age*, 72.

6. Bennett, *Unthinking Faith and Enlightenment*, 10.

7. Duerr, *Dreamtime*, 43, 45.

8. Marija Gimbutas, *The Goddesses and Gods of Old Europe: Myths and Cult Images*; Gerda Lerner, *The Creation of Patriarchy*.

9. Charlene Spretnak, "Ecofeminism: Our Roots and Flowering," 7.

10. Paula Gunn Allen, *The Sacred Hoop: Recovering the Feminine in American Indian Traditions*, 213, 214.

11. Renato Rosaldo, "Politics, Patriarchs, and Laughter," 70, 71.

12. Ynestra King, "Ecofeminism: On the Necessity of History and Mystery," 44.

13. Peggy Reeves Sanday, *Female Power and Male Dominance*.

14. Connolly, *Political Theory and Modernity*, 41–42, 44.

15. Pia M. Godavitarne, "From the Editor," 4; Carolyn R. Shaffer, "Living as Fish: Emilie Conrad Da'Oud and Continuum," 14; Starhawk, *Truth or Dare*, 15.

16. Starhawk, *Truth or Dare*, 8.

17. Tsultrim Allione, in Michele Jamal, *Shape Shifters: Shaman Women in Contemporary Society*, 44.

18. Merlin Stone, "Endings and Origins," 29.

19. Griffin, *Women and Nature*, 188 (italics in original).

20. Ibid., 186 (italics in original).

21. Lois K. Daly, "Ecofeminism, Reverence for Life, and Feminist Theological Ethics," 10.

22. Godavitarne, "From the Editor," 4.

23. Demetra George, "Mysteries of the Dark Moon," 32.

24. Christopher Jones, "Gaia: Emerging Mythology and Political Power."

25. Starhawk, *Truth or Dare*, 4–5.

26. Haraway, "A Manifesto for Cyborgs," 66.

27. Haraway, "Situated Knowledges," 581.

28. Starhawk, *Truth or Dare*, 22.

29. Haraway, "Monkeys, Aliens, and Women: Love, Science, and Politics at the Intersection of Feminist Theory and Colonial Discourse," 304.

30. Audre Lorde, "An Open Letter to Mary Daly," in Lorde, *Sister/Outsider*, 67.

31. Lorde, "Poetry Is Not a Luxury," in Lorde, *Sister/Outsider*, 36.

32. Starhawk, in Jamal, *Shape Shifters*, 121–27.

33. Godavitarne, "Light Returning: Alternative Mental Health Programs," 20–23.

34. Starhawk, *Truth or Dare*, 150, 153, 155, 156, 158 passim; for more detailed insights into daily practices in radical feminist organizations, see Wheeler and Chinn, *Peace and Power*.

35. Vandana Shiva, *Staying Alive: Women, Ecology and Development*, xiv, xvi. The foreword to this book by Rajni Kothari of the Centre for the Study of Developing Societies requires some comment. Kothari lectures feminists condescendingly about our "petit bourgeois" inclinations (xii). He counsels attention to feminism as long as it is not "just a question of women" (xii, xiii): that is, as long as it deals with the important stuff—men, for example. Talking about himself rather than about Shiva or her book, he claims the moral high ground and then accuses others (feminists) of "arrogance and insensitivity" (xiii). He buries himself unproblematically in the language of cosmic completion: women (only rural and tribal third world women are real women) "whose identity with both nature and the human community is so organic and authentic" can save us because the "deeper meanings of femininity" are "far more humane and natural" (x). "The feminine principle" can tap "principles of nature" that are more "holistic" and "inclusive" (x). For Kothari, feminism has a "natural penchant for empathy, compassion, solidarity and nurturance, particularly towards suffering humanity and the victims of history" (xii). And so on. I suspect that Kothari, a well-known Indian social scientist with leftist leanings, is brought in as a legitimating voice: not "just women" but men too can be interested in feminism (no matter how arrogantly and flippantly). Further, his casual use of heavy-handed cosmic rhetoric invokes that genre with much less reflection or qualification than Shiva displays.

I am indebted to my colleague Sankaran Krishna for an enlightening conversation about Indian social science.

36. Ibid., 194.

37. James A. Bethel, "Sometimes the Word is 'Weed'," quoted in Shiva, *Staying Alive*, 64.

38. Shiva, *Staying Alive*, 4.

39. Ibid., 46–47.

40. Ibid., xvii, 176.

41. Ibid., xviii, 223, xviii.

42. Ibid., 39.

43. Ibid., 52.

44. Ibid., 22, 28 (italics in original).

45. My thanks to Carolyn DiPalma for pointing this out.

46. Paul de Man, "The Epistemology of Metaphor," in *Language and Politics*, ed. Michael Shapiro, 201.

47. Lorde, "Uses of the Erotic," in Lorde, *Sister/Outsider*, 58.

48. Barry Lopez, *Arctic Dreams: Imagination and Desire in a Northern Landscape*, 40.

49. Griffin, *Women and Nature*, 175, 220.

50. Bennett, *Unthinking Faith and Enlightenment*, 21.

51. Griffin, *Women and Nature*, 190.

52. Connolly, *Politics and Ambiguity*, 155.

53. Kathryn Theatana, "The Priestesses of Hecate," 37; Z Budapest, "Political Witchcraft," 38.

54. Lynn Andrews, *Star Woman, Jaguar Woman, Medicine Woman, Crystal Woman, Wildhorse Woman, Flight of the Seventh Moon*. For a critique of New Age appropriations such as Andrews's, see Andrea Smith, "Indian Spiritual Abuse," 35–36.

55. Lillian Robinson, "Sometimes, Always, Never: Their Women's History and Ours," 12.

56. Riane Eisler, *The Chalice and the Blade*, 43, xvii, 44. Eisler made the financial information available at a talk she gave at the University of Hawai'i at Manoa, July 7, 1989.

57. My thanks to an anonymous reader for this insight.

58. Lorde, "Uses of the Erotic," 53, 54, 55.

59. This suggestion was made to me by T. V. Reed during conversations at the Western Political Science Association meetings, March, 1989. My own brief experience with cosmic rituals during a visit to the Seneca Falls Women's Encampment for a Future of Peace and Justice in August, 1985, was somewhat different; my impression was that most of the women either believed wholeheartedly in the incantations or else were rather embarrassed by them, but I detected little irony. Perhaps I didn't know how to look. Others have commented on the ironic moments within the antinuclear movement; see Seery, *Political Returns*, 320–33; and William Callahan's excellent discussion of Earth First! in "Another Book of Laughter and Misunderstanding: a field guide to chuckles, smiles and guffaws," 155–69.

60. For descriptions of these and other political actions, see Cook and Kirk, *Greenham Women Everywhere*.

61. Kundera, *The Unbearable Lightness of Being*, 268 (italics in original).

62. Ibid., 254.

63. The phrase "word salad" is Mike Shapiro's.

64. Starhawk, *Truth or Dare*, 3.
65. Ibid., 21.
66. I am grateful to Jane Bennett for suggesting this interpretation.
67. Starhawk, *Truth or Dare*, 124.
68. Elias, *The History of Manners*, 114.
69. Ellyn Ruthstrom, "Feeling the Power of Nature" (interview with Carol P. Christ), 23.
70. I learned this from Anne Cameron, *Daughters of Copper Woman*.
71. John (Fire) Lame Deer and Richard Erdoes, *Lame Deer: Seeker of Visions*, 152–53.
72. The phrase "temporary tourism" comes from a poem by Wendy Rose, "For the White Poets Who Would Be Indian," in *The Third Woman: Minority Women Writers of the United States*, ed. Dexter Fisher, 86–87. Thanks to Carolyn DiPalma for calling it to my attention.
73. Cameron, *Daughters of Copper Woman*, 44.
74. Ibid., 146.
75. Ibid., 151 (capitalization in original).
76. Ibid., 110.
77. Cherríe Moraga, "Refugees of a World on Fire: Foreword to the Second Edition," *This Bridge Called My Back: Writings of Radical Women of Color*, ed. Cherríe Moraga and Gloria Anzaldúa, ii.
78. Gloria Anzaldúa, "Foreword to the Second Edition," in Moraga and Anzaldúa, *This Bridge Called My Back*, iv.
79. doris davenport, "The Pathology of Racism: A Conversation with Third World Wimmin," in Moraga and Anzaldúa, *This Bridge Called My Back*, 87.
80. Ibid., 89.

Chapter Five

1. Moi, *Sexual/Textual Politics*, 111.
2. Haraway, "A Manifesto for Cyborgs," 75, 79.
3. Foucault, *The Use of Pleasure*, 5. My claim here is not that Foucault is or should be called a feminist, only that his way of framing questions is central to the inquiries of many linguistic feminists.
4. Nietzsche, *The Genealogy of Morals*, 212.
5. Foucault, *The Use of Pleasure*, 23–24.
6. Ibid., 15.
7. Ibid., 20–21, 249. The familiar narratives often prove quite difficult to dislodge, and not all attempts are successful. See, for example, Heather Findlay's argument that a developmental narrative reappears within Derrida's deconstructive schema, in Heather Findlay, "Is There a Lesbian in

This Text? Derrida, Wittig, and the Politics of the Three Women," *Coming To Terms*, ed. Elizabeth Weed, 65.

8. Foucault, *The Use of Pleasure*, 192.

9. Ibid., p. 116.

10. Ebert, "The Romance of Patriarchy," 22.

11. Cynthia Enloe, *Bananas, Beaches, and Bases*, 16. Enloe's book is fascinating in relation to the interpretation/genealogy distinction. In some ways it is unreflectively anti-genealogical: Enloe employs a non-problematized appearance-reality distinction (1) and assumes the necessity of a securely subject-centered discourse (3). These assumptions coexist with her magnificent deconstructions of the international political economy. Her text exemplifies interpretation and genealogy as contrasting dimensions of argument rather than as securely opposed categories.

12. Butler, *Gender Trouble*, 143–44 (italics in original).

13. Spivak, "Feminism and Critical Theory," 77–78.

14. Riley, *Am I That Name?*, 68.

15. Kristeva, "The New Type of Intellectual: The Dissident," in Moi, *The Kristeva Reader*, 298.

16. Irigaray, "Volume-Fluidity," in Irigaray, *Speculum of the Other Woman*, 229 (italics in original).

17. Irigaray, "The Power of Discourse and the Subordination of the Feminine," 74 (italics in original).

18. Irigaray, "The 'Mechanics' of Fluids," 106–107.

19. Shapiro, "Metaphor in the Philosophy of the Social Sciences," 195.

20. Spivak, "French Feminism in an International Frame," in Spivak, *In Other Worlds*, 148.

21. Butler, *Gender Trouble*, xi.

22. Ibid., 20.

23. Spivak, "Subaltern Studies: Deconstructing Historiography," 204.

24. Butler, *Gender Trouble*, 16.

25. Diana Fuss, "Reading Like a Feminist," 79–80.

26. Butler, *Gender Trouble*, x, 33, 138, 145 (italics in original).

27. Ibid., 139, 140.

28. Ibid., 141.

29. Ibid., x.

30. Moraga and Anzaldúa, *This Bridge Called My Back*, xxii, 15, 91; Benjamin, *The Bonds of Love*, 73, 128, 129, and 214 passim; Ruddick, *Maternal Thinking*, 112–115.

31. Trinh T. Minh-ha, *Woman, Native, Other*, 88, 89, 94.

32. Ibid., p. 94.

33. Young, "Humanism, Gynocentrism, and Feminist Politics," 179.

34. Kristeva, "The System and the Speaking Subject," 30.

35. Foucault, "A Preface to Transgression," in Foucault, *Language, Counter-Memory, Practice,* 42.

36. Foucault, "Afterword: The Subject and Power," in *Michel Foucault: Beyond Structuralism and Hermeneutics,* ed. Herbert L. Dreyfus and Paul Rabinow, 216.

37. Frye, *The Politics of Reality,* 28.

38. Irigaray, "Woman, Science's Unknown," in Irigaray, *Speculum of the Other Woman,* 21.

39. Ebert, "The Romance of Patriarchy," 35. Ebert makes her argument for the deconstruction of gender by contrasting it to the liberal humanist project of greater inclusion of women in existing institutions. But the case against "me too" feminism is a relatively easy one to make; Ebert neglects to consider the relation of her calls for ungenderedness to praxis or cosmic feminisms' calls for a women's voice. The struggle between two kinds of radical feminism is a more difficult one to resolve.

40. Ibid., 36.

41. Irigaray, "Commodities Among Themselves," 192.

42. Butler, *Gender Trouble,* 2 (italics added).

43. Ibid., 5 (first italics added; second italics in original).

44. Ibid., 5.

45. See, for example, Paul Smith, *Discerning the Subject.*

46. See, for example, Rosi Braidotti, "The Politics of Ontological Difference," in *Between Feminism and Psychoanalysis,* ed. Teresa Brennan, 91, 92; Nancy Hartsock, "Foucault on Power: A Theory for Women?" and Christine Di Stefano, "Dilemmas of Difference: Feminism, Modernity, and Postmodernism," in *Feminism/Postmodernism,* ed. Linda Nicholson, 157–75 and 63–72.

47. Butler, *Gender Trouble,* 147 (italics in original).

48. Spivak shifts to the clitoris as metonym for women, claiming that it "escapes reproductive framing." ("French Feminism in an International Frame," in Spivak, *In Other Worlds,* 151). While Spivak cannot be accused of leaving out labor in considering bodies, one might still ask her and Irigaray why women would want to be represented by any one body part.

49. Irigaray, "When Our Lips Speak Together," in Irigaray, *This Sex Which Is Not One,* 217.

50. Irigaray, "Any Theory of the 'Subject' Has Always Been Appropriated by the 'Masculine,' " 142, 143 (italics in original).

51. Irigaray, *Speculum of the Other Woman,* 365.

52. Nancy Love, "Foucault and Habermas on Discourse and Democracy," 7.

53. Haraway, "A Manifesto for Cyborgs," 75.

54. Butler, "The Body Politics of Julia Kristeva," 104, 114, 113, 117, 117.

55. Kristeva, "About Chinese Women," in Moi, *The Kristeva Reader*, 149; Butler, "The Body Politics of Julia Kristeva," 109.

56. Butler, *Gender Trouble*, 94; from an interpretive point of view, such an ideal might make Foucault worth reading.

57. Ibid., 96, 97 (italics in original).

58. Ibid., 94.

59. Ibid., 94, 98, 103.

60. Foucault, *Herculine Barbin*, xiii; Butler, *Gender Trouble*, 94, 96, 100, 105.

61. Foucault, *Herculine Barbin*, xii, xvii.

62. Foucault, *Herculine Barbin*, 26, cited in Butler, *Gender Trouble*, 97.

63. Foucault, *Herculine Barbin*, 52, cited in Butler, *Gender Trouble*, 100.

64. Foucault, *Herculine Barbin*, 39, cited in Butler, *Gender Trouble*, 102.

65. Foucault, *Herculine Barbin*, xii.

66. Ibid., xiii.

67. Apollodorus, *The Library of Greek Mythology* 3.174. Moti Shojania made this suggestion during a lively discussion of Butler and Foucault in the "Genealogy and Gender" seminar at the International Summer Institute for Semiotics and Structural Studies (ISISSS), held at the University of Hawai'i at Manoa, June 3–29, 1991. My thanks to all the members of the seminar for their contributions to this exchange, and to Christina Bacchilega for help in locating this source.

68. Sherri S. Tepper, *The Gate to Women's Country*. This interpretation of hero is particularly appropriate in light of George Bush's claims for manhood via the Gulf War, and the enormous death toll of civilians in Iraq. For discussion of these aspects of heroism, see Mehmed Ali et al., "Gender, Land, and Power: Reading the Military in Hawai'i."

69. Friedrich Nietzsche, *The Genealogy of Morals*, 153, 160, 217, 218, 242, 265 passim.

70. Michel Foucault, *The History of Sexuality, Vol. 1: An Introduction*, 159.

71. Butler also observes the nostalgia for lost *jouissance* in Lacan (*Gender Trouble*, 56).

72. Ebert, "The Romance of Patriarchy," 40.

73. Agnes Heller, *A Theory of Feelings*, 184.

74. See Butler, *Subjects of Desire,* for interesting discussion of the disputes among Lacan, Deleuze, and Foucault on the constitution of desire.

75. Kristeva, "The System and the Speaking Subject," 30.

76. Lorde, "Poetry Is Not a Luxury," in Lorde, *Sister/Outsider,* 37.

77. Mary Daly, "Be-Laughing: Nixing, Hexing and X-ing," 77.

78. Irigaray, "La Mystérique," in Irigaray, *Speculum of the Other Woman,* 191.

79. Haraway, "A Manifesto for Cyborgs," 81.

80. Irigaray, "When Our Lips Speak Together," in Irigaray, *This Sex Which Is Not One,* 212.

81. Griffin, *Women and Nature,* 195 (italics in original).

82. Irigaray, "When Our Lips Speak Together," 213.

83. In thinking about Irigaray I have benefited from Julie Wuthnow's arguments about essentialism in "Feminism and Poststructuralism: A Marriage of Convenience."

Butler also criticizes Irigaray for her totalizing stance (*Gender Trouble,* 13) and offers a fascinating comparison of Irigaray and de Beauvoir: for de Beauvoir women are the Other *within* the male system, while for Irigaray women are the Other *of* the male system (8–13). Riley characterizes Irigaray as looking for a "positive model" of femininity (*Am I That Name?,* 101, 106–7); she takes her reading of Irigaray entirely from Elizabeth Gross's representation in "Philosophy, Subjectivity and the Body: Kristeva and Irigaray," in *Feminist Challenges: Social and Political Theory,* ed. Carol Pateman and Elizabeth Gross. Via Gross via Riley, Irigaray loses the fluidity of her analysis and turns instead to a search for "models."

84. Hennessy and Mohan, "The Construction of Woman," 356–57 n. 26; 359 n. 53.

85. I see a similar dynamic in *The Feminist Case against Bureaucracy,* where I drew on Foucault to understand the productive power of discourse, but stopped at that scary point where a stable appearance/reality distinction deconstructs. Here it was Gilligan who got the last word.

86. Spivak, "A Literary Representation of the Subaltern: A Woman's Text from the Third World," in Spivak, *In Other Worlds,* 249. I will return to this argument in the next chapter.

87. See Irigaray, "Psychoanalytic Theory: Another Look," and "Così Fan Tutti," in Irigaray, *This Sex Which Is Not One,* 34–67 and 86–105.

88. Mohanty, "Under Western Eyes," passim.

89. Lorde, "Age, Race, Class, and Sex: Women Redefining Difference," in Lorde, *Sister/Outsider,* 120–21.

90. This is not to claim that linguistic feminists are always aware of irony; by definition irony is a tricky business, and can easily pass one by.

For example, in Spivak's commentary on Mahasweta Devi's "Breast-Giver," Spivak claims sophistication for her reading of a text she regards as naive and simple. Mahasweta's own reading of her text is characterized by Spivak in terms of "the pieties of a nationalist reading" ("A Literary Representation of the Subaltern: A Woman's Text from the Third World," p. 250). Meanwhile, as Christine White pointed out in our feminist theory reading group, Spivak seems to miss the humor of the story: e.g., Devi's pushing of "professional" to absurdity in characterizing Jashoda as "professional mother" (p. 222) and Kangalicharan as "'professional father" (p. 228); clever reversals of husband and wife, class and caste.

91. Butler, *Gender Trouble*, x.

92. Irigaray, "Questions," 151–52, 163 passim.

93. Butler, *Gender Trouble*, 139.

94. William Callahan, "Another Book of Laughter and Misunderstanding," 258.

95. Seery, *Political Returns*, 305–6.

96. See, for example, the reflections on writing in Moraga and Anzaldúa, *This Bridge Called My Back*; and in *The Writer On Her Work*, ed. J. Sternburg.

97. Trinh, *Woman, Native, Other*, 16–17 (italics in original).

98. Ibid., 17.

99. I am referring here to "Surname Viet, Given Name Nam," although there are stills from her other films as well.

100. Ibid., 59.

101. Ibid., 43.

102. Haraway, "Metaphors into Hardware: Harry Harlow and the Technology of Love," in Haraway, *Primate Visions*, 233.

103. Ibid., 234–35. The final sentence is a quotation from Laura Mulvey, "Visual pleasure and narrative cinema," *Screen* 16 (3): 6–18, esp. p. 14.

104. Haraway, "Metaphors into Hardware," 239.

105. Haraway, "The Bio-Politics of a Multicultural Field," in Haraway, *Primate Visions*, 275.

Chapter Six

1. The phrase "ready-made" is Trinh Minh-ha's: "Never original, 'me' grows indefinitely on ready-mades, which are themselves explainable only through other ready-mades" (*Woman, Native, Other*, 36).

2. Haraway, "A Manifesto for Cyborgs," 65–107; Haraway, "Situated Knowledges," 575–99; Trinh, *Woman, Native, Other*, 9; Teresa de Lauretis, "Eccentric Subjects: Feminist Theory and Historical Conscious-

ness," 115–50; Spivak, *In Other Worlds*; Riley, *Am I That Name?*; Butler, *Gender Trouble*.

3. Other feminist theorists have argued about the relation of the counter-subjectivity of linguistic feminism and its philosophical inspiration in some of the male postmodern thinkers to the terrain of what I am calling mobile subjectivities. With regard to Lacan, Teresa de Lauretis argues that feminism is not well served by Lacan, that the subject emerging in feminist theory is "a subject that is not divided in, but rather at odds with, language" (*Feminist Studies, Critical Studies*, 9). Diana Fuss, on the other hand, argues that "the seeds of a theory of the subject as dispersed, as multiple, can already be found in Lacan's notion of the subject as a place of contradiction, continually in a state of construction" ("Reading Like a Feminist," 87). Both Tamsin Lorraine and Jane Flax find Lacan inadequate to feminism, although Lorraine would supplement him with insights from object relations theory while Flax would replace him with the latter perspective (Tamsin E. Lorraine, *Gender, Identity, and the Production of Meaning*; Flax, *Thinking Fragments*). With regard to Derrida, Spivak has argued that he engages in an appropriation of women's voice that is unhealthy for feminism; however, she also finds his contribution significant so long as its limitations are recognized ("Displacement and the Discourse of Woman," in Krupnick, *Displacement: Derrida and After*, 184, 190; The *Post-Colonial Critic*, 45 passim). Similar debates take place with regard to Foucault; see, for example, the essays in *Foucault and Feminism: Reflections on Resistance*, ed. Irene Diamond and Lee Quinby; and Shane Phelan, "Foucault and Feminism," 421–40. Although these questions are provocative, and could be taken as yet another aspect of the man question (that asks how dependent feminism can or should be on the writings of men), they are peripheral to my inquiry. For my purposes, the important point is that mobile subjectivities have a substantial debt to these and other male postmodern thinkers, but are not reducible to that debt.

4. Connolly, *Political Theory and Modernity*, 10.

5. Seery, *Political Returns*, 56–57, 137–38.

6. Connolly, *Political Theory and Modernity*, 135 passim.

7. Jane Bennett, *Unthinking Faith and Enlightenment*, 33.

8. Harding, *The Science Question in Feminism*, 246.

9. de Lauretis, "Eccentric Subjects," 116.

10. Alcoff, "Cultural Feminism versus Poststructuralism," 435.

11. Butler, *Gender Trouble*, 112.

12. Lorde, "The Master's Tools Will Never Dismantle the Master's House," in Lorde, *Sister/Outsider*, 111.

13. Trinh, *Woman, Native, Other*, 85.

14. Ibid., 96 (italics in original).

15. Ibid., 104.

16. Butler, *Gender Trouble*, 143.

17. Haraway, "A Manifesto for Cyborgs," 93–94.

18. I am borrowing this phrase from Connolly; "antagonistic indebtedness" is Connolly's description of his own relation to Nietzsche. See *Political Theory and Modernity*, 175.

19. Haraway, "Situated Knowledges," 596.

20. I am borrowing "persistent interruptions" from Spivak, "A Literary Representation of the Subaltern: A Woman's Text from the Third World," 249; Spivak is speaking here about Marxism and feminism, but the point is a similar one.

Denise Riley also argues for a feminism that embraces the tensions between what I am calling interpretation and genealogy; but her assurance that we need these tensions, and that we need not choose between the two positions, is not accompanied by argument. Her assurances are too casual, too flip: "we needn't be tormented by a choice between a political realism which will brook no nonsense about the uncertainties of 'women,' or deconstructionist moves which have no political allegiances" (5). Yes, but how? "Instead of veering between deconstruction and transcendence, we could try another train of speculations: that 'women' is indeed an unstable category, that this instability has a historical foundation, and that feminism is the site of the systematic fighting out of that instability—which need not worry us" (5).

This "don't worry, be happy" advice just doesn't go far enough. Riley makes some welcome references to irony, calling for "a capacity for a lively and indeed revivifying irony about this 'women' who is the subject of all tongues. A political movement possessed of reflexivity and an ironic spirit would be formidable indeed" (98). Yes, of course; but isn't there a lot more to be said? I have found myself increasingly irritated with feminist theorists who make a gesture toward irony as if it were a self-evident solution to our problems, leaving me to struggle alone to figure out what that could mean, how it could work, even to come up with some examples.

21. The phrase *material-semiotic actor* comes from Haraway, "Situated Knowledges," 595.

22. Greselda Pollock, *Vision and Difference: Femininity, Feminism and Histories of Art*, 66.

23. Susan Willis, *Black Women Writing the American Experience*.

24. Spivak, "Feminism and Global Theory," in Spivak, *In Other Worlds*, 84.

25. Trinh, *Woman, Native, Other*, 66.

26. Butler, *Gender Trouble*, 148.

27. Elspeth Probyn, "Travels in the Postmodern: Making Sense of the Local," in *Feminism/Postmodernism*, ed. Linda Nicholson, 178.

28. Ong, *Spirits of Resistance and Capitalist Discipline*.

29. Probyn, "Travels in the Postmodern," in Nicholson, *Feminism/Postmodernism*, 187.

30. Rosario Morales, "We're All in the Same Boat," in Moraga and Anzaldúa, *This Bridge Called My Back*, 92 (capitalization in original).

31. Ibid., 91 (italics in original).

32. Flax, *Thinking Fragments*, 218–19.

33. Ibid., 130.

34. Spivak, "Subaltern Studies: Deconstructing Historiography," 207.

35. Riley, "Am I That Name?," 112.

36. Butler, *Gender Trouble*, 4.

37. Minnie Bruce Pratt, "Identity: Skin, Blood, Heart," in Elly Bulkin et al., *Yours in Struggle*, 11, 12, 12, 24. For another reflection on wariness of and desire for a home, see Edward Said, *After the Last Sky*.

38. I am grateful for Trinh Minh-ha's lucid struggle with the act of writing herself in the pages of *Woman, Native, Other*. She distinguishes between writing yourself and writing about yourself. The first is "a scriptive act—the emergence of the writing-self" (28); the second is the confessional, the tight constitution of an identity-claim around some supposedly secure foundation such as gender, class or color. The writer engaging in the second, perhaps in hopes of being counted oppressed enough to make claims to virtue, or honest enough to be trusted, usually ends up screening carefully the messy opacities of her life world until they fit the model and can be unveiled. I want to write about class in a way that enables me to be a writing woman, not a written woman or classed person (30). Trinh asks the question well:

Writing in the feminine. And on a colored [classed] sky. How do you inscribe difference without bursting into a series of euphoric narcissistic accounts of yourself and your own kind? Without indulging in a marketable romanticism or in a naive whining about your condition? In other words, how do you forget without annihilating? Between the twin chasms of navel-gazing and navel-erasing, the ground is narrow and slippery. None of us can pride ourselves on being sure-footed there.

(28)

Wary of the final revelation or the belated discovery of origins, I nonetheless want to attend to a rage and a longing that arrive on the scene labeled *class*. I want to prod the feminism I cherish toward greater awareness of class complexities, away from class blindness.

39. See, for example, Trinh, *Woman, Native, Other,* 43.

40. See, for example, Pratt, "Identity: Skin, Blood, Heart," in Bulkin et al., *Yours in Struggle,* 54–55.

41. Riley, "Am I That Name?," 6.

42. Shula Marks, "The Context of Personal Narrative: Reflections on 'Not Either An Experimental Doll'—The Separate Worlds of Three South African Women," in *Interpreting Women's Lives,* ed. the Personal Narratives Group, 47.

43. Barbara Cameron, "Gee, You Don't Seem Like An Indian from the Reservation," in Moraga and Anzaldúa, *This Bridge Called My Back,* 48.

44. Valerie Miner, "In a Class by Themselves," 3. In this review of *Calling Home: Working-Class Women's Writings,* edited by Janet Zandy, Miner is quoting Barbara Rosenblum.

45. Spivak, "French Feminism in an International Frame," 134.

46. Ong, *Spirits of Resistance and Capitalist Discipline,* 6. She is paraphrasing Pierre Bourdieu, *Outline of a Theory of Practice.* My thanks to Carolyn DiPalma for calling my attention to Bourdieu's argument and relating it to class.

47. For further discussion see Studs Terkel, "Who Built the Pyramids?" (an interview with Mike LeFevre) in Terkel, *Working,* 1–10; Lillian B. Rubin, *Worlds of Pain: Life in the Working Class Family;* Zandy, *Calling Home; The Common Thread: Writings by Working Class Women,* ed. June Burnett et al.; Richard Sennett and Jonathan Cobb, *The Hidden Injuries of Class.*

48. I am very grateful to Carolyn DiPalma for her insights into and interpretations of this film and its audience.

49. Anne Norton's stimulating remarks in "Response to Henry S. Kariel," 273–79, helped me to think along these lines.

50. "Ambiguous achievement" is Connolly's phrase. See "The Politics of Discourse," in Shapiro, *Language and Politics,* 144.

51. This felicitous phrase is Michael Shapiro's.

52. Callahan, "Another Book of Laughter and Misunderstanding," 258.

53. Ruddick, *Maternal Thinking,* 122, 123.

54. See Leslie Marmon Silko, *Ceremony.*

55. Fuss and Haraway come to similar conclusions from somewhat different directions; see Fuss, "Reading Like a Feminist," 89, for a brief discussion.

56. Barbara Smith and Beverly Smith, "Across the Kitchen Table: A Sister-to-Sister Dialogue," in Moraga and Anzaldúa, *This Bridge Called My Back,* 126.

57. Bernice Johnson Reagon, "Coalition Politics: Turning the Century," in *Home Girls: A Black Feminist Anthology,* ed. Barbara Smith, 359.

58. Butler, *Gender Trouble,* 15–16.

59. Kundera, *The Unbearable Lightness of Being,* 251.

60. Haraway, "A Manifesto for Cyborgs," 73. See also Nancie E. Caraway, *Segregated Sisterhood.*

61. Kundera, 256.

Bibliography

Alcoff, Linda. "Cultural Feminism Versus Poststructuralism: The Identity Crisis in Feminist Theory." *Signs* 13 (Spring 1988): 405–36.

Ali, Mehmed, Kathy E. Ferguson, and Phyllis Turnbull (with Joelle Mulford). "Gender, Land, and Power: Reading the Military in Hawai'i." Paper presented at the International Political Science Association Annual Meetings, Buenos Aires, Argentina, July 21–25, 1991.

Allen, Paula Gunn. *The Sacred Hoop: Recovering the Feminine in American Indian Traditions*. Boston: Beacon Press, 1986.

Andrews, Lynn. *Crystal Woman*. New York: Warner Books, 1988.

———. *Flight of the Seventh Moon*. New York: Harper and Row, 1984.

———. *Jaguar Woman*. New York: Harper and Row, 1985.

———. *Medicine Woman*. New York: Harper and Row, 1981.

———. *Star Woman*. New York: Warner Books, 1986.

———. *Wildhorse Woman*. New York: Warner Books, 1990.

Apollodorus. *The Library of Greek Mythology*. Trans. Keith Aldrich. Lawrence, Kansas: Coronado Press, 1975.

Barthes, Roland. *The Rustle of Language*. Trans. Richard Howard. N.Y.: Hill and Wang, 1986.

Beauvoir, Simone de. *The Second Sex*. Trans. H. M. Parshley. New York: Alfred A. Knopf, 1953.

Belenky, M. F., B. M. Clinchy, N. R. Goldberg, and J. M. Tarule. *Women's Ways of Knowing*. New York: Basic Books, 1986.

Benjamin, Jessica. *The Bonds of Love: Psychoanalysis, Feminism, and the Problem of Domination*. New York: Pantheon, 1988.

Bennett, Jane. *Unthinking Faith and Enlightenment: Nature and the State in a Post-Hegelian Era*. New York: New York University Press, 1987.

Bernstein, Richard. *Praxis and Action*. Philadelphia: University of Pennsylvania Press, 1971.

Blumenberg, Hans. *The Legitimacy of the Modern Age.* Trans. Robert M. Wallace. Cambridge: MIT Press, 1983.

Bordo, Susan. "The Cartesian Masculinization of Thought." *Signs* 11 (Spring 1986): 439–56.

Bourdieu, Pierre. *Outline of a Theory of Practice.* Trans. Richard Nice. Cambridge: Cambridge University Press, 1977.

Brennan, Teresa, ed. *Between Feminism and Psychoanalysis.* New York: Routledge, 1989.

Brown, Wendy. *Manhood and Politics: A Feminist Reading in Political Theory.* Totowa, N.J.: Rowman and Allanheld, 1988.

Budapest, Z. "Political Witchcraft." *Woman of Power* 8 (Winter 1988): 38–40.

Bulkin, Elly, Minnie Bruce Pratt, and Barbara Smith. *Yours in Struggle.* New York: Long Haul Press, 1984.

Bunche, Charlotte, et al. *Building Feminist Theory: Essays From Quest.* New York: Longman, 1981.

Burnett, June, Julie Cotterill, Annette Kennerley, Phoebe Nathan, and Jeanne Wilding, eds. *The Common Thread: Writings by Working Class Women.* London: Mandarin, 1990.

Butler, Judith. "The Body Politics of Julia Kristeva." *Hypatia* 3 (Winter 1989): 104–18.

———. *Gender Trouble: Feminism and the Subversion of Identity.* New York: Routledge, 1990.

———. *Subjects of Desire: Hegelian Reflections in Twentieth-Century France.* New York: Columbia University Press, 1987.

Callahan, William. "Another Book of Laughter and Misunderstanding: A Field Guide to Chuckles, Smiles and Guffaws." Ph.D. diss., University of Hawai'i, 1991.

Cameron, Anne. *Daughters of Copper Woman.* Vancouver: Press Gang Publishers, 1981.

Caraway, Nancie E. *Segregated Sisterhood.* Knoxville: University of Tennessee Press, 1991.

Chernin, Kim. *The Hungry Self.* New York: Times Books, 1985.

———. *The Obsession.* New York: Harper and Row, 1981.

Chodorow, Nancy. *The Reproduction of Mothering.* Berkeley and Los Angeles: University of California Press, 1978.

Cixous, Hélène, and Catherine Clément. *The Newly Born Woman.* Trans. Betsy Wing. Minneapolis: University of Minnesota Press, 1986.

Cocks, Joan. *The Oppositional Imagination.* London: Routledge, 1989.

Connolly, William E. *Political Theory and Modernity.* New York: Basil Blackwell, 1988.

————. *Politics and Ambiguity*. Madison: University of Wisconsin Press, 1987.

Cook, Alice, and Gwyn Kirk. *Greenham Women Everywhere*. Boston: South End Press, 1983.

Daly, Lois K. "Ecofeminism, Reverence for Life, and Feminist Theological Ethics." Department of Religious Studies, Siena College, Loudonville, N.Y. Typescript.

Daly, Mary. "Be-Laughing: Nixing, Hexing and X-ing." *Woman of Power* 8 (Winter 1988): 76–80.

Derrida, Jacques. *Dissemination*. Trans. Barbara Johnson. Chicago: University of Chicago Press, 1981.

————. *Spurs: Nietzsche's Styles*. Trans. Barbara Harlow. Chicago: University of Chicago Press, 1978.

Derrida, Jacques, and Christie McDonald. "Choreographies." *Diacritics* 12 (1982): 66–76.

Diamond, Irene, and Lee Quinby, eds. *Foucault and Feminism: Reflections on Resistance*. Boston: Northeastern University Press, 1988.

Di Stefano, Christine. *Configurations of Masculinity: A Feminist Perspective on Modern Political Theory*. Ithaca, N.Y.: Cornell University Press, 1991.

————. "Masculinity As Ideology in Political Theory: Hobbesian Man Considered." *Women's Studies International Forum* 6 (1983): 633–44.

Dreyfus, Herbert L., and Paul Rabinow. *Michel Foucault: Beyond Structuralism and Hermeneutics*. Chicago: University of Chicago Press, 1982.

Duerr, Hans Peter. *Dreamtime: Concerning the Boundary Between Wilderness and Civilization*. Oxford: Basil Blackwell, 1985.

Ebert, Teresa. "The Romance of Patriarchy: Ideology, Subjectivity, and Postmodern Feminist Cultural Theory." *Cultural Critique* (Fall 1988): 19–57.

Eisler, Riane. *The Chalice and the Blade*. San Francisco: Harper and Row, 1987.

Elias, Norbert. *The History of Manners*. New York: Pantheon Books, 1978.

Elshtain, Jean Bethke. *Women and War*. New York: Basic Books, 1987.

Enloe, Cynthia. *Bananas, Beaches, and Bases*. Berkeley and Los Angeles: University of California Press, 1989.

Escobar, Arturo. "Discourse and Power in Development: Michel Foucault and the Relevance of His Work to the Third World." *Alternatives* 10 (Winter 1984–85): 377–400.

Ferguson, Kathy E. *The Feminist Case Against Bureaucracy*. Philadelphia: Temple University Press, 1984.

―――. "Knowledge, Politics, and Persons in Feminist Theory." *Political Theory* 17 (May 1989): 302–14.

―――. *Self, Society, and Womankind: The Dialectic of Liberation.* Westport, Conn.: Greenwood Press, 1980.

Firestone, Shulamith. *The Dialectic of Sex.* New York: Bantam Books, 1970.

Fisher, Dexter, ed. *The Third Woman: Minority Women Writers of the United States.* Boston: Houghton Mifflin, 1980.

Flax, Jane. "Postmodernism and Gender Relations in Feminist Theory." *Signs* 12 (Summer 1987): 621–42.

―――. *Thinking Fragments: Psychoanalysis, Feminism, and Postmodernism in the Contemporary West.* Berkeley and Los Angeles: University of California Press, 1990.

Foucault, Michel. *The Archaeology of Knowledge.* Trans. A. M. Sheridan-Smith. New York: Pantheon, 1982.

―――. *Herculine Barbin: Being the Newly Discovered Memoirs of a Nineteenth Century French Hermaphrodite.* Trans. Richard McDougall. New York: Pantheon, 1980.

―――. *An Introduction.* Vol. 1 of *The History of Sexuality.* Trans. Robert Hurley. New York: Random House, 1980.

―――. *Language, Counter-memory, Practice: Selected Essays and Interviews.* Trans. Donald F. Bouchard and Sherry Simon. Ithaca, N.Y.: Cornell University Press, 1977.

―――. *The Use of Pleasure.* Vol. 2 of *The History of Sexuality.* Trans. Robert Hurley. New York: Pantheon, 1985.

Fraser, Nancy, and Linda Nicholson. "Social Criticism Without Philosophy: An Encounter Between Feminism and Postmodernism." *Communication* 10 (1988): 345–66.

Frye, Marilyn. *The Politics of Reality: Essays in Feminist Theory.* Trumansburg, N.Y.: The Crossing Press, 1983.

Fuss, Diana. "Reading Like a Feminist," *differences* 1 (Summer 1989): 77–92.

Garrod, Andrew. ed. *Learning for Life: Moral Education, Theory and Practice.* New York: Praeger, 1992.

George, Demetra. "Mysteries of the Dark Moon." *Woman of Power* 8 (Winter 1988): 30–34.

Gibbons, Michael T. "The Ethic of Postmodernism." *Political Theory* 19 (1991): 96–102.

Gillespie, Michael A. *Hegel, Heidegger, and the Ground of History.* Chicago: University of Chicago Press, 1984.

Gilligan, Carol. *In a Different Voice.* Cambridge: Harvard University Press, 1982.

Gimbutas, Marija. *The Goddesses and Gods of Old Europe: Myths and Cult Images*. Berkeley and Los Angeles: University of California Press, 1982.

Godavitarne, Pia M. "From the Editor." *Woman of Power* 8 (Winter 1988): 4.

———. "Light Returning: Alternative Mental Health Programs." *Woman of Power* 8 (Winter 1988): 20–23.

Gould, Carol, ed. *Beyond Domination*. Totowa, N.J.: Rowman and Allanheld, 1983.

Griffin, Susan. *Women and Nature*. New York: Harper and Row, 1978.

Guttentag, Marcia, and Paul F. Secord. *Too Many Women?* Beverly Hills, Calif.: Sage, 1983.

Haraway, Donna. "A Manifesto for Cyborgs: Science, Technology, and Socialist Feminism in the 1980s." *Socialist Review* 15 (March–April 1985): 65–107.

———. "Monkeys, Aliens, and Women: Love, Science, and Politics at the Intersection of Feminist Theory and Colonial Discourse." *Women's Studies International Forum* 12, no. 3 (1989): 295–312.

———. *Primate Visions: Gender, Race, and Nature in the World of Modern Science*. New York: Routledge, 1989.

———. "Situated Knowledges: The Science Question in Feminism and the Privilege of Partial Perspective," *Feminist Studies* 14 (Fall 1988): 575–99.

Harding, Sandra. *The Science Question in Feminism*. Ithaca, N.Y.: Cornell University Press, 1986.

Hartsock, Nancy C. M., *Money, Sex and Power: Toward A Feminist Historical Materialism*. New York: Longman, 1983.

Hegel, G. W. F. *The Phenomenology of Mind*. Trans. J. B. Baillie. New York: Harper and Row, 1967.

———. *Lectures on the Philosophy of History*. Trans. J. Sibree. New York: Dover Publications, 1956.

Heidegger, Martin. *Basic Writings*. Edited by David F. Krell. New York: Harper and Row, 1977.

Heller, Agnes. *A Theory of Feelings*. Assen, The Netherlands: Van Gorcum, 1979.

Hennessy, Rosemary, and Rajeswari Mohan. "The Construction of Woman in Three Popular Texts of Empire: Toward a Critique of Materialist Feminism." *Textual Practice* 13 (Winter 1989): 323–59.

Hirsch, Marianne, and Evelyn Fox Keller, eds. *Conflicts in Feminism*. New York: Routledge, 1990.

Hochschild, Arlie Russell. *The Managed Heart*. Berkeley and Los Angeles: University of California Press, 1983.

hooks, bell. "Stylish Nihilism at the Movies," Z (May 1988): 26–29.

Horowitz, Maryanne Cline. "Aristotle and Woman." *Journal of the History of Biology* 9 (Fall 1976): 183–218.

Irigaray, Luce. *Speculum of the Other Woman*. Trans. Gillian C. Gill. Ithaca, N.Y.: Cornell University Press, 1985.

———. *This Sex Which Is Not One*. Trans. Catherine Porter and Carolyn Burke. Ithaca, N.Y.: Cornell University Press, 1985.

Jamal, Michele. *Shape Shifters: Shaman Women in Contemporary Society*. New York: Arkana, 1987.

Jardine, Alice. *Gynesis*. Ithaca, N.Y.: Cornell University Press, 1985.

Jones, Christopher. "Gaia: Emerging Mythology and Political Power." Ph.D. diss., University of Hawai'i, 1989.

King, Ynestra. "Ecofeminism: On the Necessity of History and Mystery." *Woman of Power* 9 (Spring 1988): 42–44.

Kramarae, Cheris, and Paula A. Treichler. *A Feminist Dictionary*. London: Pandora Press, 1985.

Kristeva, Julia. *The Kristeva Reader*. Edited by Toril Moi. New York: Columbia University Press, 1986.

Krupnick, Mark, ed. *Displacement: Derrida and After*. Bloomington: Indiana University Press, 1983.

Kundera, Milan. *The Unbearable Lightness of Being*. Trans. Michael H. Heim. New York: Harper and Row, 1984.

Lame Deer, John (Fire), and Richard Erdoes. *Lame Deer: Seeker of Visions*. New York: Pocket Books, 1972.

Lauretis, Teresa de. "Eccentric Subjects: Feminist Theory and Historical Consciousness." *Feminist Studies* 16 (Spring 1990): 115–50.

———, ed. *Feminist Studies, Critical Studies*. Bloomington: Indiana University Press, 1986.

Lerner, Gerda. *The Creation of Patriarchy*. New York: Oxford University Press, 1986.

Lopez, Barry. *Arctic Dreams: Imagination and Desire in a Northern Landscape*. New York: Charles Scribner's Sons, 1986.

Lorde, Audre. *Sister/Outsider*. Trumansburg, N.Y.: The Crossing Press, 1984.

Lorraine, Tamsin E. *Gender, Identity, and the Production of Meaning*. Boulder, Col.: Westview Press, 1990.

Love, Nancy, "Foucault and Habermas on Discourse and Democracy." Paper presented at the annual meeting of the American Political Science Association, Washington, D.C., 1986.

Maclean, Ian. *The Renaissance Notion of Woman*. Cambridge: Cambridge University Press, 1980.

Marx, Karl, Frederick Engels, V. I. Lenin, and Joseph Stalin. *The Woman Question.* New York: International Publishers, 1951.

Mead, George Herbert. *Mind, Self, and Society.* Chicago: University of Chicago Press, 1934.

———. *Philosophy of the Present.* Chicago: Open Court Publishing Co., 1932.

Merchant, Carolyn, *The Death of Nature.* San Francisco: Harper and Row, 1980.

Mernissi, Fatima. *Beyond the Veil: Male-Female Dynamics in Modern Muslim Society.* Bloomington: Indiana University Press, 1987.

Miner, Valerie. "In a class by themselves." Review of *Calling Home: Working-Class Women's Writings,* ed. Janet Zandy. *The Women's Review of Books* 7 (September 1990): 1–4.

Mohanty, Chandra. "Under Western Eyes: Feminist Scholarship and Colonial Discourses." *Feminist Review* 30 (August 1988): 61–88.

Moi, Toril. *Sexual/Textual Politics: Feminist Literary Theory.* New York: Methuen, 1985.

Moraga, Cherríe and Gloria Anzaldúa. *This Bridge Called My Back: Writings of Radical Women of Color.* Latham, N.Y.: Kitchen Table Press, 1983.

Mulvey, Laura. "Visual Pleasure and Narrative Cinema." *Screen* 16 (3): 6–18.

Nicholson, Linda, ed. *Feminism/Postmodernism.* New York: Routledge, 1990.

Nietzsche, Friedrich. *The Complete Works of Friedrich Nietzsche,* Vol. 2, *Early Greek Philosophy.* Edited by Oscar Levy, trans. Maximilian A. Mügge. New York: Russell and Russell, 1964.

———. *The Birth of Tragedy and The Genealogy of Morals.* Trans. Francis Golffing. New York: Doubleday Anchor, 1956.

Norton, Anne. "Response to Henry S. Kariel." *Political Theory* 18 (1990): 273–79.

Ochs, Carol. *Women and Spirituality.* Totowa, N.J.: Rowman and Allanheld, 1983.

Ong, Aihwa. *Spirits of Resistance and Capitalist Discipline: Factory Women in Malaysia.* Albany: State University of New York Press, 1987.

Pateman, Carol, and Elizabeth Gross, eds. *Feminist Challenges: Social and Political Theory.* Boston: Northeastern University Press, 1986.

Personal Narratives Group, the, eds. *Interpreting Women's Lives.* Bloomington: Indiana University Press, 1989.

Phelan, Shane. "Foucault and Feminism." *American Journal of Political Science* 34 (May 1990): 421–40.

Pitkin, Hannah. *Fortune Is a Woman*. Berkeley and Los Angeles: University of California Press, 1984.

Pollock, Greselda. *Vision and Difference: Femininity, Feminism and Histories of Art*. New York: Routledge, 1988.

Powell, Chilton Latham. *English Domestic Relations 1487–1643*. New York: Russell and Russell, 1972.

Riley, Denise. *Am I That Name?: Feminism and the Category of 'Women' in History*. Minneapolis: University of Minnesota Press, 1988.

Robinson, Lillian. "Sometimes, Always, Never: Their Women's History and Ours." Stanford University Institute for Research on Women and Gender, Stanford, Calif. Typescript, n.d.

Rosaldo, Renato. "Politics, Patriarchs, and Laughter," *Cultural Critique* 6 (Spring 1987): 65–86.

Rubin, Lillian B. *Worlds of Pain: Life in the Working Class Family*. New York: Basic Books, 1976.

Ruddick, Sara. "Maternal Thinking," *Feminist Studies* 6 (Summer 1980): 342–67.

———. *Maternal Thinking*. Boston: Beacon Press, 1989.

Ruthstrom, Ellyn. "Feeling the Power of Nature." Interview with Carol B. Christ. *Woman of Power* 9 (Spring 1988): 22–24.

Said, Edward. *After the Last Sky*. New York: Pantheon Books, 1985.

———. *Orientalism*. New York: Vintage, 1979.

Sanday, Peggy Reeves. *Female Power and Male Dominance*. London: Cambridge University Press, 1981.

Savigliano, Marta. "Political Economy of Passion: Tango, Exoticism, and Decolonization." Ph.D. diss., University of Hawai'i, 1991.

Seery, John Evan. "Irony and Death (Or, Rorty Contra Orpheus)." Paper presented at the annual meeting of the American Political Science Association, Atlanta, Ga., 1989.

———. *Political Returns: Irony in Politics and Theory from Plato to the Antinuclear Movement*. Boulder, Col.: Westview Press, 1990.

Sennett, Richard, and Jonathan Cobb. *The Hidden Injuries of Class*. New York: Vintage Books, 1972.

Shaffer, Carolyn T. "Living as Fish: Emilie Conrad Da'Oud and Continuum." *Woman of Power* 8 (Winter 1988): 14–16.

Shanley, Mary Lyndon, and Carole Pateman, eds. *Feminist Interpretations and Political Theory*. University Park: The Pennsylvania State University Press, 1991.

Shapiro, Michael. "Metaphor in the Philosophy of the Social Sciences." *Cultural Critique* 2 (Winter 1985–86): 191–214.

———. *The Politics of Representation*. Madison: University of Wisconsin Press, 1988.

————. *Reading the Postmodern Polity.* Minneapolis: University of Minnesota Press, forthcoming.

————. *Language and Politics.* New York: New York University Press, 1984.

Shiva, Vandana. *Staying Alive: Women, Ecology and Development.* London: Zed Books, 1989.

Silko, Leslie Marmon. *Ceremony.* New York: Penguin Books, 1977.

Smith, Andrea. "Indian Spiritual Abuse." *National Women's Studies Action Newsletter* 3, no. 1/2 (Spring 1990): 35–36.

Smith, Barbara, ed. *Home Girls: A Black Feminist Anthology.* New York: Kitchen Table Press, 1983.

Smith, Paul. *Discerning the Subject.* Minneapolis: University of Minnesota Press, 1988.

Spelman, Elizabeth V. *Inessential Woman: Problems of Exclusion in Feminist Thought.* Boston: Beacon Press, 1988.

Spitzack, Carole. *Confessing Excess: Women and the Politics of Body Reduction.* Albany: State University of New York Press, 1990.

Spivak, Gayatri Chakravorty. *In Other Worlds.* New York: Methuen, 1987.

————. *The Post-Colonial Critic.* New York: Routledge, 1990.

Spretnak, Charlene. "Ecofeminism: Our Roots and Flowering." *Woman of Power* 9 (Spring 1988): 6–10.

Starhawk. *The Spiral Dance.* New York: Harper and Row, 1979.

————. *Truth or Dare.* San Francisco: Harper and Row, 1987.

Sternburg, J. *The Writer On Her Work.* New York: W. W. Norton, 1980.

Stone, Merlin. "Endings and Origins." *Woman of Power* 8 (Winter 1988): 28–29.

Taylor, Charles. *Hegel.* London: Cambridge University Press, 1975.

Tepper, Sherri S. *The Gate To Women's Country.* New York: Bantam Books, 1988.

Terkel, Studs. *Working.* New York: Avon, 1972.

Theatana, Kathryn. "The Priestesses of Hecate." *Woman of Power* 8 (Winter 1988): 35–37.

Trask, Haunani-Kay. *Eros and Power: The Promise of Feminist Theory.* Philadelphia: University of Pennsylvania Press, 1986.

Trinh, T. Minh-ha. *Woman, Native, Other.* Bloomington: Indiana University Press, 1989.

Tronto, Joan C. "Beyond Gender Difference to a Theory of Care," *Signs* 12 (Summer 1987): 644–63.

Walker, Alice. *In Search of Our Mothers' Gardens.* New York: Harcourt, Brace, Jovanovich, 1983.

Wayne, Valerie, ed. *The Matter of Difference: Materialist Feminist Criticism of Shakespeare.* Ithaca, N.Y.: Cornell University Press, 1991.

Weed, Elizabeth, ed. *Coming To Terms*. New York: Routledge, 1989.

Weeks, Jeffrey. *Sexuality and Its Discontents*. London: Routledge and Kegan Paul, 1986.

Wheeler, Charlene E., and Peggy L. Chinn. *Peace and Power: A Handbook of Feminist Process*. Buffalo, N.Y.: Margaret-daughters, Inc., 1984.

White, Stephen K. "Foucault's Challenge to Critical Theory." *The American Political Science Review* 80 (June 1986): 419–32.

———. "Heidegger and the Difficulties of a Post-modern Ethics and Politics," *Political Theory* 18 (1990): 80–104.

———. "Paths to a Postmodern Ethics and Politics: A Reply to Gibbons," *Political Theory* 19 (1991): 103–104.

Willis, Susan. *Black Women Writing the American Experience*. Madison: University of Wisconsin Press, 1987.

Wuthnow, Julie. "Feminism and Poststructuralism: A Marriage of Convenience." Department of Political Science, University of Hawai'i, Honolulu, December 15, 1988.

Wyschogrod, Edith. *Spirit in Ashes: Hegel, Heidegger, and Man-Made Mass Death*. New Haven: Yale University Press, 1985.

Young, Iris M. "Humanism, Gynocentrism, and Feminist Politics," *Women's Studies International Forum* 8 (1985): 173–83.

Young, Robert, ed. *Untying the Text*. London: Routledge and Kegan Paul, 1981.

Zandy, Janet, ed. *Calling Home: Working-Class Women's Writings*. New Brunswick, N.J.: Rutgers University Press, 1990.

Index

Women's experience, 2–6, 26, 85, 88, 128; with nature, 105; and politics, 91; and subjectivity, 15, 61, 69, 78

Women's voice, 3–6, 25, 102, 146; in Cixous, 16; in Gilligan, 79

Working class, 160, 161, 169; and affirmative action, 176; ambivalences of, 174–75; control over, 10; escape from, 172; and feminism, 87, 148; and op-portunity, 171–72; and oppression, 173–74; perspectives of, 168–69; white men in, 177

Wuthnow, Julie, 22, 75

Young, Iris, 58, 60, 80

Zetkin, Clara, 1, 7

Compositor:	Maple-Vail Book Mfg. Group
Text:	11/13 Caledonia
Display:	Caledonia
Printer and Binder:	Maple Vail Book Mfg. Group